Lessons from
the Intersexed

Lessons from the Intersexed

Suzanne J. Kessler

Rutgers University Press

New Brunswick, New Jersey, and London

Cover illustration: "Visit to a Family Doctor" by Norman Rockwell.
Printed by permission of the Norman Rockwell Family Trust.
Copyright © 1947 the Norman Rockwell Family Trust.

Chapter 2 was originally published as "The Medical Construction of Gender: Case Management of Intersexed Infants," in *Signs: Journal of Women
in Culture and Society* (autumn 1990):3–26.
Copyright © 1990 by The University of Chicago. All rights reserved.

Library of Congress Cataloging-in-Publication Data

Kessler, Suzanne J., 1946–
    Lessons from the intersexed / Suzanne J. Kessler.
        p. cm.
    Includes bibliographical references and index.
    ISBN 0–8135–2529–2 (cloth : alk. paper).—ISBN 0–8135–2530–6
(pbk. : alk. paper)
    1. Hermaphroditism.   2. Gender identity.   I. Title.
RC883. K47 1998   97–39342
616.6'94—dc21   CIP

British Cataloging-in-Publication information available

Manufactured in the United States of America

for Andrew
from both of us

Contents

Acknowledgments

Many thanks to my students at Purchase College who helped collect the data described in chapters two, four, and five: Eric Black, Amy Davis, Theresa Devins, Kellie Lynch, Lynne Mergler, Joyce Solano, and Jane Weider. I am also grateful to Heather Hoffman at Knox College and Elizabeth Gruskin at University of California, Berkeley, for assisting me by distributing questionnaires at their institutions, and to Peter Balsam for unselfishly taking the time to master the program that generated the figures in chapters three and five.

Faculty and graduate students at a number of seminars provided valuable feedback to me while my ideas were evolving. I particularly recognize the Women's Studies faculty at Purchase College, participants at The CLAGS Colloquium Series in Lesbian and Gay Studies, members of the Yale seminar sponsored by the Research Fund for Lesbian and Gay Studies, and faculty and students in the Social-Personality Psychology Program at the Graduate School and University Center, City University of New York. I am also indebted to Holly Devor for reading a draft of the manuscript and providing expert advice on transgender issues.

The generosity of so many intersexuals and parents of intersexed children is responsible for the emergence of this book. Many are unnamed, but I especially want to note the contributions of Martha Coventry, Sherri Groveman, Morgan Holmes, Cheri Sintes, Heike Spreitzer, Gabriella Tako, Kiira Triea, and Eileen Wells. They, of course, are not responsible for its contents and, in fact, may not agree with everything I have written.

Cheryl Chase is due special acknowledgment. Our conversations in the early 1990s, after publication of the first article I wrote on intersexuality, spurred me to reconsider my assumptions about the success of intersex surgeries. She has also helped me see that, contrary to my initial assumptions, the medical profession does not have to be the servant of an intransigent cultural ideology.

Individual physicians can be moved, and this is how politics works—one person at a time.

I could not have written this book had I not been immersed for over twenty years in the ideas that serve as its foundation. For that I thank Wendy McKenna, with whose theorizing my own is so inextricably intertwined.

Lessons from
the Intersexed

1

Introduction

Alex A. was born in 1971. He called me
to talk about what he labeled his "sexual differentiation disorder" and related his story: Alex was given a female gender assignment at birth, despite having labial-scrotum fusion. By age one or
two Alex's mother noticed that his phallus was enlarged, and by
the time he could speak, he called it "my penis." At puberty his
voice deepened, and he began to be called "he-man" by other kids.
He did not develop breasts, but by age thirteen, was menstruat-
ing irregularly from his phallus. A rural doctor put him on estrogen, and he developed small breasts but considerable axillary body
hair. In his late teens Alex was sent to an endocrinologist who
asked whether he had ever taken hormones. At that point, Alex
did not even know what hormones were. The endocrinologist said:
"I think you should change to a male" and gave him a prescrip-
tion for testosterone, but Alex never filled it. He recalls, "We were
very religious people. We [mother and I] didn't know what was
going on." Alex's mother was encouraging him to "try and grow
breasts."

By age twenty-four his breasts started to enlarge. Recently, he
saw another endocrinologist who said: "We can make you a girl"
and bolstered this suggestion with the argument, "You know,
women can even be managers now." Alex was told that his clitoris can be reduced and that an ultrasound revealed a uterus. In
spite of the doctor's recommendation, Alex does not want to go
this route. He is confused because he has always thought doctors
were gods. He feels like a male and has no idea what his diagnosis is.

Alex B. was born in 1963. At birth Alex was diagnosed with
the condition "mixed gonadal dysgenesis" and was given a male
gender assignment. Although regarded as a boy, the child was never

1

really accepted as one. Everyone in the small town knew about Alex's genital abnormality.

Now an adult woman, Alex remembers that her mother regularly examined her genitals and told her that "something like this simply was not acceptable." Yet, she remembers being content with her body. She was hospitalized at age four for reasons she still does not know. Her parents said that it was a decision by some physician they had never consulted before. Her mother had her examined at a nearby hospital at age twelve because she was not experiencing puberty. Alex had hoped for breast development and sometimes tried to pass as a female, but her parents would correct other people's view. She was given testosterone shots for one and a half years. No one explained to her what the treatment was supposedly good for, and Alex was told she should not speak of it. Treatments were stopped because they did not achieve what was desired: growth of phallic tissue. But her voice did change, and she developed facial hair and involuntary clitoral erections, all of which enormously bothered her.

At age twenty Alex left her hometown to get estrogen treatments and genital surgery. The first surgeon she went to said Alex did not have enough penile and scrotal skin to model a complete vagina and vulva. (Alex wanted to retain a functioning clitoris and put special emphasis on acceptable labia.) Her assessment is that he produced "at best a halfway aesthetically and functionally acceptable result." Although she considers the surgery as having been necessary, since she doubts whether she would have survived emotionally without it, she recognizes that she undertook it as an extreme reaction to previously extreme treatment that had been administered against her will.

One year later Alex had surgery again, urged by a physician who wanted to repair the scar tissue. Without consulting her, he tried to elongate what he felt was her too short vagina. The scar tissue rebuilt itself, and the few extra centimeters were lost again. Alex was offered a third surgery to correct these problems but turned down the offer, as well as an offer for breast augmentation. After a long period of viewing herself as "asexual," Alex began having sexual relationships with female partners. Although she had considered reestablishing a relationship with her parents, she has been unable to come to terms with their dishonesty and has completely broken off contact with them and others from her hometown.

Alex C. was born in 1960. Alex's mother went into labor too quickly to get to a hospital, so the baby was born at home in a large city. Relatives recall that her genitals were ambiguous. Her mother remembers that the doctor said she was "probably a girl." Her grandmother remembers that he said she was "probably a boy." Because of the bad weather that winter, Alex was home with her parents for a month before being seen by another physician. She was brought to the hospital due to her failing health and was diagnosed as having congenital adrenal hyperplasia (CAH). I asked her, "Were you raised as a boy that first month?" She says that no one will discuss that period with her. Alex and I agree that her current name would have been appropriate for either a male or a female.

Alex was treated by physicians continuously throughout her childhood. Blood was drawn repeatedly and her genitals were scrutinized. She claims that the endocrinologist and others at the hospital were conservative about surgery, possibly due to some bad experiences they had had. In addition, they were waiting for Alex's puberty to see whether her body would virilize further.

Alex recalls that, starting around age eight, she began getting pressured by her mother (who was being pressured by the physicians) to accept the idea of genital surgery. The argument was: Don't you want to be normal? Get married? Have babies? She remembers her answer as always being, "No." She held off until age fourteen, when both she and her mother capitulated. (By that time her father had left and her mother had remarried.) Alex was given no psychological preparation and remembers having temper tantrums in the hospital before surgery. She awoke from the surgery experiencing incredible pain.

The surgery was justified on the grounds that creating a vagina would eventually allow her to give birth. She remembers no mention of separating her scrotum to create labia or of reducing her clitoris. Her clitoris had been about three inches long and would have grown, according to her estimation, to be at the most five inches.

In spite of the surgery to create a vagina, Alex refused all physician recommendations to dilate her vagina and threw the dilators in the wastebasket. Consequently, although her vagina is of a normal length, the width has never been increased. She can barely accommodate a junior tampon. Interestingly, although her parents made her undergo the surgery, they in no way pressured her to stretch her vagina. Her mother's attitude was that now that Alex had one, she could make the decision when and if to increase its size. After Alex's first painful intercourse, she asked a physician if that was normal. Although she was assured it was not, she was not motivated to do anything to increase her vaginal capacity. She has always found intercourse painful and unsatisfactory and identifies herself as a lesbian. During sex she suffers intermittent genital pain, probably due to scar tissue and adhesions, but she is orgasmic.

Alex says that her presurgical genitals were not a problem for her or her parents. Like most CAH girls, the family was more concerned about her state of health. Her situation differs from most other CAH girls (especially children today) in that she had no surgery until puberty. She developed strategies to avoid being seen in the locker room (such as changing before the others did), but she does not recall this as a particularly big deal. Although her urethra did not run through her clitoris, but rather underneath it (much like hypospadias), she used to stand to urinate.

Unlike many other intersexed adults, Alex feels some sympathy for her mother's predicament and believes that she was as much a victim of the medical profession as was Alex. She is sure that her mother has a great deal of anger toward the physicians who never told her that her daughter's clitoris was being removed and that she would be sexually dysfunctional. At present, mother and daughter do not discuss the surgery, and Alex believes that her mother has "blocked it out."

Intrigued with Intersexuality

Who is each Alex "really"? Female or male? We tend to think that genitals, gonads, and secondary gender characteristics have some objective status and ought to be describable and describably female or male. Psychologists treat gender identity as objective. But how people categorized each Alex, as well as how the Alex's categorize themselves, seems rather elusive. Gender, that supposedly objective thing, is highly complex.

Twenty years ago, Wendy McKenna and I analyzed (among other things) the exceptional case of transsexualism in order to demonstrate how gender is socially constructed in all cases.[1] At that time, transsexualism was discussed only by transsexuals, and social constructionism was an "alternative" viewpoint. Today, transsexualism is the subject of many fine analyses,[2] and social constructionism is a mainstream theoretical perspective, grounding much of the work in Gender Studies and Queer Studies within which there is a particular interest in people who violate categories. Transsexualism, as pointed out maintains a dichotomous gender system. Other "transgressions," though, especially intersexuality and especially now, call the whole system into question.

Gender theorists are intrigued by intersexuality (often referred to as "hermaphroditism"), an idea symbolizing complexity and fluidity.[3] Television talk shows parade the real people who are living in intersexed bodies for the entertainment of an audience that is motivated like any old-fashioned side show crowd to gawk at the bizarre. Unlike a real sideshow, though, the remarkable genitals are not on view, and the audience is titillated only by the idea of intersex. Producers and consumers of pornography are intrigued by intersex genitals, it being almost incidental that they are connected to people and are usually the result of good special effects and not of actual body parts. The viewer can think: Look at how many different sexual acts can take place at the same time! I can watch "homosexual acts" without my heterosexuality being called into question (or vice versa) because the gender of those people on the screen is (in some sense) both or neither.

The theory and practice of gender reflects a completely different set of concerns for some adult intersexuals. Because they resent the shame they experienced due to the secrecy surrounding their condition and the surgeries that were performed on them as infants, they started a political movement to change medical management and to halt infant surgeries. Intersex, for them, is an identity, even if the original mark has been surgically eliminated.

All of these interests contrast with how the medical profession conceptualizes intersexuality—as a correctable birth defect. The meaning of the genital ambiguity for endocrinologists is limited to its marking of a more serious underlying medical disorder, much like a fever indicates infection. For the surgeon, the ambiguity signals an opportunity to fashion the inappropriate into the appropriate. Once the intersex marker has been corrected, the intersexed person (as intersexed) fades into the culture. The meaning of the genital variation is deflected. Physicians claim this is what the parents want. Parents are almost never heard from, but when they are, theirs is yet another perspective on this issue.

What can be learned from examining all these perspectives?

That, in essence, is the subject of this book, but before I describe its content in more detail, I will discuss yet another "case."

Virtually all academic writing on sex and gender refers to a case first described by sexologist John Money in 1972. An infant boy's penis was ablated during routine surgery to free up his constricted foreskin. The physicians, believing that he could not develop a normal male gender identity without a penis, reassigned the boy to the female gender and performed surgery to create female genitals.

The case was particularly interesting because the infant was an identical twin. This "experiment in nature" was used to test the gender socialization hypothesis. Would identical twins, one raised male and the other raised female, develop different gender identities and gender roles? Would biology (specifically prenatal hormones) be overridden by socialization?

Money's initial report was very clear.[4] Socialization ruled. The child was described as a typical little girl who could not be more different from her twin brother. The case was cited as proof of the plasticity of gender and appeared to have struck a mighty blow to biological determinism.

When Money's theory was first introduced, it impressed people in the field of psychology as very radical. Gender was not only a social construction in theory, it could literally be constructed through human intervention. The surgeons would do their part in creating the necessary genitals, and the parents would do their part by creating the appropriate social environment, one in which the child was referred to with the relevant pronoun. Gender identity and gender role would then fall into place.

Subsequent data about the twin forces us to reconsider Money's assertion. Sex researcher Milton Diamond located this twin, who Money claimed had been lost to follow-up, and reported that the child never accepted the female gender label, never acted like a "normal" girl, and at the age of fourteen requested hormones and surgery to convert him back to the male gender.[5] Surgery and hormone treatment were provided, and Joan became John. Diamond and his colleague Sigmundson concluded that the prenatal androgen that the twin had been exposed to "overrode" the socialization, proving that you cannot make a girl out of a boy or vice versa.[6] Although there are explanations other than the supremacy of biology for the failure of the twin's female gender assignment (such as inconsistent gender messages from the parents), the failure of re-assignment in this particular case is not in question.[7]

Unlike the media, my interest in this case is not whether it supports a biological or social theory of gender development but why gender theorists (including McKenna and myself) were so eager to embrace Money's theory of gender plasticity.[8] Why, also, did it become the only theory taught to parents of intersexed infants—those born with neither clearly female nor clearly male genitals, gonads, or chromosomes?

For whatever reason, gender researchers were blinded to a number of unexamined and deeply conservative assumptions embedded in Money's argument:

1. Genitals are naturally dimorphic; there is nothing socially constructed about the two categories.
2. Those genitals that blur the dimorphism belonging to the occasional intersexed person can be and should be successfully altered by surgery.
3. Gender is necessarily dichotomous (even if socially constructed) because genitals are naturally dimorphic.
4. Dimorphic genitals are the essential markers of dichotomous gender.
5. Physicians and psychologists have legitimate authority to define the relationship between gender and genitals.

Those of us who are social constructionists and have postulated the primacy of gender attribution or gender performance should have been more critical of Money's theory for putting so much emphasis on the genitals as evidence of gender.[9] We should have asked a number of questions, among them, Why did the twin boy have to be a girl if he did not have a penis?

In this book I will examine the five assumptions above and try to answer the following questions:

1. How dimorphic are genitals?
2. How successful are genital surgeries?
3. Is gender necessarily dichotomous; could it be socially constructed to be trichotomous—at least?
4. Must genitals be the essential marker of gender?
5. How does the medical profession use its authority to manage a particular version of gender?

I begin the next chapter with the last question, but before I do, one other important issue must be raised.

Meanings of Variability

We can think about variations in two very different ways. The first way is to note that most measurements of a feature cluster around the mean, thus creating a norm. The conventional medical view of intersexuality is that knowing the norms of a feature like phallic size, and knowing that most measurements cluster around the mean, validates the existence of underlying pathology when norms are not met. According to this view, genitals that vary from the norm mark a disorder (for example, an enzyme deficiency), and treatment involves correcting both the deficiency and the marker.

A second way to think about variation is to see it as validating the continuum of the feature, thus providing proof that there are arbitrary categories and subjective markers of acceptability. This is the view of gender theorists like Morgan Holmes, an intersexed woman who writes about the social construction of intersexuality. She objects to the typical medical phrase "enlarged clitoris" because it assumes that all "normal" clitorises are virtually identical in size.[10]

I have been deliberately using the term "variability" rather than the medical referent "ambiguity." As we will see in the next chapter, something needs to be done about "ambiguity," but it is less obvious what (if anything) needs to be done about "variability." Genital variability has a number of possible meanings. I will review these meanings here and consider throughout the remaining chapters which constituencies advance which meanings and how meanings gain authority.

Genitals that vary from a narrowly defined standard could have any number of different meanings:[11]

1. Your genitals signify neither of the two traditional gender categories. We need to know what gender you are, therefore we must do further testing. This meaning implies medical diagnosis but not necessarily surgical intervention.

2. We know your gender, but your genitals signify the wrong gender category. We must operate to make them conform to the right gender. The "must" implies that surgery is a medical advancement.

3. We know your gender. Your genitals, although not within the normal range for your gender now, will be in the future. We expect they will clarify on their own (for example, children with 5-alpha-reductase deficiency raised as males).

4. Your genitals are providing a clue that there is an underlying medical problem

that needs to be addressed. We prescribe (nonsurgical) treatment (for example, medication for children with the salt-losing form of congenital adrenal hyperplasia).

5. Your genitals are inferior (less functional, ugly). We pity you and suggest you have corrective/cosmetic surgery.

6. Your genitals are superior (more versatile, attractive). We envy yours and want ones like them.

7. Your genitals are just another body part that varies from person to person, like noses and ears, and it does not matter much what they look like as long as they function well. We do not think very much about yours or ours.

8. Your genitals signify something about your parents. They must have misbehaved or be genetically unsuitable. They are embarrassed by you and your genitals.

Obviously, these meanings emanate from the particular communities I mentioned earlier in the chapter. Meanings 1, 2, and 3 assume a link between genitals and gender and reflect the viewpoints of the medical establishment, which has strict criteria for genitals and technical solutions for variations. These meanings have authority, at least partly because they concretize gender. Meaning 4, although medical in its outlook, does not link the meaning to gender. This could be the primary medical attitude in a different world. Meanings 5, 6, and 7 reflect a conceptualization of the genitals as either aesthetic objects or as just another body part. Meaning 5 is promoted by some plastic surgeons, while meaning 6 is promoted by some members of the transgender community. Meaning 7 might be something worth working toward. Meaning 8 is at least part of the significance given to genital variability by some parents of intersexed infants.

One argument for reducing the number of intersex surgeries hinges on changing the meaning of variant genitals, such that a large clitoris does not necessarily mean "offense," a small penis does not necessarily mean "not a real man," and an absent vagina does not necessarily mean "not a real woman." I will discuss this further in the last chapter.

Most writings on intersexuality are either explicitly meant for medical professionals (and consequently highly technical and not analytic) or popular promotions of the status quo.[12] This book introduces and interprets the medical literature on intersexuality for scholars and students in the area of gender studies, thereby contributing to feminist theory on the social construction of gender and providing a scholarly context for understanding the contemporary intersexual movement whose goals are to halt genital surgeries on intersexed infants and bring intersexuality "out of the closet" in families confronted with a "gender crisis."

Chapter 2 describes the events following the birth of an intersexed infant. I delineate the cultural factors that influence physicians' decisions and the way physicians normalize intersexuality for parents and discuss the consequence of this management approach for the intersexed individual's family and for the two-gender classification system.

In chapter 3, I discuss the language that physicians use when they write about ambiguous genitals, and I analyze their beliefs that deviant-looking genitals require surgery. In order to understand how physicians recognize ambiguous genitals, it is necessary to consider what normal genitals are supposed to look like and how they are supposed to function. I conclude the chapter by reviewing the various surgical interventions for intersexuality, especially clitoral reduction and vaginoplasty techniques.

Chapter 4 begins with an analysis of the criteria that physicians use for determining success in cases of genital surgeries. I review the follow-up studies in medical literature and draw conclusions about the costs and benefits of doing genital surgery on infants and children. Some comparisons are made with vulvar and vaginal construction for transsexuals and for women who are recovering from gynecological cancers and have had reconstructive surgery.

The management philosophy discussed in chapter 2, because it is from the physicians' point of view, effectively ignores adult intersexuals. In chapter 5, I describe their assessment of surgical treatment, discuss the goals of the intersexual movement, and evaluate the movement's potential to alter the way physicians and parents respond to the intersexuality of children. I also characterize the parents' experience with medical professionals and with their intersexed children. In addition to analyzing medical assumptions, I draw upon data I have collected from samples of college women and men asked to reflect on genitals. What would it mean if the average person permits more genital variability than the average physician? Findings from all these sources are used to develop a thesis of how cultural understandings about gender are constructed in particular circumstances and how those understandings might be different.

In chapter 6, I connect analyses of cosmetic surgery with an analysis of intersex management, considering the consequences of either refusing surgery or demanding it without justification. I explore the meaning of genital variability and conclude with the argument that there are both practical and theoretical implications of managing intersexuality differently, were we to take genitals less seriously and to think differently about gender.

2

The Medical

Construction

of Gender

The birth of intersexed infants, babies born with genitals that are neither clearly male nor clearly female, has been documented throughout recorded time.[1] In the late twentieth century, medical technology has become sufficiently advanced to allow scientists to determine chromosomal and hormonal gender, which is typically taken to be the real, natural, biological gender, usually referred to as "sex."[2] Nevertheless, physicians who handle cases of intersexed infants consider several factors beside biological ones in determining, assigning, and announcing the gender of a particular infant. Indeed, biological factors are often preempted in physicians' deliberations by such cultural factors as the "correct" length of the penis and capacity of the vagina.

In the literature on intersexuality, issues such as announcing a baby's gender at the time of delivery, postdelivery discussions with the parents, and consultations with patients in adolescence are considered only peripherally to the central medical issues— etiology, diagnosis, and surgical procedures.[3] Yet members of medical teams have standard practices for managing intersexuality, which rely ultimately on cultural understandings of gender. The process and guidelines by which decisions about gender (re)construction are made reveal the model for the social construction of gender generally. Moreover, in the face of apparently incontrovertible evidence—infants born with some combination of "female" and "male" reproductive and sexual features—physicians hold an incorrigible belief that female and male are the only "natural" options. This paradox highlights and calls into question the idea that female and male are biological givens compelling a culture of two genders.

Ideally, to undertake an extensive study of intersexed infant case management, I would like to have had direct access to particular events, for example the deliveries of intersexed infants and the initial discussions among physicians, between physicians and parents, between parents, and among parents and family and friends of intersexed infants. The rarity with which intersexuality occurs, however, made this unfeasible.[4] Alternatively, physicians who have had considerable experience dealing with this condition were interviewed. I do not assume that their "talk" about how they manage such cases mirrors their "talk" in the situation, but their words do reveal that they have certain assumptions about gender and that they impose those assumptions via their medical decisions on the patients they treat.

Interviews were conducted with six medical experts (three women and three men) in the field of pediatric intersexuality: one clinical geneticist, three endocrinologists (two of them pediatric specialists), one psychoendocrinologist, and one urologist. All of them have had extensive clinical experience with various intersexed syndromes, and some are internationally known researchers in the field of intersexuality. They were selected on the basis of their prominence in the field and their representing four different medical centers in New York City. Although they know one another, they do not collaborate on research and are not part of the same management team. All were interviewed in the spring of 1985 in their offices. The interviews lasted between forty-five minutes and one hour. Unless further referenced, all quotations in this chapter are from these interviews.[5]

The Theory of Intersexuality Management

The sophistication of today's medical technology has led to an extensive compilation of various intersex categories based on the various causes of malformed genitals. The "true hermaphrodite" condition, where both ovarian and testicular tissue are present in either the same gonad or in opposite gonads, accounts for fewer than 5 percent of all cases of ambiguous genitals.[6] More commonly, the infant has either ovaries or testes, but the genitals are ambiguous. If the infant has two ovaries, the condition is referred to as female pseudohermaphroditism. If the infant has two testes, the condition is referred to as male pseudohermaphroditism. There are numerous causes of both forms of pseudohermaphroditism, and although there are life-threatening aspects to some of these conditions, having ambiguous genitals per se is not harmful to the infant's health.[7] Although most cases of ambiguous genitals do not represent true hermaphroditism, in keeping with the contemporary literature, I will refer to all such cases as intersexed.

Current attitudes toward the intersex condition have been primarily influenced by three factors. First are the developments in surgery and endocrinology. Diagnoses of specific intersex conditions can be made with greater precision. Female genitals can be constructed that look much like "natural" ones, and some small penises can be enlarged with the exogenous application of hormones, although surgical skills are not sufficiently advanced to construct a "normal"-looking and functioning penis out of other tissue.[8] Second, in the contemporary United States, the influence of the feminist movement has called into question the valuation of women according to strictly reproductive functions, and the presence or absence of functional gonads is no longer the only or the definitive criterion for gender assignment. Third, psychological theorists focus on "gender identity" (one's sense of oneself as belonging to the female or male category) as distinct from "gender role" (cultural expectations of one's behavior as "appropriate" for a female or male).[9] The relevance of this new gender identity theory for rethinking cases of ambiguous genitals is that gender must be assigned as early as possible if gender identity is to develop successfully. As a result of these three factors, intersexuality is considered a treatable condition of the genitals, one that needs to be resolved expeditiously.

According to all of the specialists interviewed, management of intersexed cases is based upon the theory of gender proposed first by John Money, J. G. Hampson, and J. L. Hampson in 1955 and developed in 1972 by Money and Anke A. Ehrhardt. The theory argues that gender identity is changeable until approximately eighteen months of age.[10] "To use the Pygmalion allegory, one may begin with the same clay and fashion a god or a goddess."[11] The theory rests on satisfying several conditions: The experts must

insure that the parents have no doubt about whether their child is
male or female; the genitals must be made to match the assigned
gender as soon as possible; gender-appropriate hormones must be
administered at puberty; and intersexed children must be kept
informed about their situation with age-appropriate explanations.
If these conditions are met, the theory proposes, the intersexed
child will develop a gender identity in accordance with the gender
assignment (regardless of the chromosomal gender) and will not
question her or his assignment and request reassignment at a later
age.

procedure

Supportive evidence for Money and Ehrhardt's theory is based
on only a handful of repeatedly cited cases, but it has been accepted because of the prestige of the theoreticians and its reso-
nance with contemporary ideas about gender, children, psychology,
and medicine. Gender and children are malleable; psychology and
medicine are the tools used to transform them. This theory is so
strongly endorsed that it has taken on the character of gospel. "I
think we [physicians] have been raised in the Money theory," one
endocrinologist said. Another claimed, "We always approach the
problem in a similar way and it's been dictated, to a large extent,
by the work of John Money and Anke Ehrhardt because they are
the only people who have published, at least in medical literature,
any data, any guidelines." It is provocative that this physician
immediately followed this assertion with: "And I don't know how
effective it really is." Contradictory data are rarely cited in reviews of the literature, were not mentioned by any of the physicians interviewed, and have not reduced these physicians' belief
in the theory's validity.[12]

The doctors interviewed concur with the argument that gender must be assigned immediately, decisively, and irreversibly, and
that professional opinions be presented in a clear and unambiguous way. The psychoendocrinologist said that when doctors make
a statement about the infant, they should "stick to it." The urologist said, "If you make a statement that later has to be disclaimed
or discredited, you've weakened your credibility." A gender assignment made decisively, unambiguously, and irrevocably contributes, I believe, to the general impression that the infant's true,
natural "sex" has been discovered, and that something that was
there all along has been found. It also serves to maintain the credibility of the medical profession, reassure the parents, and reflex-
ively substantiate Money and Ehrhardt's theory.

Also according to this theory, if corrective surgery is necessary, it should take place as soon as possible. If the infant is assigned the male gender, the initial stage of penis repair is usually undertaken in the first year, and further surgery is completed before the child enters school. If the infant is assigned the female gender, vulva repair (including clitoral reduction) is usually begun by three months of age. Money suggests that if reduction of phallic tissue were delayed beyond the neonatal period, the infant would have traumatic memories of having been castrated.[13] Vaginoplasty, in those females having an adequate internal structure (e.g., the vaginal canal is near its expected location), is done between the ages of one and four years. Girls who require more complicated surgical procedures might not be surgically corrected until preadolescence.[14] The complete vaginal canal is typically constructed only when the body is fully grown, following pubertal feminization with estrogen, although some specialists have claimed surgical success with vaginal construction in the early childhood years.[15] Although physicians speculate about the possible trauma of an early-childhood "castration" memory, there is no corresponding concern that vaginal reconstructive surgery delayed beyond the neonatal period is traumatic.

Even though gender identity theory places the critical age limit for gender reassignment between eighteen months and two years, the physicians acknowledge that diagnosis, gender assignment, and genital reconstruction cannot be delayed for as long as two years, since a clear gender assignment and correctly formed genitals will determine the kind of interactions parents will have with their child.[16] The geneticist argued that when parents "change a diaper and see genitalia that don't mean much in terms of gender assignment, I think it prolongs the negative response to the baby. . . . If you have clitoral enlargement that is so extraordinary that the parents can't distinguish between male and female, it is sometimes helpful to reduce that somewhat so that the parent views the child as female." Another physician concurred: Parents "need to go home and do their job as child rearers with it very clear whether it's a boy or a girl."

Diagnosis

A premature gender announcement by an obstetrician, prior to a close examination of an infant's genitals, can be problematic.

Money and his colleagues claim that the primary complications in case management of intersexed infants can be traced to mishandling by medical personnel untrained in sexology.[17] According to one of the pediatric endocrinologists interviewed, obstetricians improperly educated about intersexed conditions "don't examine the babies closely enough at birth and say things just by looking, before separating legs and looking at everything, and jump to conclusions, because 99 percent of the time it's correct. . . . People get upset, physicians I mean. And they say things that are inappropriate." For example, he said that an inexperienced obstetrician might blurt out, "I think you have a boy, or no, maybe you have a girl." Other inappropriate remarks a doctor might make in postdelivery consultation with the parents include, "You have a little boy, but he'll never function as a little boy, so you better raise him as a little girl." As a result, said the pediatric endocrinologist, "the family comes away with the idea that they have a little boy, and that's what they wanted, and that's what they're going to get." In such cases, parents sometimes insist that the child be raised male despite the physicians' instructions to the contrary. "People have in mind certain things they've heard, that this is a boy, and they're not likely to forget that, or they're not likely to let it go easily." The urologist agreed that the first gender attribution is critical: "Once it's been announced, you've got a big problem on your hands." "One of the worst things is to allow them [the parents] to go ahead and give a name and tell everyone, and it turns out the child has to be raised in the opposite sex."[18]

Physicians feel that the mismanagement of such cases requires careful remedying. The psychoendocrinologist asserted, "When I'm involved, I spend hours with the parents to explain to them what has happened and how a mistake like that could be made, *or not really a mistake but a different decision*" (my emphasis). One pediatric endocrinologist said, "I try to dissuade them from previous misconceptions and say, 'Well, I know what they meant, but the way they said it confused you. This is, I think, a better way to think about it.'" These statements reveal physicians' efforts not only to protect parents from concluding that their child is neither male nor female or both, but also to protect other physicians' decision-making processes. Case management involves perpetuating the notion that good medical decisions are based on interpretations of the infant's real "sex" rather than on cultural understandings of gender.

"Mismanagements" are less likely to occur in communities with major medical centers where specialists are prepared to deal with intersexuality and a medical team (perhaps drawing physicians from more than one teaching hospital) can be quickly assembled. The team typically consists of the original referring doctor (obstetrician or pediatrician), a pediatric endocrinologist, a pediatric surgeon (urologist or gynecologist), and a geneticist. In addition, a psychologist, psychiatrist, or psychoendocrinologist might play a role. If an infant is born with ambiguous genitals in a small community hospital without the relevant specialists on staff, the baby is likely to be transferred to a hospital where diagnosis and treatment is available. Intersexed infants born in poor rural areas where there is less medical intervention might never be referred for genital reconstruction. Many of these children, like those born in earlier historical periods, will grow up and live through adulthood with the genital ambiguity—somehow managing.

The diagnosis of intersexed conditions includes assessing the chromosomal sex and the syndrome that produced the genital ambiguity and may include medical procedures such as cytologic screening; chromosomal analysis; assessing serum electrolytes; hormone, gonadotropin, and steroids evaluation; digital examination; and radiographic genitography.[19] In any intersexed condition, if the infant is determined to be a genetic female (having an XX chromosome makeup), then the treatment—genital surgery to reduce the phallus size—can proceed relatively quickly, satisfying what the doctors believe are psychological and cultural demands. For example, 21–hydroxylase deficiency, a form of female pseudohermaphroditism and one of the most common conditions, can be determined by a blood test within the first few days.

If, on the other hand, the infant is determined to have at least one Y chromosome, then surgery may be considerably delayed. A decision must be made whether to test the ability of the phallic tissue to respond to human chorionic gonadotropin (HCG), a treatment intended to enlarge the microphallus enough to be a penis. The endocrinologist explained, "You do HCG testing and you find out if the male can make testosterone. . . . You can get those results back probably within three weeks. . . . You're sure the male is making testosterone—but can he respond to it? It can take three months of waiting to see whether the phallus responds."

If the Y-chromosome infant cannot make testosterone or cannot respond to the testosterone it makes, the phallus will not develop, and the Y-chromosome infant will not be considered to be a male after all. Should the infant's phallus respond to the local application of testosterone or a brief course of intramuscular injections of low-potency androgen, the gender assignment problem is resolved, but possibly at some later cost, since the penis will not grow again at puberty when the rest of the body develops.[20] Money's case-management philosophy assumes that while it may be difficult for an adult male to have a much smaller than average penis, it is very detrimental to the morale of the young boy to have a micropenis.[21] In the former case, the male's manliness might be at stake, but in the latter case, his essential maleness might be. Although the psychological consequences of these experiences have not been empirically documented, Money and his colleagues suggest that it is wise to avoid the problems of both the micropenis in childhood and the still-undersized penis postpuberty by reassigning many of these infants to the female gender.[22] This approach suggests that for Money and his colleagues, chromosomes are less relevant in determining gender than penis size, and, by implication, that "male" is defined not by the genetic condition of having one Y and one X chromosome or by the production of sperm but by the aesthetic condition of having an "appropriately" sized penis.

The tests and procedures required for diagnosis (and consequently for gender assignment) can take several months.[23] Although physicians are anxious not to make premature gender assignments, their language suggests that it is difficult for them to take a completely neutral position and to think and speak only of *phallic tissue* that belongs to an infant whose gender has not yet been determined or decided. Comments such as "seeing whether the male can respond to testosterone" imply at least a tentative male gender assignment of an XY infant. The psychoendocrinologist's explanations to parents of their infant's treatment program also illustrates this implicit male gender assignment. "Clearly this baby has an underdeveloped phallus. But if the phallus responds to this treatment, we are fairly confident that surgical techniques and hormonal techniques will help this child to look like a boy. But we want to make absolutely sure and use some hormone treatments and see whether the tissue reacts." The mere fact that this doctor refers to the genitals as an "underdeveloped" phallus rather than an overdeveloped clitoris suggests that the infant has been judged to be, at least provisionally, a male. In the case of the undersized phallus, what is ambiguous is not whether this is a penis but whether it is "good enough" to remain one. If, at the end of the treatment period, the phallic tissue has not responded, what had been a potential penis (referred to in the medical literature as a "clitoropenis") is now considered an enlarged clitoris (or "penoclitoris"), and reconstructive surgery is planned as for the genetic female.

The time-consuming nature of intersex diagnosis and the assumption, based on the gender identity theory that gender be assigned as soon as possible thus present physicians with difficult dilemmas. Medical personnel are committed to discovering the etiology of the condition in order to determine the best course of treatment, which takes time. Yet they feel an urgent need to provide an immediate assignment and genitals that look and function appropriately. An immediate assignment that will need to be retracted is more problematic than a delayed assignment, since reassignment carries with it an additional set of social complications. The endocrinologist interviewed commented: "We've come very far in that we can diagnose, eventually, many of the conditions. But we haven't come far enough. . . . We can't do it early enough. . . . Very frequently a decision is made before all this information is available, simply because it takes so long to make the correct diagnosis. And you cannot let a child go indefinitely, not in this society you can't. . . . There's pressure on parents [for a decision], and the parents transmit that pressure onto physicians."

A pediatric endocrinologist agreed: "At times you may need to operate before a diagnosis can be made. . . . In one case parents were told to wait on the announcement while the infant was treated to see if the phallus would grow when treated with androgens. After the first month passed and there was some growth, the parents said they had given the child a boy's name. They could only wait a month."

Deliberating out loud on the judiciousness of making parents wait for assignment decisions, the endocrinologist asked rhetorically, "Why do we do all these tests if in the end we're going to make the decision simply on the basis of the appearance of the genitalia?" This question suggests that the principles underlying physicians' decisions are cultural rather than biological, based on parental reaction and the medical team's perception of the infant's societal adjustment prospects given the way the child's genitals look or could be made to look. Moreover, as long as the decision rests largely on the criterion of genital appearance, and male is defined as having a "good-sized" penis, more infants will be assigned to the female gender than the male.

The Waiting Period: Dealing with Ambiguity

During the period of ambiguity between birth and assignment, physicians not only must evaluate the infant's prospects of becoming a good male but also must manage the parents' uncertainty about a genderless child. Physicians advise that parents postpone announcing the gender of the infant until a gender has been explicitly assigned. They believe that parents should not feel compelled to disclose the baby's "sex" to other people. The clinical geneticist interviewed said that physicians "basically encourage them [parents] to treat it [the infant] as neuter." One of the pediatric endocrinologists reported that in France parents confronted with this dilemma sometimes give the infant a neuter name such as Claude. The psychoendocrinologist concurred: "If you have a truly borderline situation, and you want to make it dependent on the hormone treatment . . . then the parents are . . . told, 'Try not to make a decision. Refer to the baby as "baby." Don't think in terms of boy or girl.'" Yet, when asked whether this is a reasonable request to make of parents in our society, the physician answered: "I don't think so. I think parents can't do it."[24]

New York State requires that a birth certificate be filled out within forty-eight hours of delivery, but the certificate need not be filed with the state for thirty days. The geneticist tells parents to insert "child of" instead of a name. In one case, parents filled out two birth registration forms, one for each gender, and they refused to sign either until a final gender assignment had been made.[25] One of the pediatric endocrinologists claimed, "I heard a story, I don't know if it's true or not. There were parents of a hermaphroditic infant who told everyone they had twins, one of each gender. When the gender was determined, they said the other had died."

The geneticist explained that when directly asked by parents what to tell others about the gender of the infant, she says, "Why don't you just tell them that the baby is having problems and as soon as the problems are resolved we'll get back to you." A pediatric endocrinologist echoes this suggestion in advising parents to say, "Until the problem is solved, [we] would really prefer not to discuss any of the details." According to the urologist, "If [the gender] isn't announced, people may mutter about it and may grumble about it, but they haven't got anything to get their teeth into and make trouble over for the child, or the parents, or whatever." In short, parents are asked to sidestep the infant's gender rather than admit that the gender is unknown, thereby collaborating in a web of white lies, ellipses, and mystifications.[26]

Even as physicians teach parents how to deal with those who may not find the infant's condition comprehensible or acceptable, they also must make the condition comprehensible and acceptable to the parents, normalizing the intersexed condition for them. In doing so, they help the parents consider the infant's condition in the most positive way. There are four key aspects to this "normalizing" process.

First, physicians teach parents usual fetal development and explain that all fetuses have the potential to be male or female. One of the endocrinologists explains, "In the absence of maleness, you have femaleness. . . . It's really the basic design. The other [intersex] is really a variation on a theme." This explanation presents the intersex condition as a natural phase of fetal development. Another endocrinologist "like[s] to show picture[s] to them and explain that at a certain point in development males and females look alike and then diverge for such and such reason." The professional literature suggests that doctors use diagrams that illustrate "nature's principle of using the same anlagen to produce the external genital parts of the male and female."[27]

Second, physicians stress the normalcy of other aspects of the infant. For example, the geneticist tells parents, "The baby is healthy, but there was a problem in the way the baby was developing." The endocrinologist says the infant has "a mild defect, [which] just like anything could be considered a birth defect, a mole, or a hemangioma." This language not only eases the blow to the parents but also redirects their attention. Terms like "hermaphrodite" or "abnormal" are not used. The urologist said that he advised parents "about the generalization of sticking to the good things and not confusing people with something that is unnecessary."

Third, physicians (at least initially) imply that it is not the gender of the child that is ambiguous but the genitals. They talk about "undeveloped," "maldeveloped," or "unfinished" organs. From a number of the physicians interviewed came the following explanations:

At a point in time the development proceeded in a different way, and sometimes the development isn't complete and we may have some trouble . . . in determining what the *actual* sex is. And so we have to do a blood test to help us. (my emphasis)

The baby may be a female, which you would know after the buccal smear, but you can't prove it yet. If so, then it's a normal female with a different appearance. This can be surgically corrected.

The gender of your child isn't apparent to us at the moment.

While this looks like a small penis, it's actually a large clitoris. And what we're going to do is put it back in its proper position and reduce the size of the tip of it enough so it doesn't look funny, so it looks right.

Money and his colleagues report a case in which parents were advised to tell their friends that the reason their infant's gender was reannounced from male to female is that "the baby was . . . 'closed up down there.' [. . .] When the closed skin was divided, the female organs were revealed, and the baby discovered to be, *in fact*, a girl." (my emphasis) It was mistakenly assumed to be a male at first because "there was an excess of skin on the clitoris."[28]

The message in these examples is that the trouble lies in the doctor's ability to determine the gender, not in the baby's gender per se. The real gender will presumably be determined/proven by testing, and the "bad" genitals (which are confusing the situation for everyone) will be "repaired." The emphasis is not on the doctors' creating gender but in their completing the genitals. Physicians say that they "reconstruct" the genitals rather than "construct" them. The surgeons reconstitute from remaining parts what should have been there all along. The fact that gender in an infant is "reannounced" rather than "reassigned" suggests that the first announcement was a mistake because the announcer was confused by the genitals. The gender always was what it is now seen to be.[29]

Finally, physicians tell parents that social factors are more important in gender development than biological ones, even though they are searching for biological causes. In essence, the physicians teach the parents Money and Ehrhardt's theory of gender development.[30] In doing so, they shift the emphasis from the discovery of

biological factors that are a sign of the "real" gender to providing
the appropriate social conditions to produce the "real" gender. What
remains unsaid is the apparent contradiction in the assumption
that a "real" or "natural" gender can be or needs to be produced
artificially. The physician/parent discussions make it clear to family members that gender is not a biological given (even though, of
course, the physicians' own procedures for diagnosis assume that
it is) and that gender is fluid. The psychoendocrinologist para-
phrased an explanation to parents thus: "It will depend, ultimately,
on how everybody treats your child and how your child is looking
as a person. . . . I can with confidence tell them that generally gender [identity] clearly agrees with the assignment." A pediatric endocrinologist explained: "I try to impress upon them that there's
an enormous amount of clinical data to support the fact that if
you sex-reverse an infant . . . the majority of the time the alternative gender identity is commensurate with the socialization, the
way that they're raised, and how people view them, and that seems
to be the most critical."

The implication of these comments is that gender identity (of
all children, not just those born with ambiguous genitals) is determined primarily by social factors, that the parents and community always construct the child's gender. In the case of intersexed
infants, the physicians merely provide the right genitals to go along
with the socialization. Of course at so-called normal births, when
the infant's genitals are unambiguous, the parents are not told that
the child's gender is ultimately up to socialization. In those cases,
doctors do treat gender as a biological given.

Social Factors in Decision Making

Most of the physicians interviewed claimed that personal
convictions of doctors ought to play no role in the decision-making
process. The psychoendocrinologist explained:

> I think the most critical factors [are] what is the possibility
> that this child will grow up with genitals which look like that
> of the assigned gender and which will ultimately function
> according to gender. . . . That's why it's so important that it's
> a well-established team, because [personal convictions] can't
> really enter into it. It has to be what is surgically and
> endocrinologically possible for that baby to be able to make

it. . . . It's really much more within medical criteria. I don't
think many social factors enter into it.

While this doctor eschews the importance of social factors in gender assignment, she argues forcefully that social factors are extremely important in the development of gender identity. Indeed,
she implies that social factors primarily enter the picture once the
infant leaves the hospital.

In fact, doctors make decisions about gender on the basis of
shared cultural values that are unstated, perhaps even unconscious,
and therefore considered objective rather than subjective. Money
states the fundamental rule for gender assignment: "Never assign
a baby to be reared, and to surgical and hormonal therapy, as a boy,
unless the phallic structure, hypospadiac or otherwise, is neonatally of at least the same caliber as that of same-aged males with
small–average penises."[31] Elsewhere, he and his colleagues provide specific measurements for what qualifies as a micropenis: "A
penis is, by convention, designated as a micropenis when at birth
its dimensions are three or more standard deviations below the
mean. . . . When it is correspondingly reduced in diameter with
corpora that are vestigial, . . . it unquestionably qualifies as a micropenis."[32] A pediatric endocrinologist claimed that although "the
[size of the] phallus is not the deciding factor, . . . if the phallus is
less than two centimeters long at birth and won't respond to androgen treatments, then it's made into a female." There is no clearer
statement of the formula for gender assignment than the one given
by one well-published pediatric surgeon: "The decision to raise
the child with male pseudohermaphroditism as a male or female
is dictated entirely by the size of the phallus."[33]

These guidelines are clear, but they focus on only one physical feature, one that is distinctly imbued with cultural meaning.
This becomes especially apparent in the case of an XX infant with
normal female reproductive gonads and a "perfect" penis. Would
the size and shape of the penis, in this case, be the deciding factor
in assigning the infant as a "male," or would the "perfect" penis
be surgically destroyed and female genitals created? Money notes
that this dilemma would be complicated by the anticipated reaction of the parents to seeing "their apparent son lose his penis."[34]
Other researchers concur that parents are likely to want to raise a
child with a normal-shaped penis (regardless of size) as "male,"
particularly if the scrotal area looks normal and if the parents have

had no experience with intersexuality.[35] Elsewhere, Money argues
in favor of not neonatally amputating the penis of XX infants since
fetal masculinization of brain structures would predispose them
"almost invariably [to] develop behaviorally as tomboys, even when
reared as girls."[36] This reasoning implies first that tomboyish behavior in girls is bad and should be avoided and second that it is
preferable to remove the internal female organs, implant prosthetic
testes, and regulate the "boy's" hormones for his entire life than
to overlook or disregard the perfection of the penis.[37]

The ultimate proof to the physicians that they intervened appropriately and gave the intersexed infant the correct gender assignment is that the reconstructed genitals look normal and
function normally in adulthood. The vulva, labia, and clitoris
should appear ordinary to the woman and her partner(s), and the
vagina should be able to receive a normal-sized penis. Similarly,
the man and his partner(s) should feel that his penis (even if somewhat smaller than the norm) looks and functions in an unremarkable way. Although there are no published data on how much
emphasis the intersexed person, him- or herself, places upon genital appearance and functioning, physicians are absolutely clear
about what they believe is important. The clinical geneticist said,
"If you have . . . a seventeen-year-old young lady who has gotten
hormone therapy and has breast development and pubic hair and
no vaginal opening, I can't even entertain the notion that this young
lady wouldn't want to have corrective surgery." The urologist sum-
marized his criteria: "Happiness is the biggest factor. Anatomy is
part of happiness." Money states, "The primary deficit [of not having a sufficient penis]—and destroyer of morale—lies in being unable to satisfy the partner."[38] Another team of clinicians reveals
its phallocentrism and argues that the most serious mistake in
gender assignment is to create "an individual unable to engage in
genital [heterosexual] sex."[39]

The equation of gender with genitals could only have emerged
in an age when medical science can create genitals that appear to
be normal and to function adequately, and an emphasis on the
good phallus above all else could only have emerged in a culture
that has rigid aesthetic and performance criteria for what constitutes maleness. The formulation "Good penis equals male; absence of good penis equals female" is treated in the literature and
by the physicians interviewed as an objective criterion, operative
in all cases. There is a striking lack of attention to the size and

shape requirements of the female genitals, other than that the clitoris not be too big (see chapter 3) and that the vagina be able to receive a penis (see chapter 4).[40]

In the late nineteenth century, when women's reproductive function was culturally designated as their essential characteristic, the presence or absence of ovaries (whether or not they were fertile) was held to be the ultimate criterion of gender assignment for hermaphrodites. As recently as 1955, there was some concern that if people with the same chromosomes or gonads paired off, even if they had different genitals, that "might bring the physician in conflict with the law for abetting the pursuit of (technically) illegal sex practices."[41] The urologist interviewed recalled a case from that period of a male child reassigned to "female" at the age of four or five because ovaries had been discovered. Nevertheless, doctors today, schooled in the etiology and treatment of the various intersex syndromes, view decisions based primarily on chromosomes or gonads as wrong, although, they complain, the conviction that the presence of chromosomes or gonads is the ultimate criterion "still dictates the decisions of the uneducated and uninformed."[42] Presumably the educated and informed now know that decisions based primarily on phallic size, shape, and sexual capacity are right.

While the prospects of constructing good genitals is the primary consideration in physicians' gender assignments, another extramedical factor was repeatedly cited by the six physicians interviewed—the specialty of the attending physician. Although intersexed infants are generally treated by teams of specialists, only the person who coordinates the team is actually responsible for the case. This person, acknowledged by the other physicians as having chief responsibility, acts as spokesperson to the parents. Although all of the physicians claimed that these medical teams work smoothly, with few differences of opinion, several of them mentioned decision-making orientations that are grounded in particular medical specializations. One endocrinologist stated, "The easiest route to take, where there is ever any question, . . . is to raise the child as female. . . . In this country, that is usual if the infant falls into the hands of a pediatric endocrinologist. . . . If the decision is made by the urologists, who are mostly males, . . . they're always opting, because they do the surgery, they're always feeling they can correct anything." Another endocrinologist concurred: "[Most urologists] don't think in terms of dynamic processes. They're interested in fixing pipes and lengthening pipes, and not dealing with hormonal, and certainly not psychological issues. . . . 'What can I do with what I've got?'" Urologists were defended by the clinical geneticist: "Surgeons here, now I can't speak for elsewhere, they don't get into a situation where the child is a year old and they can't make anything."

Whether or not urologists "like to make boys," as one endocrinologist claimed, the following example from a urologist who was interviewed explicitly links a cultural interpretation of masculinity to the medical treatment plan. The case involved an adolescent who had been assigned the female gender at birth but was developing some male pubertal signs and wanted to be a boy. "He was ill-equipped," said the urologist, "yet we made a very respectable male out of him. He now owns a huge construction business—those big cranes that put stuff up on the building."

Postinfancy Case Management

After the infant's gender has been assigned, parents generally latch onto the assignment as the solution to the problem—and it is. The physician as detective has collected the evidence, as lawyer has presented the case, and as judge has rendered a verdict. Although most of the interviewees claimed that parents are equal participants in the whole process, they gave no instances of parental participation prior to the gender assignment.[43] After the physicians assign the infant's gender, the parents are encouraged to establish the credibility of that gender publicly by, for example, giving a detailed medical explanation to a leader in their community, such as a physician or pastor, who will explain the situation to curious, casual acquaintances. Money argues that "medical terminology has a special layman's magic in such a context; it is final and authoritative and closes the issue."[44] He also recommends that eventually the mother "settle [the] argument once and for all among her women friends by allowing some of them to see the baby's reconstructed genitalia." Apparently, the powerful influence of normal-looking genitals helps overcome a history of ambiguous gender.

Some of the same issues that arise in assigning gender recur some years later when, at adolescence, the child may be referred to a physician for counseling.[45] The physician then tells the adolescent many of the same things his or her parents had been told years before, with the same language. Terms like "abnormal," "disorder," "disease," and "hermaphroditism" are avoided; the condition is normalized and the child's gender is treated as unproblematic. One clinician explains to his patients that sex organs are different in appearance for each person, not just those who are intersexed. Furthermore, he tells the girls "that while most women menstruate, not all do . . . that conception is only one of a number of ways to become a parent; [and] that today some individuals are choosing not to become parents."[46] The clinical geneticist tells a typical female patient: "You are female. Female is not determined by your genes. Lots of other things determine being a woman. And you are a woman but you won't be able to have babies."

A case reported by one of the pediatric endocrinologists involving an adolescent female with androgen insensitivity provides an intriguing insight into the postinfancy gender-management process. She was told at the age of fourteen "that her ovaries weren't normal and had been removed. That's why she needed pills to look normal. . . . I wanted to convince her of her femininity. Then I told her she could marry and have normal sexual relations. . . . [Her] uterus won't develop but [she] could adopt children." The urologist interviewed was asked to comment on this handling of the counseling. "It sounds like a very good solution to it. He's stating the truth, and if you don't state the truth . . . then you're in trouble later." This is a strange version of "the truth," however, since the adolescent was chromosomally XY and was born with normal testes that produced normal quantities of androgen. There *were* no ovaries or uterus. Another pediatric endocrinologist, in commenting on the management of this case, hedged the issue by saying that he would have used a generic term like "the gonads." A third endocrinologist said she would say that the uterus had never formed.

Technically, these physicians are lying when, for example, they explain to an adolescent XY female with an intersexed history that her "ovaries . . . had to be removed because they were unhealthy or were producing 'the wrong balance of hormones.'"[47] We can presume that these lies are told in the service of what physicians consider a greater good—keeping individual/concrete genders as clear and uncontaminated as the notions of female and male are in the abstract. One clinician suggests that with some female patients it eventually may be possible to talk to them "about their gonads having some structures and features that are testicular-like."[48]

This call for honesty may be based, at least partly, on the possibility of the child's discovering his or her chromosomal sex inadvertently from a buccal smear taken in a high school biology class. Today's litigious climate may be another encouragement. In sum, the adolescent is typically told that certain internal organs did not form because of an endocrinological defect, not because those organs could never have developed in someone with her or his sex chromosomes. The topic of chromosomes is skirted. There are no published studies on how these adolescents experience their condition and their treatment by doctors. An endocrinologist interviewed mentioned that her adolescent patients rarely ask specifically what is wrong with them, suggesting that they are accomplices in this evasion. In spite of the "truth" having been evaded, the clinician's impression is that "their gender identities and general senses of well-being and self-esteem appear not to have suffered."[49]

Lessons from Intersex Management

Physicians conduct careful examinations of the intersexed infant's genitals and perform intricate laboratory procedures. They are interpreters of the body, trained and committed to uncovering the "actual" gender obscured by ambiguous genitals. Yet they also have considerable leeway in assigning gender, and their decisions are influenced by cultural as well as medical factors. What is the relationship between the physician as discoverer and the physician as determiner of gender? Where is the relative emphasis placed in discussions with parents and adolescents and in the consciousness of the physicians? It is misleading to characterize the doctors whose words are provided here as presenting themselves publicly to the parents as discoverers of the infant's real gender but privately acknowledging that the infant has no real gender other than the one being determined or constructed by the medical professionals. They are not hypocritical. It is also misleading to claim that the physicians' focus shifts from discovery to determination over the course of treatment: first the doctors regard the infant's gender as an unknown but discoverable reality; then the doctors relinquish their attempts to find the real gender and treat the infant's gender as something they must construct. They are not medically incompetent or deficient. Instead, I am arguing that the peculiar balance of discovery and determination throughout treatment permits physicians to handle very problematic cases of gender in the most unproblematic of ways. This balance relies fundamentally on a particular conception of "natural."[50] Although the "deformity" of intersexed genitals would be immutable were it not for medical interference, physicians do not consider it natural. Instead, they think of, and speak of, the surgical/hormonal alteration of such "deformities" as natural because such intervention returns the body to what it ought to have been if events had taken their typical course. The non-normative is converted into the normative, and the normative state is considered natural.[51] The genital ambiguity is remedied to conform to a "natural," that is, culturally indisputable gender dichotomy. Sherry Ortner's claim that the culture/nature distinction is itself a construction—a product of culture—is relevant here. Language and imagery help create and maintain a specific view of what is natural about the two genders, and I would argue, about the very idea of gender—that it consists of two exclusive types: female and male.[52] The belief that gender consists of two exclusive types is maintained and perpetuated by the medical community in the face of incontrovertible physical evidence that this is not mandated by biology.

The lay conception of human anatomy and physiology assumes a concordance among clearly dimorphic gender markers—chromosomes, genitals, gonads, hormones—but physicians understand that concordance and dimorphism do not always exist. Their understanding of biology's complexity, however, does not inform their understanding of gender's complexity. In order for intersexuality to be managed differently than it currently is, physicians would have to take seriously Money's assertion that it is a misrepresentation of epistemology to consider any cell in the body authentically male or female.[53] If authenticity for gender resides not in a discoverable nature but in someone's proclamation, then the power to proclaim something else is available. If physicians recognized that implicit in their management of gender is the notion that finally, and always, people construct gender, as well as the social systems that are grounded in gender-based concepts, the possibilities for real societal transformations would be unlimited. Unfortunately, neither in their representations to the families of the intersexed nor among themselves do the physicians interviewed for this study draw such far-reaching implications from their work. Their "understanding" that particular genders are medically (re)constructed in these cases does not lead them to see that gender is *always* constructed. Accepting genital ambiguity as a natural option would require that physicians also acknowledge that genital ambiguity is "corrected," not because it is threatening to the infant's life but because it is threatening to the infant's culture.

Rather than admit to their role in perpetuating gender, physicians "psychologize" the issue by talking about the parents' anxiety and humiliation in being confronted with an anomalous infant. They talk as though they have no choice but to respond to the parents' pressure for a resolution of psychological discomfort and as though they have no choice but to use medical technology in the service of a two-gender culture. Neither the psychology nor the technology is doubted, since both shield physicians from responsibility. Indeed, for the most part, neither physicians nor parents emerge from the experience of intersex case management with a greater understanding of the social construction of gender. Society's accountability, like their own, is masked by the assumption that gender is a given. Thus, the medical management of intersexuality, instead of illustrating nature's failure to ordain gender in these isolated, "unfortunate" instances, illustrates physicians' and Western society's failure of imagination—the failure to imagine that each of their management decisions is a moment when a specific instance of biological "sex" is transformed into a culturally constructed gender.

Most people assume that the boundary between "female" and "male" is clear. But is the boundary between female and male genitals so obvious that when physicians encounter a "problem" genital they know it? Would anyone know it? What is never directly addressed in the intersexuality management literature is how easy or difficult it is to recognize ambiguous genitals. Once physicians see ambiguous genitals, what feelings are evoked, and what means are at physicians' disposal to "correct" the "problem"? These are questions I will consider in the next chapter.

3

Defining and

Producing

Genitals

Obstetricians do not stand at the delivery table with ruler in hand, comparing the genitals they see with a table of values.[1] They seem to know ambiguity when they see it. In the medical literature on intersexuality, where physicians communicate their findings and their assumptions, the phrase, "ambiguous genitals" is used freely with no apparent need to define what "ambiguous" means in this context. One could say that ambiguous genitals are described ambiguously. It is not uncommon to read statements like, "Their [intersexed] external genitals look much more like a clitoris and labia than a penis or scrotum."[2] One surgeon writes, without further specification, that the tip of the phallus should be the "expected size for the patient's age."[3] Another states that the need for surgery "must be judged on the basis of the size of the shaft and glans of the clitoris in relation to the size of the patient and the interrelationship of the labia, mons veneris, and pubis."[4]

One way to interpret this vagueness is that the ambiguity is so obvious that a physician who has seen scores of genitals has no need to validate the obvious. But the nonmedical reader is left wondering to what extent genitals must be ambiguous before they are seen to be in need of "correction." There are, of course, normative data on genital size, shape, and location,[5] but I will delay a discussion of specifications in order to consider the meaning of genital variations for physicians, as projected through their justifications for surgery and their descriptions of aberrant genitals.

Genital Intolerance

Physicians describe all genital surgery on intersexed infants as necessary. Yet there are at least three categories of distinguishable genital surgery:

1. that which is *lifesaving*—for example, a urethra is rerouted so that the infant can pass urine out of his or her body;
2. that which *improves the quality of life*—for example, the urethral opening is redesigned so that a child can eventually urinate without spraying urine on the toilet seat; and
3. that which is *aesthetic*—for example, the small penis is augmented so that the (eventual) man will feel that he looks more manly.

Nowhere in the medical literature on intersexuality are these different motivations alluded to.[6] In fact, although variant genitals rarely pose a threat to the child's life, the postdelivery situation is referred to as a "neonatal psychosexual emergency," seeming to require life-saving intervention.[7]

Few arguments are put forth in defense of performing surgery on intersexed infants. When pressed for a reason, physicians assert that "normal" genitals will maximize the child's social adjustment and acceptance by the families. Physicians claim they are acting in the interest of parents, who are motivated by a desire to protect their child from teasing.

Teasing is not an insignificant construct in theories about gender. Philosopher Ellen Feder exposes the way psychiatry uses testimony about teasing not only to justify treatment of Gender Identity Disorder in children but also to define it. Feder notes that what alarms teachers and parents about a child's cross-gender behavior is not the behavior per se but the other children's reactions to it. Teasing and name-calling are one of the manifest symptoms of child gender disturbance. Children on the playground are treated "as a kind of natural tribunal," and the medical profession imbues this with authority, rather than treating the teasing and the institutions that tolerate it as in need of correction.[8] Obviously, the same could be said of the management of intersex. Much is made of the possibility of teasing, but documentation is not provided for how teasing has negatively impacted those rare people whose intersexed genitals were not "surgicalized." Nor is there a discussion in the medical literature about procedures for counteracting (or curing) the teasing.

One endocrinologist and intersex specialist, in defending current practices, says that not doing surgery would be unacceptable to parents because "some of the prejudices run very deep."[9] Implicit in this defense is that the genitals themselves carry the burden of evoking acceptance. There is no sense that the burden is or ought to be on people to learn to accept the genitals. As one intersexual said, "It's difficult to be Black in this culture, too, but we don't bleach the skin of Black babies."[10]

An argument for surgery that is grounded in prejudice overlooks the fact that many bodily related prejudices have been moderated. More people than ever before discuss their cancer histories in public, are open about their AIDS status, and admit to having had an abortion. These changes have required a different way of talking, and it can be argued that the mere fact of talking differently has helped create changes in the way people think about cancer, AIDS, and abortion. Rather than assuming that physicians (like anyone else) are primarily motivated by greed and the power to impose their definitions on the ignorant, we could be more generous and assume that they (like anyone else) find it difficult to imagine new ways of talking in familiar situations. In chapter 6, I propose some new ways for physicians to talk differently about intersexuality, predicated on more comfortable attitudes about variant genitals.

Current attitudes about variant genitals are embedded (not too deeply) in medical reports and offer insight into the late-twentieth-century medical management of intersexuality. Feelings about larger-than-typical clitorises are illustrated by these representative quotations (my emphasis):

> The excision of a hypertrophied clitoris is to be preferred over allowing a *disfiguring and embarrassing* phallic structure to remain.[11]

> The anatomic *derangements* [were] surgically corrected. . . . Surgical techniques . . . remedy the *deformed* external genitals. . . . [E]ven patients who suffered from major clitoral *overgrowth* have responded well. . . . [P]atients born with *obtrusive* clitoromegaly have been encountered. . . . [N]ine females had persistent phallic enlargement that was *embarrassing* or

offensive and incompatible with satisfactory feminine presentation or adjustment. [After] surgery no prepubertal girl . . . described *troublesome* or painful erections.[12]

Female babies born with an *ungainly* masculine enlargement of the clitoris evoke grave concern in their parents. . . . [The new clitoroplasty technique] allow[s] erection without cosmetic *offense*.[13]

Failure to [reduce the glans and shaft] will leave a button of *unsightly tissue*.[14]

[Another surgeon] has suggested . . . total elimination of the *offending* shaft of the clitoris.[15]

[A particular surgical technique] can be included as part of the procedure when the size of the glans is *challenging* to a feminine cosmetic result.[16]

These descriptions suggest not only that there is a size and malformation problem but that there is an aesthetic and moral violation. The language is emotional. Researchers seem disgusted. The early items on the list suggest that the large clitoris is imperfect and ugly. The later items suggest more of a personal affront. Perhaps the last item says it most transparently: the clitoris is "challenging."[17]

A social psychologist should ask: How were embarrassment and offense displayed? If the clitoris is troubling, offending, and embarrassing, who exactly is troubled, offended, and embarrassed and why? Not only are these questions not answered by intersex specialists, they are not even asked. A comment from an intersexed adult woman about her childhood is a relevant counterpoint: "I experienced the behavior of virtually everyone towards me as absolutely dishonest, embarrassing." Her comment reminds us that objects in the world (even non-normative organs) are not embarrassing; rather, people's reactions to them are. Another intersexual woman's "uncorrected" clitoris was described by her sexual partner as "easy to find."[18] Whether a clitoris is easy to find is arguably of some importance in sexual interactions, but it is not a criterion that physicians use for determining the suitable size for a clitoris.

An unexceptional quotation about the clitoris further substantiates the physicians' attitude:

The clitoris is not essential for *adequate* sexual function and sexual *gratification* ... but its preservation would seem to be *desirable* if achieved while maintaining *satisfactory* appearance and function. ... Yet the clitoris clearly has a relation to erotic stimulation and to sexual gratification and its presence is desirable, even in patients with intersexed anomalies if that presence does not interfere with *cosmetic, psychological, social and sexual* adjustment.[19] (my emphases)

Using my emphases as a guide, the alert reader should have some questions about the above quotation: Is "adequate sexual function" the same as "gratification"? If not, then which refers to the ability to orgasm? Why is the presence of the clitoris only desirable if it maintains a satisfactory appearance (whatever that is) and does not interfere? Lastly, how are the four different adjustments assessed and ranked, and is the order accidental?

Compared to language describing the larger-than-average clitoris, the language describing the small penis is less emotional but no less laden with value judgments. Common descriptors for the small penis are "short, buried, and anomalous." Sometimes there is a discussion about whether the microphallus is normally proportioned or whether it has a *"feminine stigmata* typical of intersexuality" indicative of *"arrested (feminine) development"*[20] (my emphases).

The emotionality in the case of the small penis is reserved for the child "who cannot be a boy with this insignificant organ. . . . They *must* be raised as females. . . . They are *doomed* to life as a male without a penis."[21] This last quotation suggests, as I showed in chapter 2, that if the penis is small enough, some physicians treat it as though it does not actually exist. Given its size, it does not qualify as a penis, and therefore the child does not qualify as a boy. "Experience has shown that the most *heartbreaking* maladjustment attends those patients who have been raised as males in the vain hope that the penis will grow to a more masculine appearance and size 'at a later date'"[22] (my emphases).

Physicians do not question whether a large clitoris ill prepares a girl for the female role. The emphasis is more on its ugliness. In contrast, physicians' descriptions of the micropenis are tied quite explicitly to gender role (my emphases): "Is the size of the phallus ... *adequate* to support a male sex assignment? [If not], those patients [regardless of genotype] are *unsuited* for the masculine role."[23] A ten-year-old boy (with a microphallus) considering sex change was given testosterone ointment, after which he *"reaffirmed his allegiance to things masculine."*[24] "The sexual identification of the patients by their parents seemed less ambiguous following [testosterone] treatment, and the parents encouraged *more appropriate male behavior* in the patients following treatment."[25] "After Barbara's sixteenth birthday, her penis developed erections, she produced ejaculations, and she found herself feeling a *sexual interest in girls."*[26]

The penis needs to be large enough to support masculinity (in the eyes of the parents and the child). If it is really a penis, it will push the child toward the "male" gender role, even, as the last example shows, if the child is a girl.

Given the pejorative language used to portray the large clitoris, and the pitying language applied to the child with the small penis, it is not surprising that genital surgery in these cases is described as necessary. It is affirmed as necessary, though, not because anyone (or any one profession) has deemed it so but because the genital, itself, requires the improvement. The quotations below (my emphases) establish that the organ carries the message itself; there is no messenger:[27]

> Given that the clitoris *must* be reduced, what is the best way to do it?[28]

> When the female sex is assigned, an operation on the clitoris together with other *necessary* procedures to modify the genitalia becomes *necessary* for the establishment of proper psychological and social adjustment.[29]

> The size of an enlarged clitoris *demanding* clitorectomy cannot be stated in exact measurements.[30]

> The child with hypertrophy of the clitoris will *require* corrective surgery to achieve an acceptable functional and cosmetic result.[31]

Where does the clitoris get its right to demand reduction? Presumably from nature. If it is an affront to nature, it is understandable why the language used to describe it is so emotional. Unlike the large clitoris, which is too big for its own good, the micropenis is too small for its own good and "demands" to be made into a clitoris. However, although it is widely assumed that men with micropenises are unhappy—and should these men be lucky enough to have female partners, they, too, will be unhappy—there is evidence to the contrary.[32] The physicians' assertion that penises of insufficient length are "inadequate" implies that penises that fall within the measurement range are adequate. Adequacy as a physical measurement rather than an interpersonal negotiation is a neat way of side-stepping a difficult social-psychological determination. (It is probably not irrelevant that the vast majority of genital surgeons are male.)

To summarize, the medical point of view is that large clitorises and small penises are wrong and need to be, in the words of medical management, "corrected."[33] The term "correction" not only has a surgical connotation but a disciplinary one as well.[34] In this, as in all important enterprises, words matter. An intersexed woman chastised me for the title of a paper I wrote, "Creating Good Looking Genitals in the Service of Gender."[35] "Fact is," she said, "they don't create, they destroy."

Who has the power to name? Physicians talk about "medical advancements in surgical correction," but some people subjected to such surgeries (as I will discuss in chapter 5) refer to them as "genital mutilations." Those opposed to male circumcision contribute to the argument about the power to name genital interventions. They refer to the penis with a foreskin as the penis in its natural, *intact* state and write about circumcision as *amputation*. In their graphic descriptions, they refer to the *"stripping* of the glans" and even *"skinning* the infant penis alive" (my emphases), instead of the benign "snipping" of the foreskin. If, as happens on rare occasion, a male is born without a foreskin, it is noted in his records as a birth defect called aposthia, suggesting that the foreskin should have been there all along. It is a peculiar body part that should have been there only to be removed. Why, too, does the medical profession refer to the natural bonds between the foreskin and the glans of the newborn as "adhesions," since the ordinary meaning of adhesions is "unwanted and unhealthy attachments which often form during the healing process after surgery or injury"?[36] Why do physicians write about "a more natural appearance of a penis without the foreskin," when what they really mean is "nicer looking"?[37]

"Mutilation," a word we usually apply to other cultures, signals a distancing from and denigration of those cultures, and reinforces a sense of cultural superiority. One culture's mutilation is another's ritual. The manner in which intersex management is medically ritualized protects it from claims of mutilation until one moves outside the medical culture and takes a different perspective. Compare the terminology of medical professionals (top row) with that a medical outsider might use (bottom row):

Language Comparison

Presurgical genitals	Intervention	Postsurgical genitals
"deformed"	"create"	"corrected"/ "normal"
"intact"	"destroy"	"damaged"/ "unnatural"

Defining the Penis and Clitoris[38]

Before pursuing the issue of ambiguity, some details about genital specifications must be discussed. Most neonate penises range between 2.8 and 4.5 centimeters in length and .9 and 1.3 centimeters in width.[39] The median length is about 3.5 centimeters.[40] Although there is some discussion in the literature about how penile measurements should be made (flaccid, stretched, or erect), the consensus is that flaccid penile lengths vary too much and therefore are not a reliable measure, and that there is a correlation between the fully stretched penis and the erect length.[41]

Standards for penile diameter or circumference also depend on whether the penis is measured relaxed, erect, or stretched. Because penile diameter is not a reliable measure, the definition of normal sized is based on length, not width, although the two are correlated. Usually, the shorter the penis, the smaller the diameter of the shaft and the shorter the overall body length.[42] One researcher is exceptionally clear about why it is necessary to have genital norms: "There is no need to stress the importance of having mean values and [a] range of measurements of normal genitals in the newborn infant. These can be most helpful in those cases in which the infant is suspected of having genitals of abnormal size."[43]

When is a penis too small? "A micropenis is . . . defined as having a stretched length of less than two and a half standard deviations below the mean for age or stage of sexual development." Statistically, any measurement that falls more than two and a half standard deviations below the mean is smaller than 99.4 percent of a normally distributed population.[44]

In general, medical standards permit infant penises as small as 2.5 centimeters (about one inch) to mark maleness, but usually not smaller. One influential and highly published surgeon writes that she is concerned about penises that are smaller than 2.0 centimeters at birth, and she reassigns the infant to the female gender if the phallus (no longer a penis) is less than 1.5 cm. long and .7 wide. She believes that a male infant needs a penis of a certain size in order to be accepted by family and peers. Yet she believes that infants with a form of pseudohermaphroditism known as 5–alpha-reductase deficiency should be raised as males, in spite of the fact that their penises are not "male-like" at birth and will not become "male-like" until puberty.[45] Clearly, to accept a small penis in this case, it is only necessary that the physician and the family expect that the infant will eventually have a penis of the proper size. If the parents of children with 5–alpha-reductase deficiency are capable of ignoring the materiality of their child's genitals in the anticipation of ones that more customarily match the child's gender assignment, why could not *most* parents? I will consider in a later chapter the implications of some parents being able to reinterpret the meaning of their infant's genitals and some physicians justifying early surgery on the basis of the parents' assumed inability to tolerate atypical genitals.

A micropenis is not simply a small phallus. By some criteria, it must have a urethra and a meatus.[46] According to this definition, a phallus without a urethral tube, *no matter what the size*, is a clitoris. One exception to this rule, which makes the rule clearly a social construct and not a law of nature, is the penis created for the female-to-male transsexual. Surgeons perform a technique called "metoidioplasty," which transforms the transsexual's clitoris into a penis by first treating it with testosterone and then "severing the suspensory ligaments that hold the clitoris in a position tucked under the pubic bone." This is followed by repositioning the clitoral crura forward and covering the exposed tissue with a flap of abdominal skin.[47] The result is a reasonable-looking penis, yet one that would have been considered unacceptably small by physicians if it were to have developed naturally on an XY person. The transsexual is capable of having erections and orgasms but cannot urinate through this penis, as the urethra is not rerouted. (Although being able to urinate in a standing position is the rationale for performing most penile surgeries [see chapter 4], this is apparently not a requirement for transsexual men.) This distinction illustrates a point I have been making: that what counts as a "definitive" gender marker varies with context and that these variations are typically permitted to "pass" with little acknowledgment of gender's constructed nature.

Not only is the fact of a urinary outlet on the glans of the penis an issue, its location on the glans is of critical importance to urologists. The "normal" penis is described as one with a meatus in the center of the glans. The "normalcy" of this location is drawn into question by a study that measured the meatal location in 500 men who had never had penile surgery and had been admitted to a hospital for the treatment of prostate and bladder conditions.[48] Only 55 percent of the men in this sample had a meatus located at the tip—where it supposedly belongs. The authors of the study recognize that surgery might not be necessary for many males whose meatus is not in the "desired location," but they do not pursue the deeper issue of who desired this location and why.

Penises with the meatus not in this location are referred to as "hypospadiac." If the hypospadias is "minor," the meatus is merely off center or on the underside of the glans; if major, the meatus might be a larger-than-usual opening underneath the penile shaft. John Money refers to this as an "open gutter" in the "female position."[49] In the most severe cases, the urethra is entirely absent. Although hypospadias is estimated as occurring in one in every 200 male births, it is much more rarely (one in 10,000 births) a sign of an underlying intersex condition.[50] Technically, the diagnosis of hypospadias is made only if the infant's scrotum is fused and contains both testes—in other words, if the infant has already been determined to be 100 percent male.

As I explained in chapter 2, intersex managers operate as though size were the only critical feature in categorizing the phallus and assigning gender. Whether one categorizes penises and clitorises according to size or urethral tubing and meatal position is arbitrary, but using the urethral tube and meatus standard might help parents accept daughters with large clitorises. (In the last chapter, I will suggest other ways to help parents understand their children's atypical genitals.)

In spite of one writer saying, "The size of an enlarged clitoris . . . cannot be stated in exact measurements,"[51] there are published norms for the clitorises of fetuses, infants, and adults.[52] This was not always so. A 1916 medical text gives size ranges for the penis and testicle, but not for the clitoris.[53] Tables of normative clitoral values appeared only in the late 1980s, more than forty

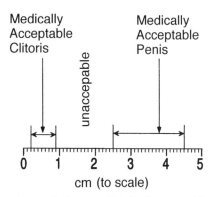

Medically Acceptable Clitoris

Medically Acceptable Penis

unaccepable

0 1 2 3 4 5

cm (to scale)

Figure 1. Ranges of Medically Acceptable Infant Clitoral and Penile Lengths

years after similar values for penile sizes.[54] In one contemporary report, the clitoral length of eighty-two neonates ranged from .2 to .85 centimeters, and the clitoral width ranged from .2 to .6 centimeters.[55] Some researchers factor length and width to compute a "clitoral index."[56] A clitoral index comparison of "normal" infants and those with a form of intersexuality called congenital adrenal hyperplasia (CAH) noted measurements over nine times greater among the infants with CAH.[57]

How big must a clitoris be before physicians decide it is too large? In one study, infant clitorises that were reduced ranged from 1.5 centimeters to 3.5 centimeters prior to surgery.[58] In spite of there being a table of standards, physicians are more likely to refer to the average clitoris in food terminology, such as a pea or small bean.[59] In general, medical standards do not allow clitorises larger than .9 centimeters (about 3/8 of an inch). Figure 1 indicates standard clitoral and penile lengths for infants, revealing that intermediate area of phallic length that neither females nor males are permitted to have.

Not all pediatric surgeons who treat the intersexed are aware that there are published guidelines for clitoral size. One physician who has operated on intersexed infants for over twenty years was not—he told an interviewer that "overall appearance is most important."[60] We can only speculate about whether greater dissemination of information about the normal range for clitoral size would increase or decrease the number of clitoral reductions. Some have argued that universal standards would permit more "consistent guidelines for gender assignment,"[61] but it seems likely that if clitoral sizes are publicized and treated as guidelines, even more surgeries will be performed. Perhaps without a standardized set of ranges, physicians have been accepting more variability. I will explore these possibilities further in the last chapter, where I discuss the future of genital surgery.

Unlike the reluctance of medical personnel to wait and see if the girl "grows into" her clitoris, nature is more likely to be permitted to run its course in terms of the labia. For example, if the prepuce adheres to the clitoris of a small child, this is not considered to be of clinical significance, since it is assumed that separation will occur spontaneously with androgen production at puberty. "An attempt to strip the prepuce from the underlying tissues is not only meddlesome but painful."[62]

Despite the fact that the degree of labial-scrotal fusion is an important criterion for determining that genitals are ambiguous, there is scant discussion in the medical literature of how "normal" labia and scrotum ought to look. Unlike the relatively narrow standards for clitoral size, labial variation seems to be more permissible.[63] Texts say that the labia should not be completely fused, but a minor degree of posterior fusion is tolerable, and the labia majora are not required to completely cover the minora. Even a hundred years ago, medical texts acknowledged labia variability: "The extension backward of the labia minora varies very much. In some women they go back to the middle line, so as to form a complete ring inside of that formed by the labia majora. In others they do not even reach the level of the meatus urinarius."[64]

Looking at Genitals with Expectations

Ambiguity is at least partially determined by factors such as who is looking, why they are looking, and how hard they are looking. Intersex specialists warn against jumping to conclusions about what is there and what is not.[65] For example, physicians are cautioned about using testosterone in "treating [an] infant or young boy with a normal-size penis which *appears* [my emphasis] small because it is partially buried in the prepubic fat pad."[66]

How hard one "looks" at genitals and what one "sees" is not constrained by the optic nerve but by ideology. Given gender socialization, boys probably look at each others' genitals more than girls do. This is not because boys' genitals are objectively more obvious than girls' but because "male" genitals have a different sociological import.[67]

Not all parts of "male" genitals are equally important. The cultural meaning of the penis so overshadows the scrotum (fused or not and filled or not) as a gender marker, that scrotal "imperfection" is generally irrelevant. A writer who interviewed Roger Gorski, a physician/researcher at the University of California, Los Angeles, reported that Gorski showed him a close-up photograph of a child's genitals and asked, "What sex is it?" The writer, seeing a penis "plain as day," said confidently that it was a boy. "Gorski's eyebrows shot up. 'Where are the testicles?' he asked. I looked closer. Oops."[68] Gorski was using the photograph to show how the genitals of a genetic female with CAH can be affected, but the example illustrates as well how the average (nonmedical) person, even one who is interviewing a doctor about genitals and gender, can accept a missing scrotum as reasonable.

What one sees when one looks at a clitoris betrays as much about the viewer's assumptions as about the clitoris. One urologist, who was adamant about the need to reduce a girl's larger-than-typical clitoris, told a reporter that he worried about the effects on her when the girl's parents and caregivers saw her spend her early life with *"a big huge phallus in the lower end of the abdomen."*[69] Readers will recall that this "enormity" is likely to be about an inch in length. The atypical clitoris, as it is photographed for medical texts (brightly lit in a tight "close-up," with the labia held wide apart), is more conspicuous than it might otherwise seem—certainly more than it is in almost all real-life circumstances.

The fact that "looking" matters is supported by the invention of a surgical technique that involves recessing the enlarged clitoris beneath the labia so that it can no longer be seen. As I will discuss later in this chapter, one problem with this technique is that the "buried" clitoris swells during sexual arousal and produces a painful erection. At what cost is the clitoris required to be an internal organ? In older drawings of the female organs, the clitoris is portrayed as internal, like the bladder, uterus, and cervix.[70] More recent sketches treat it as an external part of the genitals.[71] Clitorises are not protruding more than they used to. Rather, public discussions of female sexuality in the last thirty years have helped evolve a public meaning for the clitoris.

Labia, in contrast, do not (yet) have much of a public role in

Western cultures. The less delineated and meaningful a body part is, the more variability is tolerated. One surgeon who does genital reconstruction for women who have had genital cancers believes that

> if one expects to see something and what one sees falls into that realm, then the mind says it's normal. . . . In genital reconstruction, there is usually only a labia majora made because people are not that sophisticated and require a labia minora, and that is much more difficult to construct. . . . You could fool most of the people most of the time. . . . [Patients] are unaware that if they don't have [a labia minora] it's not normal. And their partners, male or female, are not that sophisticated to see that they're missing it. M. Butterfly is a perfect example. . . . If you can give someone a hair escutcheon— the triangular shape—and you can give someone lips that provide a certain fullness, and a vagina, then you have accomplished a tremendous amount. . . . Most of them are thrilled to not only have the function but the appearance that to them looks like someone they've seen in a locker room or looks like a picture they've seen in a magazine.[72]

How much of the physician's deemphasis of the labia minora is due to current surgical limitations, and how much to the assumption "out of sight, out of mind," is left to speculation. It is obvious, though, that looking at labia in this way, much like an everyday person, and not as someone with stringent "ideals," promotes a degree of tolerance not extended to other genital parts but that might serve as a model for how to think about them. In chapter 6, I suggest that Western culture's lack of interest in the labia minora (in contrast to the meaningful and damaging interest given them in some African and Middle Eastern cultures) might be drawing to an end.

Types of Surgical Procedures for Unacceptable Genitals

One problem with analyzing intersex management as an example of the *social* construction of gender is that the *surgical* construction of gender is overlooked. As social constructionists, we can successfully show how "females" and "males" are created through rules for seeing gender, but we have not grappled with a more material issue. Concretely, in what ways does the medical profession strive to produce "female" and "male" genitals? Before describing some surgical techniques, I will define some relevant terms.

"Genitoplasty" is any surgery on the genitals. The terms "clitoroplasty" and "phalloplasty" refer to a number of different techniques involving surgery on the phallic tissue. If the infant is given a female gender assignment, either term might be used, but if the infant is given a male gender assignment, only the term phalloplasty is applied. Clitoroplasty is often accompanied by "monsplasty" or "labioplasty," surgery on the labial-scrotal tissue.

There are different clitoral surgical options and no medical consensus on how much of the enlarged clitoris need be removed by a variety of "trimming and wedging techniques" in order to make it a "suitable" size.[73] Some physicians argue for amputation of all erectile tissue ("clitoridectomy" or "clitorectomy"), claiming that retention of even just the glans is complicated by tissue sloughing.[74] Those in favor of this complete extirpation claim that to do less is a halfway measure "because this allows the bulk of the clitoral shaft and both corporal extensions to remain (and) . . . such tissue can become turgid and painful."[75] A medical justification is not always offered; sometimes the physician recommends clitoridectomy only because it produces a more satisfactory appearance.[76]

Within the last twenty years, those who are opposed to clitoridectomies have developed other techniques, "clitoral reductions" or "resections."[77] One procedure developed by Judson Randolph and his associates attempts to preserve erectile tissue when the elongated shaft is excised and the reserved glans is grafted onto the stump.[78] Modifications of these procedures continued into the 1980s.[79]

More recently, surgeons have developed a technique whereby a cut is made through the midline of the clitoris, and outer tissue is spread back to form the labia.[80] The clitoris is sutured to the pubic bone, and it retains its blood supply and nerve function. Surgeons using electrodes in the operating room to measure nerve impulses in the clitoris claim that sensation is preserved with this technique. As I will discuss below, critics question what this actually means in terms of the intersexed person's experience.

Some clitoroplasty techniques do not involve amputation of any part of the clitoris. In 1961, John Lattimer developed a procedure called "clitoral recession," which reduces the apparent size of the enlarged clitoris by "burying the erectile shaft" under a fold of skin so that only the glans is visible.[81] There are reports in the medical literature of the recession failing to produce a sufficiently small clitoris and the patient eventually requiring clitoral amputation.[82] "In an(other) apparent attempt to avoid pubic bulging," "clitoral plication," or a folding of the clitoral shaft, was proposed.[83] Like the recession technique, this kind of procedure is said to be better suited for relatively mild cases of clitoromegaly (enlarged clitoris).

How is it determined which of the various clitoroplasty procedures will be used? Randolph regrets that there are no size criteria by which clitoridectomy or one of the less severe operations is chosen.[84] Authors of a prestigious reference text caution that a decision on the type of clitoroplasty should not be made until "the clitoris reduce(s) in size to a definite, although limited, degree after the infant has been placed on an appropriate and adequate regimen of steroid replacement."[85]

These kinds of discussions make it appear that surgeons unhurriedly and rationally evaluate the individual infant's genital potential and all the surgical possibilities and then select the most appropriate course of action. It is more likely that they routinely carry out the procedures developed at their hospital or promoted as "standard" by their colleagues. One critic of intersex management reports that half a dozen intersex surgeons she spoke with in 1994 were uniformly ignorant of the Randolph technique. The Lattimer technique is more common at the hospital where it was developed, even though the surgeons admitted they had no long-term data on the procedure, explaining that "the surgery was too new, and humans take such a long time to reach sexual maturity."[86] The Lattimer technique was described in a 1961 issue of The Journal of Urology.[87]

Some intersexed females are born with incomplete, imperfect, or absent vaginas and undergo some kind of vaginoplasty to correct this. Vaginal anomalies range from what is considered the "mild end" of the spectrum—girls with a "low vagina"—to the "severe end"—a very high vagina located above the level of the external urethral sphincter.[88] A number of the different vaginoplasty techniques performed on intersexed girls were developed on male-to-female transsexuals.

The neovagina can be lined with either the girl's own skin

taken from another part of her body (e.g., abdomen, intestine, buttocks) or other biological material, for example placental membrane. Some methods take advantage of an internal cavity that
already exists, while others create a semiexternal sheath from partially sutured labia. As with clitoroplasties, the popularity of various vaginoplasty techniques varies by geographic locale.[89]

Debates regarding vaginoplasty are not just about which technique to use but when the surgery should be done—before the age
of two, in middle childhood, or even as late as puberty. More physicians are recognizing that there are good reasons to delay surgery until puberty, after the girl's pelvis has finished growing and
she is old enough to change dressings, dilate her vagina, and apply
topical estrogen cream daily in order to keep the vagina from clos-
ing up. Another advantage to delaying the surgery is that the
amount of dense scarring is reduced.[90]

In spite of these and other reasons to postpone vaginoplasty,
some surgeons are still advocating what is called a one-step or
"unified" procedure for infants: clitoroplasty, labioplasty, and vaginoplasty.[91] A typical rationale for vaginoplasty in the first few weeks
of life is: "The psychological advantage to the parents and children is enormous."[92] With no evidence supplied, the sense one
gets is that if the vagina is constructed before the girl reaches an
age of awareness, she will either never discover that she was not
born with a vagina (unlikely, given the lengthy dilation routine) or
be compensated by the surgically constructed vagina for the one
she was not born with.

As an alternative to surgery, some physicians advocate a nonsurgical method of expanding a vagina called "pressure dilation."
This involves the insertion of a solid plastic dilator into the vagina for fifteen minutes twice a day for months or years.[93] Some
children are dilated by their parents. Others, whose vaginas are
surgically reconstructed, are hospitalized once a year for dilation
until the age of fourteen.[94]

What about the males? Although there are phalloplasty techniques designed to increase the size of the penis and to improve
penises that are irregular (for example: bent, buried in an abnormally developed prepuce, or with the glans not proportional to the
shaft),[95] the most common type of penile surgeries are not for small
or misshapen penises but for those penises whose urethral opening
is not in the typical location—the center of the glans tip. For all
degrees of this condition, called "hypospadias," physicians

normally recommend one of many different surgical procedures.[96] Hypospadias, like genital "abnormalities" of the female, is described as "a surgical challenge, although it is routinely repaired with great success."[97]

Just how much success surgeons can claim is the subject of the next chapter, but before considering that, I want to discuss an issue that troubles philosophers more than physicians or people in everyday life—"realness." It is worth thinking about whether surgeons (even though they take their work seriously) believe they are making authentic genitals. The language they use, especially to refer to the construction of female genitals, is revealing (my emphases):"The complete absence of a vagina necessitates creative surgical reconstruction to *simulate a vagina.*"[98] The technique "produces tissue that *looks like labia.*"[99] Surgeons resection the enlarged phallus, "thereby reducing its size and recessing it in the mons to *resemble* a clitoris."[100] Use an interior flap of mucous membrane for fashioning a *"cosmetic clitoris"* which "is not expected to have any function."[101]

One male-to-female transsexual expresses her sense of genital inauthenticity when she says, "I find it hard to relate to having a vagina. I wonder if vaginoplasty is a purely cosmetic reshaping of the penis, which is not in any real way connected to a real vagina. Even when I hear about post-op orgasms I think, 'Is this just a male orgasm coming from a reconstructed penis?'"[102]

Although deficient, surgically constructed female genitals may have a genuineness that surgically constructed male genitals never will, perhaps because subtraction produces something more real than addition. Some physicians express themselves as though they believe that underneath all the female's genital tissue (in the shape of a phallus and scrotum) there are real labia and a clitoris struggling to emerge from the surgical knife. One surgeon in describing his technique makes it appear as though his role is to merely push and prod and help the rightful genitals emerge. "It is best to *strike a happy medium* and let the mucous membrane edge and skin edge *seek their own union* after *proper positioning* of the glans and skin have been *arranged*"[103] (my emphases). In contrast, the work of phalloplasty for both intersexed infants and transsexual adults is described as dreadfully difficult. In the case of female-to-male sex reassignment surgery, "there remains an implicit privileging of the phallus, a sense that a 'real one' can't be made, but only born."[104]

Undeniably, the act of surgery itself confers some amount of "realness." For reasons that deserve some analysis, body parts created by putting plastic inside the skin (for example, silicone breasts, vulva molds, or penile implants) are treated as more real than (without benefit of a surgeon) attaching the plastic outside the skin (for example, falsies or dildoes). At what point do surgically constructed genitals become real and not a mere resemblance or simulation? After the operation is concluded? After a diaper is changed and no questions are asked? After the genitals are used?

If intersex surgeries are routinely performed, even though there is an underlying suspicion that real ones cannot be made and even though the surgical consequences are far from ideal, the social constructionist is left with an even greater appreciation for the culture's interest in enforcing dichotomous gender with dimorphic genitals. By the end of the following chapter, readers should be asking what the cost is of the demand that genitals be made "normal."[105]

4

Evaluating

Genital

Surgery

"It is important that we as gynecologic surgeons know our surgical anatomy and the limits of our surgical armamentarium."

—Stephen H. Cruikshank, M.D., 1993

A baby was born in 1959 with an enlarged clitoris. She was named Laura. At puberty her voice began to deepen, and although she developed breasts, her clitoris grew. She kept the clitoral growth a secret from her parents, who considered her a tomboy. "Laura" is now an adult male named Larry. Larry computes that he has and always had more male characteristics (chromosomes and organs) than female, carefully emphasizing, "It's *not* that I was both sexes and I *decided* to be male" (his emphasis). He claims to have always felt like a male. Medical examinations revealed what he referred to as "underdeveloped gonads," and he asserts he was born with a penis and a vaginal orifice. As an adult, he has had over twenty genital surgeries to make his genitals look as male as possible, and he plans to have his urethra totally reconstructed. According to Larry, he can "function sexually" as a male, but is sterile.

Determining the success of intersex surgeries depends on how one weighs the various functions of genitals. As I explained in chapter 2, at birth genitals are for the purpose of assigning gender. In that sense they are for the physician and the parents. Later, genitals are for sexual pleasure and in that sense are for oneself and one's sexual partner. Very occasionally in adulthood, genitals are for reproduction and the perpetuation of the family and species. Inasmuch as genitals are treated as semipublic signs of maleness or femaleness, they are for identity development and social acceptance. Finally, given the relationship of sexual/reproductive and urinary structures, genitals are also for urination.

These biological and cultural functions of the genitals are not of equal or undisputed importance. Surgeons, given the authority to physically construct genitals, clearly weigh certain genital uses disproportionately. As I will show, criteria for success rest, at least partly, on assumptions about what and whom genitals are for. It will be evident that the consequences of surgeons' judgments are more than theoretical.

Evaluating Genital Surgery on Females

Surprisingly, in spite of the thousands of genital operations performed every year, there are no meta-analyses from within the medical community on levels of success. Surgeons describe, rather impressionistically, their own handful of patients not "lost to follow-up," and typically evaluate their own invented procedure, rarely comparing across procedures and never comparing results with a control sample—the intersexed who did not receive surgery. What makes it even more difficult to draw conclusions is that it is nearly impossible to tell across studies whether the same small group of patients at different ages is being discussed.

In spite of these difficulties, I reviewed twelve clitoroplasty and vaginoplasty follow-up studies published between 1974 and 1995.[1] Most reports were written by the developers of specific surgical techniques who also assessed the results of their own procedures. Others were independent comparisons of different surgical techniques.

In addition to examining the medical literature of follow-up studies on the success of intersex surgery, I am drawing upon three other sources:

1. reflections from adults who had been surgically "corrected" as children (in none of the follow-up studies is there any indication that a criterion for success includes the intersexed adult's reflection on his or her surgery);

2. conversations from transsexuals about their genital surgery; and
3. medical reports and interview data from physicians who treat women with genital cancers.

It is not easy to extract from the medical studies exactly what criteria are used to measure success. The language is so vague as to be mystifying: "[The surgery] yield[ed] an *acceptable* appearance and in most instances *satisfactory* sexual adjustment . . . leading to an *improved* psychologic base"[2] (my emphases). For whom is it acceptable? In what sense is the sexual adjustment satisfactory? How is improvement assessed and what is the comparison level or population? Physicians also write, "Complications have been minimal"[3] or "There were no deleterious psychological responses to the operation"[4] or "Most of these walking mosaics of sex manage to survive this adversity."[5] Even recent reports are susceptible to a criticism about vagueness: The clitoroplasty is a "relatively simple procedure [that] gave very good cosmetic results . . . and quite satisfactory functional results."[6] The reader searches in vain for any assessment by which that was determined.

The criteria that were repeatedly (albeit vaguely) mentioned can be grouped into four categories: clitoral appearance, clitoral sensitivity (sexual responsivity), vaginal size, and complications.[7]

Clitoral Appearance
How genitals look is not of trivial concern to surgeons. In fact, it is the first criterion mentioned in most of the reports. One surgeon evaluated anatomical results as "excellent" if there was a "normal or near normal anatomic appearance"; "satisfactory" if the "genital contours . . . are compatible with life as a female but [there was] . . . some degree of protrusion of the clitoris or some enlargement of the glans when the labia are retracted"; and "unsatisfactory" if the "persistent phallic enlargement . . . was embarrassing or offensive and incompatible with . . . feminine presentation or adjustment." Neither exact physical nor psychosocial measurements were offered.[8] (Over a fourth of the children in another sample required a second clitoroplasty in order to achieve even a satisfactory rating.)[9]

In their list of conclusions, the surgeons emphasize the importance of clitoral appearance by claiming that "most [patients] have made a satisfactory [psychological] adjustment if the anatomic appearance of the clitoris is perceived as acceptable." The authors, however, provide no evidence for this correlation, and a careful reading of the article in no way indicates that the girls themselves rated the clitoris's acceptability. In fact, the authors state that "most children were unaware of the nature or function of the clitoris and had little comprehension of the nature of their corrective surgery."[10]

What is considered passable anatomy, though, is occasionally peculiar. One group of surgeons writes, "Gross appearance of the external genitalia was *acceptable*, although on close examination the lack of the clitoris was obvious"[11] (my emphasis). (Similarly, in another study the eight patients who received clitoridectomies were rated as having "a satisfactory cosmetic result.")[12] An accompanying photograph of the vulva clearly missing a clitoris and labia minora is provided as evidence of this satisfactory result. Insofar as genitals are external and merely a public marker of gender, one might argue that the lack of a clitoris and labia minora is acceptable or satisfactory, at least to the surgeon, if not to the woman herself. This distinction is not addressed in the literature.

There is only a glimmer of recognition that surgeons may be inappropriately emphasizing cosmetic success. "It has become obvious to all workers in this field that sexual function and psychosocial adjustment are the main goals for these patients, rather than simple assessment of their genital appearance."[13]

Lest there be any doubt about whom the genitals are for, one team of researchers justifies doing surgery by saying that it "relieves parental anxiety about the child with relatives and friends."[14] Another surgical group is even more explicit in concluding that "for a small infant, the initial objective is an operation to feminize the appearance of the baby to make it acceptable to the parents and family."[15] It is not uncommon for follow-up reports to include the observation that "the parents were satisfied with the results of the genital surgery."[16]

Clitoral Sensitivity/Sexual Responsivity

Do the various genital surgeries preserve sexual responsivity? Although a criterion in most follow-up studies is "creat[ing] a clitoris with normal sensation," what this means is either not explicitly addressed or handled in a problematic way.[17] Throughout the decades of intersex surgeries, sexual responsivity has mainly been assessed by self-report. More recently, researchers have measured calibrated nerve-conduction responses to electrode stimulators.

What about self-reports? From the way the "results" are reported, it is difficult to ascertain the formality with which interviews were conducted, and one gets the sense that patient remarks were collected rather casually. Outcomes are mixed. One research group writes, "Adolescent girls who engaged in masturbation or sexual intercourse experienced enjoyable sensations. . . . All six of the young women who had engaged in sexual intercourse . . . reported achieving orgasm in response to clitoral stimulation."[18] Another's analysis of twelve clitoral revisions, all but one of which had been rated satisfactory in terms of appearance, revealed that in only five was erectile function and sexual gratification confirmed.[19]

Other researchers, who appear hesitant to ask their patients straightforward questions, display their naiveté when they describe why erotic response cannot be assessed: "[Some patients] of marriageable age are still single, and any relevant conclusion regarding the erotic response of the glans is hard to determine."[20]

One of the follow-up studies that Anne Fausto-Sterling and Bo Laurent analyzed indicated that "patients who have undergone [clitoridectomy] show ambivalence toward sexual activity as well as sexual inhibition."[21] In another study, the authors state, "It has been established that the clitoris is not necessary for *satisfactory sexual gratification*"[22] (my emphasis), leaving the reader to wonder if this is a euphemism for orgasm or whether it is a (poor) substitute for it.

John Money, in making decisions regarding whether to assign an intersexed infant as male or female, downplayed sexual responsivity as a criterion for females but not for males. "Although surgical intervention (to create a female) requires extensive resection of tissue, including reducing a grossly enlarged clitoris, erotic sensitivity, although perhaps lessened, is not lost and orgasm is typically possible later in life."[23] In arguing against assigning an XY intersexed infant to the male gender, Money says, "For an individual with this anomaly, the penis is too short for sexual intercourse, and its erectile response is inadequate. The fluid of ejaculation is minimal or absent. Pleasant erotic feeling is not missing, but it does not reach the full climactic peak of orgasm."[24]

Intersexed adults provide ample anecdotal evidence that their early genital surgery left them sexually impaired. Some report genital insensitivity and/or pain and many are unable to experience orgasm, but not all physicians are sympathetic: After examining an intersexed woman's genitals, one physician characterized them as "an area a couple of centimeters in diameter with no feeling and everything else is fine. You'll get someone to hold you nice and you'll be ok."[25]

What about physiological measurements? A recent study that measured pudendal-evoked potentials before and after erectile tissue from the enlarged clitoris had been removed touted the surgical procedure because it preserved nerve conduction in five of six intersexed infants. The authors were cautious in extrapolating from this finding when they said that the technique "*may* permit normal sexual function in adulthood"[26] (my emphasis).

Cheryl Chase, the founder of the Intersex Society of North America (ISNA), an organization that advocates less surgery for intersexed infants (and will be discussed in the next chapter), is not impressed by the new technology that demonstrates how clitoral nerve conduction is preserved. She cites the cases of intersexed women whose electrodiagnostic tests showed normal nerve firing, and yet they either have the complete absence of genital sensation and great difficulty reaching orgasm or intense genital pain following sexual stimulation. Chase points out that measurements of the pudendal nerve were obtained from infants during surgery before the wound was closed and that there is no follow-up data on whether the nerve remains intact during the process of healing. Because so much tissue is removed during the clitoral reduction, it is unlikely, believes Chase, that sensory receptors are intact.[27]

The authors of the paper reporting this "breakthrough" methodology defended themselves by making the obvious point that sexuality depends on social and emotional factors as well as anatomical ones and that even some women who have not had genital surgery are anorgasmic. They reiterated their original cautionary assertion, that although their technique preserves nerve conduction, it "does not guarantee normal adult sexual function."[28]

Some of the technical problems of clitoroplasties and vaginoplasties for intersexed infants are relevant for women with genital cancers.[29] Although, for these women, gender is not problematic, medical criteria for successful surgery, as in the intersexed cases, reflect cultural values about the importance of genitals and what constitutes legitimate femaleness.

Inasmuch as physicians who do reconstructive surgery on women with genital cancers mention clitoral functioning, they acknowledge that clitoridectomies (even when there is an attempt to rebuild the clitoris) are disastrous to the woman's sexual responsivity.

One plastic surgeon said:

> We will go to any pains not to take off the clitoris, even if we're doing surgery for vulvic [sic] cancer. . . . We used to do radical vulvectomies which included removal of the whole clitoris . . . but the years have shown that you don't need to do that kind of mutilating surgery. . . . The other problem is that when you do those deeper pelvic operations you've interrupted the innervation of nerves that run from those structures so you may physically have a clitoris . . . but it doesn't function.

Comments like that one make sense out of unamplified assertions in the oncology literature that, as a consequence of genital surgery, libido and coitus frequency are reduced.[30]

One gynecological oncologist designed a new technique of limited vulvectomy because one of his patients refused to have her clitoris removed, which was at that time a conventional step in the vulvectomy procedure. This illustrates the difference between operating on an infant who cannot make her wishes known (and whose clitoris is in some sense not yet relevant to her parents) and a vocal adult woman with a sexual history to reflect upon in planning her sexual future.[31]

Vaginal Size

Despite all the discussion in the medical literature about the cosmetic appearance of the reduced clitoris, many researchers consider that the ultimate criterion of whether the intersexed female has been successfully treated is if her vagina is the right size and can function successfully.[32] A "successful vagina" is one that is capable of, if not "orgasmic" intercourse, at least nonpainful intercourse with a "normal-size" penis.

In one of the studies that followed up more than a few intersexed women, the authors asked, "Is the vaginal opening adequate for sexual intercourse?"[33] Twelve of the fifty-two who had been judged by their physician as having an adequate vagina did not engage in "sexual activity." If they had adequate vaginas, why, the authors pondered, were the women not "having sex?"[34] In addition, they wondered why the twenty-eight with inadequate vaginas elected not to seek additional surgery to enlarge the capacity of their vaginas. This reader of the article wonders at the authors' wonder.

Even though the vaginas were deemed "adequate" by the physicians, there is no assurance that they were judged adequate from the women's point of view. Or perhaps they were adequate in a dimensional sense, but not a necessary organ for their sexual activity. Only four of the women in this sample reported being lesbians, but we have no way of knowing how easy the physicians made it for the women to discuss their lesbianism with them.[35] (I am not assuming that only heterosexual women use their vaginas in their sexual activities, but I will wait until chapter 5 for a full discussion of genital functioning and sexual orientation.)

Furthermore, the way the questions were asked and the data interpreted masks the possibility that many of the intersexed women might have been lesbian or bisexual. The phrases "heterosexual activity," "sexual intercourse," and "sexual experience" are often used interchangeably.[36] Researchers might mistakenly conclude that women are not sexually active if they report not using their vaginas in sexual intercourse, as if sexual intercourse were the only sexual activity one could do with a male or female partner.

If, however, we accept that many of the women were not hiding their lesbianism but were asexual, even though they have "adequate" vaginas, this can be seen as additional evidence of medical mismanagement. Of what consequence to one's sexuality is an early history of scores of physicians examining, poking, and photographing one's genitals from birth through adolescence? One intersexed woman recalls, "For the first seven years of my life, I was passed from doctor to doctor, and I remember that they all wanted to do the same thing: look up my crotch."[37] This kind of experience is confirmed by a psychoendocrinologist who has treated hundreds of intersexed children. "I think that [repeated genital exams] has bad consequences. I can't prove it, but I think so, . . . and I personally feel that excess genital exams . . . is a form of abuse."[38]

Add to this the necessity of daily vaginal dilation, without which the neovagina would close up. Nowhere in the medical management literature is there a discussion of the repercussions of repeated vaginal dilation of a daughter by her parents. What meaning does the intervention have for inserter and insertee? Does the body part lose all its sexualized connotations or is it experienced by the girl as a violation by her parents—indeed, as sexual abuse? Even adult women recovering from vaginal cancer and who need to dilate their new vaginas are unlikely to emerge from the several months of using a stent emotionally unscathed.

Assessments of vaginal constructions for women after cancer surgery are bleak, although this is undoubtedly compounded by psychological and physical issues regarding the cancer itself. In one study two years after vaginoplasty, fewer than half of the couples reportedly had a complete "sexual rehabilitation," although it is unclear what sexual rehabilitation means.[39] Was intercourse possible? Was it enjoyable? By both partners? The sexual outcome is hedged: "Eventually the vaginal cavity is epithelized completely and a return to normal coital activity is *appropriate.* . . . The sensitivity to pressure was excellent, but tactile sensitivity was diminished"[40] (my emphasis).

Physicians who treat women with genital cancers contrast what they see as the difficulty in creating satisfactory-looking genitals for their patients, whose tissue has been damaged by radiation therapy, with the ease in creating genitals for the intersexed. One refers to intersex surgery as follows: "So you create a vagina which is no big deal. You create a cavity, line it with some skin which you can take from the buttocks or the thigh and you have a functional vagina." That this is an overly positive assessment of vaginoplasty for the intersexed is evident from the findings from six different follow-up studies:

More than half of the eighty intersexed patients had what was described as an "inadequate" introitus. The researchers admitted that "it was disappointing."[41]

In fifteen of twenty-three who had vaginal reconstruction during infancy, "the vagina was functionally inadequate."[42]

"In only four of the nine patients [gynecologically examined] were the genitalia functionally normal."[43]

"Review of the results of introital operations done early in childhood has been discouraging. Of the two methods used, the results are equally bad in both."[44]

"[Of] the eight adult patients who underwent extensive vaginal as well as clitoral surgery, . . . sexual function has ranged from satisfactory to poor."[45]

Three of the nine adult women "are not sexually active. Two

of them have stenosis of the introitus but have not yet accepted the advice to have a secondary enlarging procedure."[46]

An intersexed woman with androgen insensitivity reports that "after two late vaginoplasty operations, [I] still have only a short, partly 'externalised' [sic] vagina. . . . Infertility has been the least of my problems."[47] Another woman with androgen-insensitivity syndrome (AIS) countered her surgeon's statement that a woman have a marriage proposal as a precondition for vaginal construction with the comment that her "wedding would have had to have happened in the aneasthetic [sic] room and the honeymoon in the recovery ward, because the neovagina shrank back to its preoperative state within the ensuing 1–2 weeks."[48] A surgical consultant told one intersexed woman that her vagina was technically excellent and should be adequate (even though it was only six centimeters in length), but she and her sexual partner found this not to be so.[49]

Complications in Clitoral and Vaginal Surgery

There is little discussion of clitoral surgery complications, and whatever is mentioned is referred to as "minimal."[50] In a 1987 follow-up of ten patients, the authors report "no episodes of glans sloughing, flap necrosis, urinary tract infections, wound infections [or] stress incontinence."[51] Given the number of genital surgeries performed yearly, though, one would not want to draw conclusions on the basis of ten cases. Vaginal surgery, in comparison, is described even by the surgeons as problematic. Almost all intersexed who had vaginal surgeries in infancy are diagnosed with stenosis, a narrowing of the vaginal canal requiring, according to the surgeons, further surgery.[52] Additional complications include scarring, growth of hair at the introitus, and a high percentage of urinary-tract complications.[53] In an independent review of eight studies of vaginoplasty, the researchers noted multiple references among the sixty cases to scarring, residual pain, and high frequencies of postoperative complications requiring additional surgeries, all resulting in a relatively low level of reported sexual activity.[54] A recent study concludes that neither of the two vaginoplasty "procedures is entirely satisfactory. . . . Both procedures may lead to neovaginal stenosis, inadequate length, poor lubrication, or all three."[55] Because of these kinds of problems, some surgeons "limit vaginoplasty to a simple cosmetic procedure and delay definitive vaginoplasty."[56]

Five mothers of intersexed daughters provide firsthand reports that confirm these complications and convey more of a flavor of the interventions:[57]

> [She] continues to have problems with scar tissue causing a blockage to the vaginal opening, and infections usually build up behind it. Aside from two other reconstructive surgeries, she has been for repeated day surgeries (cystoscopies, vaginal dilations, removal of scar tissue, etc.). . . . In an attempt to stop the growth of scar tissue, my husband and I had to catherterize [sic] [her] vagina twice a day for two weeks. . . . Poor [girl] is so scared of her 'tube'. . . . She just keeps saying it hurts, and it gets worse when she has to go to the bathroom. . . . [The surgeon] aspirated inside but found no sign of infection, so at that point, we still don't know what's wrong.

> The scar tissue problem is getting better. [The doctor] thought we could wait another year before checking again. . . . She's going to need one more reconstructive surgery because she still has a bit of loose skin in the vaginal area. [The doctor] left it that way because it allowed him the use of that tissue for grafting the skin in the vaginal opening while trying to correct the scar tissue problem.

> [She] has still been so sick, I think we're on #7 bladder infection and 1 kidney. She has never been like this ever, except since her last surgery (3 months ago). Now she has a super swolin [sic] labia. The flap of skin on the outside is so swollen and cherry red. Obvious[ly] a serious infection. Maybe the stitches? . . . She has taken antibiotics since [the surgery] but still [the infections] reoccur.

> When she was five years old she had peritinitis [sic] because her vaginal opening was so small she got an infection and it spread through her system.

> [T]he stitches [are] not taking. . . . [She] keeps pulling at something.

Even though more recent reports suggest that newer techniques produce fewer complications, intersexed women with stenosis do not always accept the advice to have a secondary enlarging procedure, a procedure that some authors claim is "not a big undertaking" and that they assert is not emotionally disturbing.[58] None of the twenty-one females with an inadequate introitus in one follow-up study sought additional plastic surgery. Some said they believed that nothing beneficial could be done to correct their abnormality.[59] What does it mean that some patients are not compliant with their physician's recommendations to have additional surgeries, or to be available for follow-up investigations, or even to dilate their vaginas after surgery? How much noncompliance is there, and is this greater than patient noncompliance in other medical conditions? One physician interviewed said:

> I have seen patients who were not properly counseled, who rejected the wearing of a stent [dilator], who just couldn't get it in. If it was in, they couldn't take it out. I remember several youngsters when I was in training who had to come back here and go under anesthesia and have the stent reinserted because we were afraid that if we didn't get the stent in, the vagina was going to collapse and the whole process would be for nil, and there are such patients who require a certain maturity, a certain stability, whom one needs to evaluate very carefully.

Physicians admit that few adolescent girls are capable of taking the initiative in asking for a vaginoplasty and that dilating the vagina seems also to be "quite a psychological burden."[60] It must be a psychological burden for parents also, but this is never discussed in the medical management literature. Discussions with parents attest to it though. One mother of a young girl who had undergone clitoroplasty, but not yet vaginoplasty, told me that she hopes the physicians will not recommend vaginal surgery until much later. She had talked to another mother whose eighteen-month-old intersexed infant was pulling out her eyelashes and biting her nails in response to the dilation. When the mother discontinued the dilation, the pulling and biting stopped. The mother that I spoke with cannot imagine having to dilate her daughter. She compared it to child abuse. "Wouldn't you think that it's the same thing in the kid's head? Here's somebody sticking something in me." Do physicians suppose that a young child understands that a painful, humiliating procedure done for "appropriate medical procedure" is not sexual abuse? One adult intersexual woman writes, "My decision to drop all medical care [at age seventeen] was the direct result of the humiliation and obfuscation I had been subjected to over the prior seven years."[61]

When noncompliance is mentioned in the medical literature, it is discussed as reflecting poorly on the patient rather than on the procedure. Noncompliance is described as unfortunate because it interferes with the surgeon's opportunity to do his job and "fix it" once and for all or with the researcher's ability to get accurate follow-up statistics. One set of authors, after admitting that they judged one-fourth of their sample as having unsatisfactory anatomic results, add that "perhaps the *saddest figure* is found in the four patients lost to follow-up"[62] (my emphasis). It is as though the loss happened to the physicians rather than being something that the procedures, themselves, might have created. One clinician who is critical of the medical management of the intersexed sets the record straight: "We, as caregivers, are the ones who lost them."[63]

When researchers report that a patient "has adamantly refused further surgery in spite of disfiguring prominence of her clitoris,"[64] possible meanings of that refusal are unexamined. Was the initial surgery experienced as mutilating? Was the consequence sexual muting? Was the experience of having one's genitals poked and peered at too objectifying?

That patients and parents even refuse initial surgeries is imbedded into medical reports, usually without comment. For example, a discussion of a fourteen-year-old girl who reportedly had a successful vaginoplasty concludes with the comment: "Despite a large clitoris, she does not wish any modifications to be made."[65] Fausto-Sterling cites two of Hugh Hampton Young's cases describing parents who were advised to have the children surgically normalized.[66] Both sets of parents refused and, following initial examinations, "never returned." Although Hampton Young describes these as cases of "resistance," considering the quality of genital surgery, especially decades ago, one could just as easily label them cases of "assertion" or "preservation."

A Different Source of Data on Female Genital Surgery: Male-to-Female Transsexuals

Given the problems with intersex genital surgery, the topic of genital surgery on transsexuals is being introduced for several reasons. In some respects the quality of the surgery itself is a relevant comparison, even though adult bodies present different kind of challenges than infant bodies. More significant than the surgical comparisons, though, are the assumptions about the genital-gender relationship that a study of transsexual surgeries reveals.

Genital surgeries on male-to-female transsexuals, in contrast to those performed on intersexed infants, have been refined over decades by surgeons conferring directly with their patients. One might think that surgeries on fully grown bodies ought not be fraught with some of the problems that plague infant surgeries.[67] Is that so, and what criteria do physicians (and transsexuals) use to assess the success?

The impetus for one recent follow-up study was the paucity of data on orgasmic responsivity of postoperative transsexuals.[68] In their review of earlier research, the authors refer to such nebulous criteria as "satisfactory results," with no indication whether the measure was vaginal capacity, genital appearance, sexual sensitivity, or something else. In their own follow-up of fourteen male-to-female transsexuals, only four reported being orgasmic after surgery, even though ten had been orgasmic prior to surgery. Many of the nonorgasmic, however, claimed to have "sexual satisfaction." Those who were dissatisfied with their vagina claimed it was too shallow or required additional cosmetic surgery. Only one-third of the transsexuals in one sample had functional vaginas after vaginoplasty.

In another recent study of transsexuals, six months after surgery only slightly more than half had "normal" sexual intercourse; most said they had "the sensation of 'orgasm.'"[69] One has to wonder whether "sensation of orgasm" (especially with orgasm put in quotation marks) is equivalent to orgasm. The author is mystified as to why intercourse had not been engaged in by the remaining sample of transsexuals despite their having what was judged to be very adequate vaginas. As with the intersexed population, there is no acknowledgment that sexual behaviors other than intercourse may be preferred or that the transsexual's partner is not a man.

Sixty-four transsexuals were interviewed by another researcher, and most reported being pleased with the surgical results, saying they were reliably orgasmic.[70] The author cautions that these high claims "reflect a wide range of respondent interpretation of orgasm" and suggest a need to promote a particular image of the postsurgical transsexual to the general public—the image of a real woman. The transsexuals claimed more satisfaction with genital feeling during coitus than with genital function, the latter being the ability of the vagina to contain a penis comfortably. Yet, the author fails to draw any implications about the quality of the vaginoplasties from the repeat genital surgeries undergone by transsexuals in this sample. We might speculate whether they are searching for perfect-looking or perfectly functioning genitals and whether they are willing to trade the second for the first.

On the internet newsgroup TRANSGEN, transsexuals trade advice about passing as women and air complaints about surgeries they have had. In the remarks excerpted here, the participants, operated on by a surgeon who probably does more "sex-change" operations than any other surgeon in the United States, reveal that the 1990s is not an era in which genital surgery has been perfected.

R: My state of mind is such that I can't imagine really wanting to have sex *even if I could.* . . . I think I can have orgasms. (her emphasis)

V: I call myself an asexual nymphomaniac. . . . [T]he entire extent of getting sexually aroused is a slight tingling that lasts for maybe all of 3 seconds . . . then it's gone for another month or so.

R: My roommate in the hospital was having sex with her boyfriend six weeks after surgery.

V: Did she know she was doing it, in other words, could she feel it? I had sex with my husband a couple of months after my surgery. But, as I've said before, my response was to ask him if he was in yet. Also, I'm sure you could have had sex six weeks after your operation too . . . if you had found a man that was less than 2 inches in diameter, which isn't hard . . . I kept wishing for an inflatable dilator . . . because I was so swollen that I was too small for the hard one—talk about pain!!! I eventually got a speculum and used that to open myself up far enough to accept [the surgeon's] hard dilator. . . . The dilator that he started me out on had to be at least an inch in diameter. . . . I never got up to the two-inch dilator (I had to stop dilating in order to heal—doctor's orders), but I did get to the one just before it, and it felt like that one was hitting on my bones. I'm surprised at the requirement for the two-incher . . . especially since most men aren't two inches in diameter, and few women use dildoes that large. . . . [I used to douche with Clorox Bleach and water . . . but] I have difficulty getting a douche nozzle in anymore. . . . It will take only a simple z-plasty to widen my vaginal opening.

R: There was no way [the dilator] was going to fit inside me—my vaginal entrance was too small, and no amount of painful stretching would make it go in.

V: People I've spoken to, even people who had the surgery five years ago, have had infections—regardless of how minor. . . . I had a massive infection and . . . my clitoris was rotting away.

R: For a month or two early in the healing process I had trouble with my urine stream. It came out in all kinds of weird directions, like straight up.

V: Yeah, right after my surgery, my urine "stream" was more like something that comes out of a sprinkler. . . . Right now scar tissue is covering my urethral opening, so the only way urine has of getting out is the trench in the erectile tissue. But the scar tissue is also twisting the erectile tissue. I also have scar tissue inside my urethra. . . . Urine started coming out from above my clitoris. So sometimes I can't urinate at all, and when I do, I can go only little capfuls at a time, and that shoots all over the place. When I urinate, I have to stick my head between my knees, and sometimes the stream will still hit me in the foot. My husband has to frequently cathertize [sic] me in order to avoid infection, and because sometimes I simply can't urinate.

R: I have an ongoing problem with a smelly discharge from my vagina. . . . My gynecologist has prescribed various things for it, but they only partially work.

V: I used to lay [sic] on the couch and put my legs over my husband's shoulders. He would then use a washrag to clean me out like a drinking glass! . . . Also, in the relative scheme of things SRS [sex reassignment surgery] seems pretty mild compared to some other surgical procedures done every day. I mean, flaps, skin grafts, genitourinary surgery, intestinal surgery, and SRS on babys [sic] with poorly defined genitalia are done all the time without extraordinary complication rates. Could it be that a baby whose genitalia rots away because of a poorly performed SRS [to correct poorly defined genitalia], a man whose penis rots away from a poorly performed prostate surgery, or a woman whose genitalia rot away because of a poorly performed hysterectomy would all be able to find a lawyer and a sympathetic jury, so shortcuts are taken on us? Please help me understand.

R: The extreme soreness faded over a period of about two months. . . . The numbness faded much more slowly. I still have some slight numbness in that area, but I mostly don't notice it. . . . [The surgeon] said the tightness was caused by a muscle that was stretched around the opening.

V: Most of the pain that I have now comes from the shrinking scar tissue. It has twisted and is pulling on and squeezing my erectile tissue. It is also pinching nerves. . . . I've spoken to people who had surgery 5 years ago and they say they still numb. . . . Are you sure that you haven't just gotten used to [the numbness]?

R: I don't know how much of [my problem] is his [the surgeon's] fault.

V: All of it. Unless you went against his orders, which it doesn't sound like you did, your results are in his hands. That's why he went to school and why he is getting paid. There is too much blaming of the victim in this community.

R: I don't remember what [the surgeon] himself told me, but I don't think there were any promises of perfection.

V: I asked him if it was true that my results would be so good that a gynecologist [wouldn't be able to tell I was a TS]. And he said yes. . . . He also told me that the two possible complications were a fistula, which he claimed happens in only 1 percent of his patients, and vaginal stenosis, which he blamed on his patients. After I went back to the gender clinic I got a copy of [his] records. There he claims to have warned me about everything that I complained to the gender clinic about—and not the things that he did warn me about but that I wasn't suffering from. . . . I'm surprised at all of the information that I am able to get now because of my bad results that I wasn't able to get before my surgery.

R: I've already had enough surgery in that part of my body to last me for the rest of my life.

V: I hear ya sister, and amen!!!. . . . You refer to your results as "semi-ok," I call mine bad.[71]

Data from transsexuals, both formal and informal, suggest that despite years of surgical "advancements" and ready access to verbal feedback from highly motivated adults, genital functioning is still imperfect. One famous surgeon repeatedly asserted at a 1995 international conference that his male-to-female surgeries could fool a gynecologist, as though how the genitals look to a professional is the paramount criterion.

Evaluating Genital Surgery on Males

As I mentioned in chapter 2, in cases of intersex when there is genital ambiguity, the infant is usually given a female gender assignment. There are circumstances, however, when the XY infant has a well-formed phallus with the size potential to sustain a male gender assignment.

Most boys with micropenises are treated with testosterone rather than with surgery. The hormone-induced enlargement, however, just initiates premature penile growth, leaving the adult male with essentially the same-size penis he had as a child. The penis does not grow twice and the dictum "Those who are born with a micropenis die with one" still holds.[72] The argument in favor of early hormone treatment is that as a result "the boy has greater self-confidence in the locker room or in normal childhood hetero-sexual rehearsal play . . . [and] the worries of the parents are al-layed."[73] Presumably, having grown up with this confirmation of his masculinity, he will be in a better position to face life as an adult male with a micropenis. (Given the number of references in the medical literature to the "locker room," one might think that boys and men spend most of their waking hours there.)

Most surgeons (as opposed to endocrinologists) favor surgery over hormone therapy for males with micropenises. In the words of one renowned surgeon: "These guys [for whom hormones have not spurred enough penile growth] sometimes try to kill them-selves."[74] The documentation for disproportionate numbers of sui-cides among men with micropenises is not provided.

As with clitoral repair, surgeons often promote their own tech-nique as resulting in fewer complications, a more pleasing appear-ance, and "the avoid[ance of] the psychological trauma of repeated hospitalization and operations on a sensitive organ."[75] The authors of one follow-up report conclude that "hypospadias repair remains a matter of individual surgical preference, and excellent results have been reported with diverse techniques."[76] In spite of these so-called excellent results, physicians have coined the term "hy-pospadias cripples" to refer to males whose penises do not look or function better after "corrective" surgery.[77] Most of the criticism is leveled at surgical procedures from earlier decades, but even recent "advancements" in the 1990s are described as having high complication rates.[78]

A follow-up study of boys who underwent surgery between 1985 and 1992 to correct severe hypospadias concluded that there was a high incidence of fistulas, with almost half requiring sec-ondary operations.[79] Although surgery was described as producing excellent cosmetic and functional results, as with surgery on fe-male genitals, no criteria for excellent functioning were provided. One assumes that since the boys are still young, urinary and not sexual functioning is what was meant. It is rare that boys are fol-lowed into adulthood, so claims about long-term cosmetic and functional excellence need to be considered with caution.

Unlike surgeries performed to straighten the penis or to cover exposed mucous membrane, none of the 150 different surgical techniques to repair hypospadias are medically necessary to reduce pain or prevent illness.[80] Males with hypospadias do not suffer from renal anomalies in greater proportion than the general population, and a urologist who performs hundreds of these surgeries admitted in a public forum that many minor forms of glans hypospadias "do not need to be repaired."[81]

Why then are they? The parents' needs are alluded to as often as the boys'. One surgeon writes that when a child's penis is malformed and surgery is needed to correct it, parents will be "comforted" by its normal shape and size.[82] Another asserted publicly that the most grateful parents he has encountered are those whose son's penis was given a normal appearance.[83]

By far the most common reason for performing hypospadias surgery is to permit a boy to stand when he urinates. Physicians who advocate hypospadias repair for this reason, as though this were an essential biological mandate, ignore the historicity of urinary postures. Also, boys who cannot urinate in what is referred to as the "male manner" are said not to be able to "demonstrat[e] their prowess at urinating at certain distances in competition with other boys . . . which could lead to competence anxieties related to their penis."[84] It needs to be emphasized that the surgeries, by and large, are not performed in order to allow the male to urinate, which would be a medical emergency, but to allow him to urinate in a culturally sanctioned position.

One woman who writes about the social construction of intersexuality complained that her son's preschool teacher was trying to teach him to stand up and "pee like a big boy" whereas she, the mother, considered standing to urinate just an excuse for men to spray urine all over the bathroom floor. She relates her attitude to the rationale for hypospadias surgery by imagining a physician saying, "You can't be a real male . . . unless you can behave like a complete jackass while using the toilet, so we're going to have to remove the skin from your forearm to construct a barely functioning urethra for you so that you can also behave like a pisshead."[85]

An analysis of five recent follow-up studies of hypospadias repair revealed similarities to the literature on clitoral repair.[86] Criteria for success are only vaguely alluded to, with reports noting whether the urinary function after surgery is "satisfactory" or "unsatisfactory." (In the studies reviewed, approximately three-fourths of the penises were judged "satisfactory" for urination.) The one study that provided any criteria for assessment mentioned the force, quality, and direction of the urinary stream. "Of major importance to a concentrated, 'riffled' urinary stream is a vertical meatus with well-opposed meatal lips."[87] There is the same concern for "appearance" as in genital surgery on females. Although two-thirds of the 345 patients were judged by the physicians as having a good- or satisfactory-looking penis, a group of researchers who have examined hundreds of boys and men with hypospadias claims that the "surgery never produces a perfectly normal penile appearance."[88] In this typical sample, adult males with hypospadias had on the average more than three surgeries.

Who instigates the secondary and tertiary surgeries that so many of these boys undergo? The answer is of more than academic interest, since it is well known that the rate of complications increases with each surgical procedure performed.[89] The rationale for many of the hypospadias surgeries is to repair complications produced by previous surgeries.[90] One study noted that the parents were more pleased by how their son's penis looked than the surgeons, so it may be that parents are not the ones to instigate additional surgeries.[91]

Physicians debate what is a reasonable success and complication rate for hypospadias surgery.[92] They balance the increased risk of surgery against the psychological risk to the family and the infant from delaying it.[93] They make all these determinations without considering what is a reasonable argument for surgery in the first place. Although physicians concede that age of hypospadias repair is "dictated by social criteria," there is no acknowledgment that the surgery itself is dictated by nonmedical concerns.[94] How does one balance the need for a "concentrated, riffled urinary stream" against the psychological effect of repeated surgeries and separations from parents, not to mention urinary tract infections, fistulae (holes), hair growth inside their new tubes, and scar tissue?[95]

Because follow-up studies are not long-term and patients are rarely assessed after early childhood, the one recent large-scale study on genital perceptions of a large number of hypospadiac men and boys is worth a thorough consideration.[96] The males' satisfaction with specific features of their penis after surgery were compared to ratings from an age-matched sample of males surgically treated for an inguinal hernia. The comparison group was not males with hypospadias who had not had surgery, probably because there are so few who have not. Several findings are particularly relevant.

Even after surgery, the hypospadiac males were less satisfied with the position of their meatus than was the comparison group, but the feature of their penises they were most dissatisfied with and self-conscious about was its circumcised appearance. Was this, the authors speculate, because the circumcised penis seems smaller or because the loss of the foreskin was perceived as a defect? Many of the men and boys reported having received comments on their penile appearance in locker rooms, but the researchers do not mention whether these comments were about the circumcised aspect of the penis or some other feature.

It is relevant that the data were collected in The Netherlands, where circumcision is uncommon. In contrast, a study conducted in the United States found that boys who were circumcised were more satisfied with their penises than were the uncircumcised males, who were in the minority. The authors of Dutch study suggest that parents and patients be informed that after surgery the penis will look circumcised and that a circumcised nonhypospadiac penis (of which they have seen few) and a circumcised hypospadiac penis look very similar. In other words, they need to be taught what a penis can look like.

The authors conclude that "the ability of patients with hypospadias to cope with their somewhat different penile appearance is positively related to genital perception."[97] The males with hypospadias who thought their penis looked different from other males after surgery had a more negative perception of what their penis looked like. "Factors that might negatively affect genital perception of patients with hypospadias [are] unrealistic expectations of the cosmetic results of surgery, the parents' anxieties about their son's . . . sexual . . . functioning and fertility, or the parents' negative perception of their son's penile appearance."[98] If physicians addressed those factors (especially considering that the hypospadiac penis is not completely "normalized" by surgery), the surgery might be obviated in many if not most cases.

Some adult intersexuals who have had a bad experience with hypospadias surgery concur. One who was born with a small penis and complete hypospadias had ten "reconstructive" surgeries by the time he was eighteen. Doctors told him that another six operations would have him "in ship shape," but instead he opted to have the penis removed and is now living as a woman. Another wrote, "Hermaphrodites, beware. . . . [A]ny surgeon's promise of beautiful looking and feeling genitals is probably exaggerated, and you would be better off not to have surgery at all."[99]

Testimonies like that give credence to the argument that most hypospadiac penises should be left "uncorrected," at least until after puberty, when physical development is complete and the young man is able to make a decision for himself, weighing the emotional impact of impaired erotic sensation against the emotional impact of having a penis that "looks different." In chapter 5, I will pursue the question of whether hypospadias is (in many, if not most, cases) a cosmetic difference that could be tolerated.

It is interesting to compare hypospadias repair to phalloplasty for female-to-male transsexuals. Female-to-male transsexuals, unlike the parents of intersexed boys, are cautioned to be realistic in their expectations. "Make no mistake, once you have undergone one of these surgical procedures you have altered your body. The skin will experience a wound. . . . The surgeon works with flesh, and we have to acknowledge that the flesh we bring in is our own, and it may not present the ideal working conditions for the surgeon."[100]

Most female-to-male transsexuals are so convinced that the surgical options are poor that they limit intervention to life-long hormone treatment, bilateral mastectomy, and hysterectomy. In anthropologist Holly Devor's sample of thirty-nine transsexual men, only 15 percent chose genital surgery.[101] Granted, it would be more convenient in today's society to have one's lower body match one's upper body and public and private identities, but most of these men seem not to be driven by this. If others were not afraid of being "caught" with the wrong genitals, probably more would opt not to have one of the expensive, risky, and generally unsatisfactory phalloplasty techniques.

What Motivates Genital Surgeries?

A noncritical reading of the medical literature would lead to the conclusion that genital surgery on the intersexed is routine, postsurgical genitals can pass inspection, and medical complications are few. If only patients and parents would comply with tedious postsurgical procedures and physicians' suggestions to have whatever additional surgeries are prescribed, the consequence would be good-enough genitals for both public inspections and private matters.

A careful analysis of follow-up studies, however, argues for a moratorium on infant intersex surgeries. Not all intersexed adults who are critical of intersex surgeries believe that the solution is better surgical techniques or more tightly controlled follow-up investigations. By focusing on the problems with specific surgical techniques or inadequate follow-up studies, some critics of intersex management fear they are providing consent to do the surgeries, "in pursuit of perfecting the technique" without questioning the reason for the procedures.[102]

Why have the limitations and complications of clitoroplasty, vaginoplasty, and phalloplasty, as demonstrated by the follow-up data, not put a brake on surgical gynecology or urology? What accounts for the surgical momentum? There are, I believe, at least two powerful forces: commitment to the concept of medical advancement and that of dimorphic genitals.

In the previous chapter, I discussed how medicine portrays itself as obeying nature's command to reduce large clitorises. Medicine, as the servant not only of nature but of technology, portrays itself as becoming more and more "advanced" as physicians become more and more wise. Through technology they have become better readers of nature's pattern. The following quotes from the medical literature testify to this advancement (my emphases):

> *Progress* in diagnosis has so improved that an appropriate sex assignment can be made promptly and accurately [and] a more *orderly* surgical approach has developed.[103]

> The surgical management . . . is receiving increased attention as clinical *insight*, directing the assignment of sex, *gains refinement*.[104]

> The tragedies of yesteryear . . . rarely occur . . . [Now gender assignment] can be issued with *confidence*.[105]

> Previously the *ideal* management of the enlarged phallus associated with . . . intersex disorders was unknown.[106]

> [There have been] improved results since 1975 [due to] *newer improved* operative techniques.[107]

Surgical interventions are presented as progressive, and surgeons are presented as more and more skillful, insightful, and confident about gender. For example, authors of recent publications call the earlier use of clitoridectomy "unfortunate."[108] Another writes that preserving the sensitive tip is "more according to nature's pattern."[109] What are the links between discerning nature's pattern, developing new technologies, and evolving beliefs about gender? Why was nature's pattern hidden for so many years? Physicians lament the techniques of yesteryear and proclaim the need for careful follow-up studies.[110] Pediatric endocrinologist Gary Berkowitz from Johns Hopkins admitted to a reporter, "There are lots and lots of opinions and precious little data."[111] Surgeons are more likely to admit the drawbacks of current surgical techniques in informal discussions and private letters than in publication. A urologist from a major medical center in a small discussion with adult intersexuals warned that "there's a steep learning curve" for surgeons operating on intersex infants.[112] Another highly respected surgeon who developed a clitoral recession technique recommended in a personal letter to an intersexed woman that she exercise extreme caution about subjecting herself to future reconstructive surgeries.[113]

> "Every generation of medical intersex specialists has characterized the work of the previous generation as terrible. . . . I have no doubt that, twenty years from now, the next generation of medical intersex specialists will be shaking their heads over the 'terrible' price that was exacted on intersexed children by the surgeries of the early 1990s."[114]

This "terrible price" is not widely acknowledged, though. For example, Fausto-Sterling asserts that clitoridectomies grew out of fashion in the 1960s as physicians became educated about the clitoral basis of female orgasm. Yet instead of admitting that clitoridectomies had been wrong and even damaging, the literature just suddenly changed.[115] Medical "advancements" proceed with little recognition that today's advancements will be tomorrow's problems.

One can complain about the medical profession and call individual physicians or the entire enterprise misogynistic and arrogant. Similarly, one can complain that parents of intersexed infants are overly obsequious toward medical authority, but as I contended at the end of chapter 2, if culture demands gender, physicians will produce it, and of course, when physicians produce it, the fact that gender is "demanded" will be hidden from everyone.

The prevailing medical viewpoint is that genital surgery on intersexed infants, although not problem-free, is inarguably worthwhile. Parenting a female with clitoral insensitivity and vaginal complications is seen as preferable to parenting a female with a larger-than-typical clitoris and a smaller-than-typical vagina. Parenting a male with a scarred and insensitive penis is seen as preferable to parenting a male with a normally functional (but small) one or one that does not permit a direct urinary stream. Nowhere in the medical literature is there an acknowledgment that these are value judgments.

But what about constituencies that have different value judgments? When we look at intersexuality not from the physicians' point of view but from the former patients' and the parents'—two groups whose views about intersexuality have been molded by medical management (although not always as the physicians intended)—an even more complicated picture emerges. We will see in the next chapter what intersexuality looks like to people who have other-than-medical commitments.

5

Questioning

Medical

Management

"To find one's gender ambiguous or shifting is as cruel a blow as could befall one's ego. It's as close as any of our children might come to the nightmare experienced by Gregor Samsa, of Franz Kafka's terrifying story *Metamorphosis*, who wakes up one morning to find himself transformed into a human size insect."

—Jared Diamond, 1992

Toby was born with nonstandard genitals. Raised as a girl until age twelve, Toby lived as a boy for the next five years and has presented him/herself as "neuter" since then. In 1987, Toby attempted to start a support group of like-minded and like-bodied people. The group was called "Finding Our Own Ways," and an initial newsletter was sent from the Midwest to potential members. As Toby conceived it, the group's purpose was to provide a forum for people who think of themselves as neuter and/or asexual and who wish to make (nonsexual) connections with others, to "discover and explore ways of being ourselves, in a setting free of pressure to define ourselves in terms of maleness or femaleness . . . to support . . . nontraditional gender identification as legitimate and non-pathological, and [to provide] a source of education for the public and professionals."[1] Part of the accompanying manifesto read, "I am a complete person. If I am a man or a woman, my manhood or womanhood is in no way diminished by my disinterest in sexual activity. If my genital anatomy is other than male or female, this is not a defect or a deformity; I am as I am meant to be. I affirm my capacity to be whole as an asexual person."[2] Toby claimed there were somewhat fewer than two dozen members of the support group but no other "neuters." It is unclear what response Toby got to his/her solicitation for new members and newsletter subscriptions. No second issue of the newsletter was forthcoming, and I have heard nothing more from Toby or this embryonic movement.

Five years later, Cheryl Chase, an intersexed woman, founded the Intersex Society of North America (ISNA), dedicated to the cause of asserting hermaphroditic identities and halting genital surgery on intersexed infants and children unless absolutely necessary for their physical health and comfort. Over the next few years, Chase wrote letters to various popular magazines and professional journals, receiving little acknowledgment from professionals but a few responses from other intersexed. "Many intersexuals are so isolated, traumatized, and fearful that they . . . take months to years to screw up the courage to respond," Chase told me. With the evolution of the Internet, she made contact with dozens of intersexuals and the professionals who work with them.

Nearly two years after her initial "feelers," in the winter of 1994, Chase distributed hundreds of copies of a newsletter called *Hermaphrodites with Attitude,* in which she reported having received hundreds of inquiries, leading to a mailing list of intersexuals in five countries and fourteen U.S. states. At the same time, Chase called the first of many ISNA face-to-face meetings. Early in 1996, ISNA got its own Web page, and later that year members of the group staged a public demonstration at the annual meeting of the American Academy of Pediatrics, the purpose being to increase the visibility of the intersexed and to force physicians to recognize that their patients are not satisfied.

By then Chase claimed nearly 100 intersexed correspondents, including people with every major intersex condition: androgen-insensitivity syndrome (AIS), true hermaphroditism, Klinefelter's syndrome, progestin virilization, mixed gonadal dysgenesis, and congenital adrenal hyperplasia (CAH). Most, but not all, had been born with variant genitals; some had undergone genital surgery; others had lived with their genital variability. Virtually all, however, had complaints and welcomed the existence of the organization.

By 1997, the primary efforts of ISNA had shifted from recruiting and supporting members to directly influencing the medical community. In the spring of 1997, ISNA members picketed Columbia Presbyterian Hospital in New York City, where intersex surgeries are performed. It was featured prominently and sympathetically in the *New York Times* and *Newsweek*.[3] Weeks later, Chase's story and ISNA's goals were spotlighted on national television during a "Dateline NBC" segment. An intelligently crafted strategic plan to use the media and personal contacts to convert physicians, one at a time, was paying off. ISNA representatives were being invited to professional meetings and were being written about in professional newsletters. Physicians were asking that their colleagues rethink their stance about intersexuality, a possibility that I did not imagine when I first began writing about intersex in the late 1980s.

Simultaneous to ISNA's development, support groups for intersexuals were forming in Canada, Europe, Asia, Australia, Japan, and New Zealand. In Germany, a group of intersexuals, using some of the same strategies as ISNA, established a peer support and advocacy group. The initial name of the group, Intersex Support Network Central Europe, was later changed to Genital Mutilation Survivor's Support Network and Workgroup on Violence in Pediatrics and Gynecology, reflecting the fury of its political evolution.

A self-help group in England, originally organized for parents of children with androgen-insensitivity syndrome, eventually began to attract women with androgen insensitivity. The Androgen-insensitivity Syndrome Support Group (AISSG) published its first newsletter, *ALIAS*, in early spring 1995 and listed goals similar to ISNA's: to reduce secrecy and stigma surrounding AIS, to develop enlightened support within the medical community for young people with AIS and their parents, and to provide a network of information (including personal contacts) for those with AIS. By mid-1996, Sherri Groveman, a member from the United States, had publicized the existence of AISSG by writing directly to over 300 physicians and scores of organizations and by posting notes in medical journals. The result was several new calls every week.

Although there are some differences among the intersex advocacy groups, most members criticize the way their intersexuality was and is handled and argue that there needs to be a break in "the vicious cycle in which shame [about variant genitals] produces silence, silence condones surgery, and surgery produces more shame (which produces more silence)."[4] Intersexuals urge parents of newly diagnosed intersexed infants not to inflict unnecessary surgery on their infants, not only because erasing the variant genitals ruins sexual responsivity but because the meaning of the surgery gives rise to a secret in the families that has long-term, detrimental consequences.

In the five years between Toby's failure to organize asexual neuters and Chase's success in creating a political movement of sexual hermaphrodites, something significant had happened, electronic communication being only part of the story. The social construction of gender had become mainstream theory, and transgender culture was creeping inward from the margins of society to make its presence felt on daytime talk shows.[5] Theory and politics were both grappling with the issue of the gender dichotomy. How real is it and how necessary? In this chapter, I will elucidate the intersexuals' view on genital dimorphism and the gender dichotomy as well as present evidence that people do learn to see the dichotomy by learning to see the dimorphism, all of which suggests that a gender dichotomy is not a necessary feature of human life.

The Intersexual Agenda

The primary item on the intersexual agenda is decreasing if not ceasing genital surgeries on intersexed infants. To this end, members of ISNA have been trying to link their concerns about nonconsensual intersex surgeries with the international battle against female genital mutilation. In 1997 press releases, ISNA cleverly began to refer to intersex surgeries as "IGM" to heighten the association with "FGM," a widely understood abbreviation of female genital mutilation.

Although much has been written about African and Middle Eastern female genital mutilation in the last few years, none of the North American activists, including novelist Alice Walker, author of *Possessing the Secret of Joy*, have been willing to consider genital mutilation of the intersexed as a related issue. Fran Hosken, author of *The Hosken Report: Genital and Sexual Mutilation of Females*, wrote Cheryl Chase, "I am really dealing with quite a different topic from what you are interested in—that is, we are not concerned with biological exceptions, but rather with the excuses that are used to mutilate female infants which are both colorful and imaginative."[6]

The distinction between "biological exceptions" and "cultural excuses" makes sense only on the most superficial level. Presumably, broadening the scope of the complaint to include intersex surgeries would be seen as diluting the argument and would mean confronting the American medical establishment at a time when it needs to be wooed.

Chase, with two professionals, wrote a letter to the editor of *The New England Journal of Medicine* in response to an article on female "circumcision." They linked genital mutilation in Africa and surgical treatment of intersexed children, referring to both as "culturally determined practices of harmful genital surgery" and explaining that cultural practices are continually contested and renegotiated. As evidence, they pointed to the gay rights struggle as having successfully effected profound social changes. They called on physicians to rethink the logic of genital surgery on infants who cannot give informed consent. Their letter was never printed.

Members of ISNA believe that the final version of the congressional bill to ban female genital mutilation in the United States is worded in such a way that it could include genital surgery on intersexed infants. It reads in part: "Whoever knowingly circumcises, excises, or infibulates the whole or any part of the labia majora or labia minora or clitoris of another person who has not attained the age of 18 years shall be fined under this title or imprisoned not more than 5 years, or both." It goes on to say that "a surgical operation is not a violation of this section *if the operation is necessary to the person's health and is performed by a person licensed as a medical practitioner in that state.*"[7] (my emphasis) The successful application will depend on marshaling enough evidence to demonstrate that intersex surgery, in many if not most cases, is not necessary for the child's health. Tactically, intersexual activists should preemptively claim that the bill covers surgery of intersexed infants, which would force physicians to refute that interpretation.[8]

A subsection of the bill mandates that statistics be compiled on the number of girls under eighteen years old in the United States who have been subjected to genital mutilation. This is encouraging to members of ISNA. As the U.S. government seeks to limit (if not outlaw) genital mutilation of girls, the explicit connection between what is referred to as "ritualized cutting" and presumably nonritualized intersex surgery will continue to be made. It remains to be seen whether the reporting of statistics on intersex surgeries will be mandated under the authority of this bill. Without mandated reporting, it is almost impossible to answer accurately the question: How many intersexed infants are born each year in the United States, and what percentage of them are surgically altered?[9]

The war on genital mutilation is viewed as a women's issue. There is, though, a parallel (albeit more marginal) movement to fight the circumcision of male infants. Among a number of national and international groups, the most vocal is NOHARM—National Organization to Halt the Abuse and Routine Mutilation of Males—which advocates "for those who wish to be actively involved in the fight for universal genital integrity."[10] The director of UNCircumcising Information and Resource Center published a book that details the history and myths surrounding circumcision and techniques for restoring the foreskin. The book is sprinkled with hundreds of testimonials from men who regret having been circumcised as infants, some of whom had their foreskins restored and are delighted with the results.[11]

The anticircumcision position is articulated in the rhetoric of other social movements. Just as adults have "come out of the closet" regarding the physical and sexual abuse they experienced as children, the leaders of the uncircumcising movement are trying to raise the nation's awareness of another "very old and hidden crime against children" and to "restore a sense of wholeness" to those who had been cut.[12] Who has rights over one's body? Making analogies to both slavery and abortion, Jim Bigelow argues that one's body is one's own, and no one—whether parents, medical professionals, or religious practitioners—has the right to make a circumcision decision on behalf of the infant. "The male foreskin is the only organ of the human body of either sex over which parents are 'given such authority."[13] Presumably Bigelow is referring to conditions in countries where female circumcision is not common. He suggests filing civil rights class action suits against hospitals or linking up with proposed legislation to outlaw female genital mutilation.[14]

Yet Bigelow does not see any connection between infant circumcision and infant intersex surgery. "No one has the right to alter or amputate any part of [the boy's] genitals unless he was born with an obvious birth defect which requires radical and immediate treatment."[15] Bigelow's complaint about male circumcision duplicates the intersexuals' argument. "They [parents] are making a decision that they believe they *must* [his emphasis] make so that it can be done 'at the right time' if it's going to be done. And they have been assured by the system that it is their decision to make."[16] He neglects to see that this is also true of intersex surgery.

As conservative as Bigelow believes the medical community to be, The American Academy of Pediatrics' (AAP) policy on male circumcision, if applied to intersexed infants, would be a step in a progressive direction. The AAP admits that circumcision of the male has both advantages and disadvantages, and it recommends that parents consider not only medical factors but also aesthetics, cultural prescriptions, and social pressure. Parents of intersexed infants, in contrast, are not told that these are important factors to consider before committing their children to surgery.

The eventual success of the anticircumcision movement will at least partly hinge on convincing others that circumcision is elective, more akin to ear piercing than to appendectomy, and infants are not capable of electing anything. (Even readers of "Dear Abby," according to Bigelow, are conceding that ear piercing ought to be left up to the girl herself.)

Those who are fighting against ritual genital cutting of girls and boys are not arguing that the genitals should not be altered because they have a privileged meaning related to gender, but because they are a part of the body, like any other part that does not deserve to be destroyed. New ways of thinking about genitals need to be promulgated, including not encumbering them with extra meaning. This may mean taking genitals less seriously, a point I will develop in chapter 6.

Intersexual Identity

There are two radical corollaries to the argument that genital surgeries ought not to be performed on infants, based on the assumption that the surgeries limit gender options. One is that intersexed adults who were surgically altered and were not permitted an intersexual identity in childhood should "come out" as intersexual persons in adulthood. The second is that, from this point on, children born with "unacceptable" genitals should be permitted to develop an intersexual identity.

Much of the language of intersexuals has decidedly been formed by the history of the gay movement. Cheryl Chase compares coming out as intersexual in the 1990s with coming out as gay in the 1950s, when early activists proposed considering homosexuality a valid difference, not an illness, sin, or crime.[17] She reasons that just as homosexuality has come to be understood, at least by some people, as a social construct, intersexuality, too, can be reinterpreted from thinking of it as a monstrous condition to thinking of the management of intersexuality as monstrous. Alice Dreger's scholarship on how hermaphrodites in medieval Europe were not pathologized bolsters Chase's views on the historicity of intersexuality's meaning.[18] To Chase, the parallel with the destructive force of homophobia is obvious; it is social intolerance rather than individual pathology that is traumatic to an adolescent coming to terms with intersexuality.

The following quotations from two intersexuals display not only their anger but their acceptance of intersexuality as a permanent feature of themselves, even if in the eyes of the medical profession they were "repaired":[19]

> Parents have to decide whether they want an "aesthetically acceptable" [child] or a "happy, healthy, and intact" child. Before allowing them to decide in favor of the former, the child should better be adopted by someone else who is more tolerant, or even killed. . . . [I] think I was born at the wrong time and at the wrong place, but definitely not the "wrong way."

> It is that lie, that there is something so terribly wrong with us, that we need to be ashamed because we do not conform to sex polarity, that our biology is different. . . . It's the shame that the medical treatment instills. . . . It's the "private distress" that they insist our parents have. But godammit, why the fuck should I have been grateful? They steal our ability to feel that we have the right to unconditional love.

Some intersexuals, because of the response of others to their genitals or because of their knowledge of having been treated as neither completely female nor male, have developed what they refer to as an "intersexual identity." This identity, which begins as a private experience, is then promoted as a public category. My use of the term "intersexual" throughout this chapter to refer to intersexed adults reflects their choice of label, which is meant to replace "intersexed," a medical diagnosis applied by outsiders. On the surface, the distinction in terminology might seem trivial, but the power to label and ultimately rethink the meaning of that label is obvious. Whether "intersexual" becomes legitimated, just as "gay" replaced "homosexual" first by gays and then by much of the larger culture, remains to be seen. That not all intersexuals consistently use "intersexual" instead of "intersexed" (see below) reflects, I believe, not so much ideology but an exuberance in being able to utter either term out loud with ownership and pride. It is perhaps a first step in ultimately switching from "intersexed" to "intersexual" or for using "intersexed" to refer to the body and "intersexual" to the identity.[20] "If we can create a proud, public intersexual identity, we will be in a better position to fight with the gender nazis who are mutilating intersex infants. . . . I never was a male or a female. If the surgeons had not intervened I would have been an intersexual improperly assigned male, rather than an intersexual improperly assigned female."

Several intersexuals, in discussing the genital surgery they underwent, refer to it as their "sex change." They experience the childhood transfer as going from the category "intersexed" to the category "intersexed woman," a fine distinction perhaps, but one that suggests the psychological tenacity of their intersexuality and their profound loss. "I have managed to calm down my murderous rage at [the] professionals, but probably I'll never get over what my parents did to me by trying to kill me off."

This validation of intersexuality is revealed in the way some intersexuals experience their genitals not as a clitoris, a penis, or even as microphallic tissue. "I wish there was a way of talking . . . without intrinsically distorting things by misinterpreting them in terms of either male or female." Another objects to applying the term "phallic clitoris" to a larger-than-typical clitoris because that assumes that the appropriate place for a phallus is on the male. Intersexuals' clitorises "are not phallic, they are phalluses in themselves, however decidedly different from the male penis." She names this appendage that was removed from her the "phalloclit."[21] A third intersexed woman refers to her surgically removed (larger-than-typical) clitoris as her "lost penis," not because she believes herself to be male but because she does not believe that penises naturally mark maleness. Chase, again showing the influence of the gay movement on her conceptualization of intersexuality, calls intersexed genitals "queer genitals."

The intersexed identity is not adopted for political reasons but is a direct outgrowth of surgical experiences.[22] This is ironic since one argument surgeons make for surgical intervention as early in infancy as possible is that "tangible evidence of abnormality is . . . removed before any questions arise in the child's mind."[23] For some intersexuals, genital surgery creates rather than erases their intersexuality. One argues that the "corrected" intersexual must not only face chronic depression as a consequence of "desperately wishing for the return of body parts" but must deal with the identity issue. Chase concurs: "What we share is an experience . . . of object [under the knife]. . . . We need to assert . . . an intersex identity in order to . . . protest the way that we have been treated, to expose the harm done to us and to try to prevent it from continuing to be done to those intersexuals who come after."

In an earlier analysis of the relationship between genitals and gender, Wendy McKenna and I discussed "cultural genitals," those which a "person feels entitled to and/or is assumed to have."[24] The cultural genitals (not some configuration of biological material) are the foundation for any gender attribution made. "Lee is assumed to have a penis; Lee is a male." The way some intersexuals talk about their genitals, it is obvious that their private identities (although usually not the gender attributions made to them) are grounded in the genitals they no longer have. One intersexual says that others might assume she has female genitals, but because her physical genitals were removed, she does not feel entitled to the genitals constructed in their place. According to her, she is "a person possessing no 'cultural genitals' at all."

The degree to which intersexual groups are taken seriously by physicians depends to some extent on whether, as *intersexuals*, they are advocating changes in medical management. Because members of AISSG primarily identify themselves as "intersexed women," who are motivated to improve their condition as women (including encouraging improvements in vaginoplasty techniques), and not as "intersexuals," who question the gender categories, they have garnered more respect from the medical profession. Members of ISNA, who are organized around their "spoiled identity," have been routinely snubbed by medical schools, medical conferences, and medical journals.[25] They are proclaiming a common identity that medicine presumably obliterated decades ago. In contrast, members of AISSG have had their positions received with greater tolerance.[26] The androgen-insensitivity diagnosis, around which they are organized, was conferred upon them by physicians, and their "complaints" are seen as legitimate, given that the mere fact of their coming together validates the medical diagnosis. Those who organize around "intersexuality," however, are challenging not merely a management style (including a surgical style) but the right of the profession to manage them at all. They are also, by virtue of not being limited to a specific diagnosis, demonstrating that intersexuality is not as rare as physicians maintain.

One might think that women with androgen-insensitivity syndrome are not inclined to think of themselves as "intersexual" because they are medically classified as pseudohermaphrodites and not "true" hermaphrodites. This distinction comes from the medical profession and is not, I believe, of psychological import. Whether one's gonads are an ovotestes mixture or, instead, clearly one or the other, is probably less meaningful than what one's genitals look like or used to look like before surgery. The distinction between pseudo and real is unlikely to be what distinguishes members of AISSG from members of ISNA since the latter are also mostly pseudohermaphrodites, true hermaphroditism being extremely rare.

A journalist interviewed some surgeons at Johns Hopkins Medical Center about their views on intersexuals who belong to groups like ISNA. These physicians believe that intersexual activists are "a self-selected group brought together through their negative experiences."[27] It would be difficult to argue that those who make up the intersexual movement represent all those who have been given an intersexed diagnosis. (One member of ISNA reports that two devout Christians who showed some interest in the organization stopped participating in on-line discussions and were never heard from again.) That there are those with an intersex diagnosis who have lives and concerns that could not be more different from members of ISNA is reflected in the following remarks from two intersexed women who wrote to a parent of an intersexed child:[28]

> I work as a Sales Representative in a bank and I have been married for almost three years. I do all the things that anyone else does. People do not even know that I have Congenital Adrenal Hyperplasia [CAH] unless I tell them. . . . [T]hen they are surprised.

> I personally have done real well with my condition. The older
> I have gotten the better it has been. . . . [I] have been married
> 1 year & 7 months. . . . [My gynecologist] said I will have to
> be put on fertility drugs to get pregnant. I haven't done that
> yet. I may try next year.

According to one political intersexual, those intersexed who
are satisfied with their medical treatment and are leading conventionally gendered lives are "playing a game called 'gender separation' and 'keeping a normal image.'" Needless to say, not everyone
would see it that way. The fact that most intersexed people, including those in and out of intersexual groups, are living mani-
festly functional lives as assessed by psychological, social,
educational, and economic measures, does not mean that the genital surgeries and parental treatment they received had no effect
and that gender is completely nonproblematic for them. One group
of women with CAH whose clitorises had been recessed in combination with vaginal reconstruction differed from a matched sample
of women in liking less to touch themselves, feeling less erotic,
and being less sexually active. The authors concluded that their
patients had developed successful coping strategies and were able
to view their lives as satisfying, yet they admitted that the data
showed a high negative correlation between the number of surgical and clinical complications and quality of life.[29]

We might not expect those intersexed whose intersexuality
was eliminated by successful medical management to step forward and refute the claims of the political intersexuals. After all, a
successful treatment might have made them oblivious to any connection they might have with those who have publicly identified
themselves as intersexual, and certainly would not motivate them
to "go public" with a refutation. But physicians have countered
intersexuals' claims with nothing more than generalities. No documentation (anonymous or otherwise) has been offered of adult
intersexed who are pleased with their treatment.

Some intersexuals seem to be asking for the recognition of a
third gender category, the basis for membership being the possession (or past possession) of other-than-typical genitals, gonads, or
chromosomes. For some, gender has been problematic from the
time of birth; others are irregularly gendered in a more cloaked
manner—for example, they are chromosomal mosaics, neither
completely XX nor XY.

Not all intersexuals are promoting third-category status; rather, they are proposing that their intersexuality be legitimated by the use of "intersexual" as a modifier. The adjective "intersexual" would be coupled with femaleness or maleness much like "diabetic man" or "tall, blond woman." The modifier would clue others to the current (or past) mixture of the person's gender markers and the particularity of this characteristic for whatever it suggested. The public/performative gender would be "female" or "male," although the presentation might be coded to alert others to the intersexual status.

What are the grounds for claiming an intersexual identity either as a third category or as a modifier of one of the two standard genders? Those who underwent genital surgery, those who evaded it, and those who did not need it could be "intersexual" if they shared the consciousness of being differently gendered. According to Morgan Holmes, an intersexed member of ISNA Canada, the fact that one's adult body is no longer intersexed, having been altered in infancy to look female or male, does not militate against one's *identity* being intersexed. She points out that the medical diagnosis and consequent surgery help create the intersex category and thus the identity. She asks: "Was I intersexed before I was medicalized?" and compares herself to a woman friend with a three-and-a-half-inch clitoris that escaped "correction."[30] Holmes's friend refuses the intersex label for herself, claiming that this would be an additional burden, making her even more of an outsider than her lesbianism already does. I suspect that her rejection of the label has more to do with a lack of identity fit. She was not diagnosed; she was not "surgicalized;" she does not feel like an intersexual. Holmes's own argument confirms this: "It is partly in the naming that bodies become intersexed."[31]

Medical professionals name intersexuality in order to eradicate it, but this apparently backfires in many cases. The intersexual community names intersexuality to affirm the identity that the medical management created. One intersexual woman says, "Intersexed is a new self-label. I have arrived at this naming through my association with the Intersex Society of North America. . . . It seems to me that intersexed is a good neutral, collective term that associates me with those who share my specific physical difference."

Holmes writes about intersex being both a "natural occurrence" and a construction of medical/social interests.[32] While the latter is clearly true, in what sense is intersex natural? Genital, gonadal, and chromosomal variants are evident (if we look for them), but that does not make the category intersex "natural."

In a provocative set of articles, biologist Anne Fausto-Sterling, although not arguing for the "naturalness" of intersex categories, argues for legitimizing them, which, she claims, would help disrupt gender and dissolve gender oppositions.[33] It is true that validating alternative genitals validates alternative "sexes" and damages the privilege of "female" and "male." But the issue is gender and not "sex." The limitation with Fausto-Sterling's proposal is that legitimizing other sets of genitals still gives genitals (albeit in more than two forms) primary signifying status and ignores the fact that in the everyday world gender attributions are made without access to genital inspection. There is no sex, only gender, and what has primacy in everyday life is the gender that is performed, regardless of the flesh's configuration under the clothes.[34] It is difficult to accept the argument that the intersex category is legitimate and that genitals do not or should not matter. Intersexuals and their supporters want to decouple genitals and gender, but the "legitimacy" argument reinforces the relationship. They accuse others of taking genitals too seriously, but like medical professionals, their own response contributes to the seriousness. A more radical intersexual agenda would make intersex identities moot. There would just be women with large clitorises or fused labia or men with small penises or misshapen scrota—phenotypes with no particular clinical or identity meaning. Holmes considers this possibility when she calls the intersexual movement "a utopian project which can envision its own obsolescence."[35]

Both the medical community and the intersexual community claim intersexuality, the former as a health condition to be remedied and the latter as an identity to be promoted. How is it possible that medical and transgender communities recognize intersexuality in their own ways, and how might it be possible not to recognize it at all? Is there evidence that people learn to see dimorphism and, alternatively, that they could learn not to see it? Once genitals were no longer recognized as being of two distinct forms, "female" and "male" as dichotomous categories would likewise become difficult to see.

The Parents' Perspective[36]

In ancient Rome it was considered an ill omen to give birth to an intersexed child. The child was exposed to the elements and left to die. In the late twentieth century the meaning and consequences of genital ambiguity are less harsh. Nevertheless, intersexuality in a family creates an unusual drama. One intersex specialist described the case of a girl who was brought to the hospital because her father had attempted to rip off with his fingers the girl's enlarged clitoris.[37] The family of another intersexed child reportedly was so distraught about the infant's condition that the grandmother "considered committing suicide with the baby."[38] Are these spectacular examples typical or are they aberrant cases used to justify the current medical treatment of intersexuality?

Some parents are anguished after consenting to genital surgery, when they reflect upon their "giving in" to physicians. One regretful mother who authorized three surgeries on her son's penis wrote, "I will explain to my child . . . I did the best I could with the information at hand. My son will know I am human, I make mistakes, and I love him. Hopefully he will know I didn't intend harm but I was not informed." A father who precipitously consented for his infant's penis and testicles to be removed on the first day of life, while the physicians were performing other surgeries for some life-threatening conditions, is tormented by thoughts that his (now) daughter will never forgive him for castrating her.

These kinds of accounts are rarely published. As I discussed in chapter 2, in medical reports of intersexuality the parents of the infant are in the background, referred to, "educated," but not heard from. Insofar as we learn anything about the parents' reactions from the physicians, it is, at best, a filtered version, and we are still left with questions. For example, articles invariably refer to parents' negative emotional state (my emphases):

> The erected clitoris in such patients clearly suggested a penis and was a source of *embarrassment* for mother and child.[39]

> The existence of a normal-sized penis in patients assigned a male role is *comforting* to the parents even when hypospadias is present. Conversely, female babies born with an ungainly masculine enlargement of the clitoris evoke *grave concern* in their parents.[40]

John Gearhart, a surgeon at Johns Hopkins Medical Center, claims that "the mother especially finds [not doing surgery] worrisome. She says, 'This really bothers my husband and I [sic]. We'd like to fix this'"[41] (my emphasis). Quotations like these leave us with more questions than answers. How are anxiety and embarrassment displayed and are these the prevailing emotions?

One of the few articles in the management literature that goes beyond these vague, undocumented allusions reports interviews with twenty mothers of intersexed children. "Marital harmony was strained at the time of diagnosis in fourteen cases and there were five divorces, as a result."[42] A second period of family crisis was at the time of surgery. There was a temporary rejection of children by fathers, and some mothers reported their husbands were opposed to surgery, but the authors never describe what form the paternal rejection or apathy takes. Are we to conclude that fathers, in general, are more likely to be ambivalent about surgery than mothers, and if so why? Does it matter whether the surgery is on a girl or a boy? Is the stress any different than what families confront in other severe medical problems? Since physicians and not parents are the ones who publish articles, it is important to listen to how parents experience their child and their education from the physicians.

In chapter 2, I showed how physicians normalize intersexuality for parents and keep gender from being problematic by locating the problem in the genitals. Direct data from parents illustrate this. One mother gave birth to what doctors told her was a girl. The morning after the delivery, she was told they were not sure whether the baby was a female because they could not find a vaginal opening. "Your baby knows what he [sic] is and will tell us after we run some tests." This, she said, put her at ease, and she has subsequently used that phrase herself to explain the process of gender assignment. The way she put it to me was, "It's our job to figure [the gender] out." When I introduced myself to another mother as a social psychologist interested in situations when children are born with ambiguous genitals and "there might be a need for a gender decision to be made," she countered with, "There isn't a decision that's made. They are born with ambiguous genitalia, but they are *female*; they are definitely *female*" (her emphases).

The parents' perspective helps us see that one of the ways physicians normalize the intersex condition and keep the infant's

gender from being problematic is by first teaching parents to see
the genital ambiguity and then by teaching them to see the ambiguity as not important. It is merely a genital ambiguity, and a correctable one at that.

The following examples are taken from letters written by
mothers of intersexed children, some of whom appear to have initially experienced their infants as "perfect" and were taught by
the doctors that what looked like perfection was not; other mothers seem to have continued to experience their infants as "perfect," despite atypical genitals.

> My son was born 5 months ago and was pronounced to be a
> "girl" at birth—it wasn't until the next morning that they
> found no vaginal opening and knew something was wrong.
> After chromosome tests, ultra-sounds, blood work, etc. . . . [h]e
> was [found to be] a perfect male, but his testes never dropped
> to form [a] scrotum and he had an under-developed penis. We
> were very lucky that my son had no other problems.

> She was born perfectly healthy and looking like a girl—but
> she had skin fusion, and no opening to her vagina, which her
> urologist wants to correct soon.

> We thought we had two perfectly healthy children. The bomb
> fell when I took [my daughter] to her two-week check-up.
> Her pediatrician discovered that she had no vaginal opening.
> He very gently told me that she had what was called "am-
> biguous genitalia."

These are all interesting examples of "perfect." In the first
case he is a perfect male in spite of an absent scrotum and a small
penis; in the second case, she is "perfect" too, although she will
"need" genital surgery; in the third case, the supposed ambiguity
of the girl's genitals has no bearing on her perfection.

Some infants who are eventually labeled "intersex" are at first
taken to be normal from the parents' (untutored) perspective. Although the parents needed to be educated about their child's medical abnormality, from a "looks" point of view, what they saw looked
normal to them. Each of the following examples suggests that parents rely on the physicians not only to tell them what gender their
child is but to tell them whether the child's genitals look good
enough.

When Marlee was born we had no idea there was anything wrong with her. . . . They told us she was a girl, then a boy, and then they were not sure. . . . After two weeks in ICU they found out she was a girl. . . . She has had two surgerys [*sic*] already.

Rob is now much more irregular than he was before surgery. Before surgery he was changed by baby-sitter and church workers and no one ever expressed feelings there was something "wrong" with him.

They told me they weren't sure if Noreen was a boy or girl. A few hours later they told me she was a girl. Her vagina was very swollen. . . . So far they said she will not need surgery yet. *They say* she looks okay. [my emphasis]

In another family, the "perfect" baby girl was taken home soon after birth only to be returned to the hospital six weeks later with breathing difficulties. The mother reports, "They told us she may possibly be a boy. Her clitoris was enlarged but her vagina had only closed partially. However the "lips" that overlap the vagina had not formed. . . . Tests proved she was definitely a girl, and a very slight operation around one year old opened her vagina to the proper length. That was all the surgery she needed. The large clitoris now seems smaller as her new body has grown around it."

There are two important points about this last example. First, this girl with an enlarged clitoris and unusual labia was unremarkable to these parents and presumably to the physician who delivered her until it was discovered a month and a half later that she had congenital adrenal hyperplasia (CAH). Secondly, clitoral surgery was averted by just waiting long enough for the body to grow, a management strategy that was more common in previous generations before the current philosophy of intersex management.

One woman, now married, recalls, "Doctor thought I was a boy, they did [a] test and confirmed I was a girl. But I never had any surgeries. . . . My parents wouldn't have wanted to go through it."

"Our daughter was born in 1956. . . . [She] had a large clitoris and the Dr. said they'd just 'cut it off' when she got older. Thank God the cortisone took care of that."

A past director of the Magic Foundation, a national organization created to provide services for the families of children who have a growth disorder condition (one of which is CAH), has known parents who have elected not to have surgery performed on their daughters and admits that such a decision works out, especially when a particular doctor feels that the family should wait and see what happens. In one medical case of an XY infant diagnosed with partial androgen-insensitivity syndrome and given a female gender assignment shortly after birth, the authors report that "the mother had not fully comprehended the nature of the syndrome, but had understood that her child would grow up as female. The clitoral enlargement was not deemed disturbing."[43]

The mother of a son diagnosed as having a form of male pseudohermaphroditism with adrenal insufficiency, described his penis to me as "underdeveloped" and said his testes had not descended. Although the urologist where the baby was born told her to raise the child as a female, physicians at a university hospital where the baby was sent for further examination encouraged her to raise the child as a male in accordance with his chromosomes and despite the small penis. Like most parents of an intersexed infant, her concerns about gender were quickly supplanted by her medical concerns, for example what kind of hormones and surgery he might need. The boy was treated with testosterone, there was some penile growth, and his first surgery created a new urethral opening. The second surgery was described by the mother as "cosmetic" to reconstruct the scrotum to look "more like a scrotum." According to the mother, the doctors say, "He's gotten as normal looking as he can." Although this mother remembers being shocked when she was told about her son's condition, she now suspects that genital abnormalities are more common than people think. It is unclear whether that suspicion has permitted her to accept her son's irregular penis more easily or whether the belief in genital variability is a consequence of that acceptance.

She told me that "thirty years ago they would have kept him a girl," apparently unaware that, even today, it is common to give a female gender assignment to an infant with a small phallus. Although most of her son's doctors have been supportive of the assignment decision, others reportedly were "appalled." Her family too has been understanding, except for a grandmother who had a lot of problems dealing with "that part of the body."

The supposedly embarrassing problem of a micropenis seems not to be much of a problem for this mother. All of her comments about her son's penis and scrotum are about what it looks like currently. She says nothing about her concerns about how his genitals will function, what they will eventually look like, or whether he will have reproductive capacity. One urologist told her she might not want her son to see pictures of penises until later, since it might make him feel inadequate. She told me that she did not take his remarks seriously. She sent me an audiotape of a favorite song called "It's Only a Wee-wee, so What's the Big Deal."

In describing the life of an intersexed cousin who was never surgically altered, one woman explained to me, "Her father thought she was perfect—made by God."[44] How is it that some children, even though their genitals deviate from the norm, manage to live regular lives without genital surgery? How many surgeries might be avoided if physicians would just wait and let nature take its course—"nature" being either the body changing on its own and/ or the parents and child coming to accept the genitals as a reasonable marker of the child's gender? One mother of an intersexed son wrote me, "I know I would have at least considered hearing the 'no surgery' option . . . but that is currently not available to new parents in the isolation that doctors create."

Given that some intersexed infants have medical problems not directly related to genitals, physicians could capitalize on the parents' attention to these issues and deemphasize genitals. It is clear from parents' letters that much of their initial shock, sadness, and fear was related to the medical emergencies associated with their child's CAH. If we take on face value what they said they were worried about, they are concerned with (in order of emphasis): whether their child will die from dehydration due to a salt imbalance, the long-term effects of steroid treatment, whether their child will remember to take medications as she/he gets older, and how tall their child will eventually be (some types of CAH cause early, accelerated bone growth that eventuates in the end of growth before the children reach what would have been their adult height).

Less frequently cited concerns include whether their child will weigh too much as a consequence of the medications, have the characteristic "moon face" of CAH children, be too dark-complected or too hairy, be able to reproduce, and whether they will meet other children with the same condition. The parents worry that they may never overcome feelings of loneliness resulting from being the only one they know who has to face this situation, and that they in some way contributed to the disorder by taking drugs or alcohol, smoking, or exposing themselves to toxic substances. The mothers wonder if they should take medication during another pregnancy to help prevent having a second child with CAH. Like other parents, their main worry is what the future will bring for their children.

One might argue that parents express so little concern about their intersexed children's genitals because that part of the problem was already taken care of by the surgeons. It is at least possible, though, that some parents considered their child's genitals the least of their problems, in spite of all the physicians' allusions to the parents' embarrassment. How astute are physicians in assessing what is of greatest concern to their patients and families? Women diganosed with androgen-insensitivity syndrome (AIS) report being more preoccupied with their lack of pubic hair, their memories of having been lied to and put on display for medical students, and their difficulty talking to relatives who they suspect might also have AIS than with what they call "nonissues" such as XY chromosomes, testes, and infertility, the features of their condition focused on by medicine and psychology.[45]

There is no question that parents who are preoccupied with many of the health issues surrounding having a child with an intersex diagnosis are motivated to collaborate with the physician and see the genital surgeries as necessary, relatively simple, and curative. In the words of one mother, "The plastic surgeon *erased* any physical sign of her enzyme deficiency" (my emphasis). A mother who knows a number of parents with intersexed children told me, "There's quite a bit of concern [about gender] initially until they find out that through surgery it can be corrected." The equating of gender with genitals in that quotation is blatant and provides, from the parents' point of view, evidence for the arguments I made in chapter 2: parents are dependent almost entirely on members of the medical profession for an interpretation of the situation, and early surgery masks the problematic nature of gender.

Parents are provided with a comprehensive treatment plan involving medication and surgery that is presented as imperative and non-negotiable. The medical view is the authoritative view, and the parents adopt it, adding to it their own private concerns. Genital surgery within the first year helps resolve at least part of the parents' anxiety about their children's health. One mother expressed this directly when she wrote to another mother, "I have to admit I was a little bit surprised that your doctor would hold off on [your daughter's vaginoplasty] until puberty. I guess having [my daughter's] done so early in her life has made this so much less emotional and stressful."

Even though most of the parents' letters were extraordinarily lengthy and detailed—often two to three single-spaced, typed pages—in almost all there were only cursory descriptions of the genitals and the surgery. Each example below is from a different letter and displays the full extent of that parent's discussion about the child's genitals and the surgery:

> She was born with ambiguous genitalia and had corrective surgery when she was eight weeks old.

> At eight months she had a clitoral reduction. She's also had her vagina opening made.

> They just tucked some of [her clitoris] behind her pelvic bone, I believe. The next operation she might have to have some cutting done (I think) of her clitoris.

> She had a clitoral recession at eighteen months. Though there has been only a little talk of it, we understand that her uterus and vagina are normal.

> [She] had surgery done when she was fourteen months old. They reduced her clitoris but it was very minor. Other than that she's only had her vaginal opening stretched.

Those few parents who expanded on the genital ambiguity and surgical repair focused disproportionately on how the genitals look rather than on what the child might be experiencing or how her genitals might function in the future. I indicate this not to allege that the parents are malevolent but to show how they are mirroring the physicians' main criterion for success.

One mother's comment on her daughter's surgery was, "They did a cliterus [sic] reduction and you can't tell any difference between her and any other girl. They did a great job."

After a six-year-old girl's second clitoroplasty and labioplasty, her mother writes, "It looks better than it did, but my husband thought maybe another operation, but I think it's fine like it looks now! . . . Lately she's been saying it hurts down there. . . . It looks fine on the outside. . . . I'd say all in all [she] did very well with the surgery."

If "looks" matter, what should one be able to see if one looks? One set of parents told me that their daughter's reduced clitoris is so receded under the hood that it cannot be seen. Their pediatrician admitted he could not find it, and the urologist promised that when the vagina was constructed at puberty, the clitoris would be "pulled down." The parents seem unconcerned about sexual functioning, but, in passing, the mother said that her daughter's genitals "don't look quite right, not normal." After describing the labia minora as too long and a lump that "might be scar tissue," she concluded her assessment with, "It looks ok . . . I guess as normal as surgery can do." In spite of this lukewarm assessment, she evidenced no regret about having had the surgery done.

In the previous chapter, I described a clitoroplasty technique that involved hiding the clitoris beneath folds of skin. In the words of one mother, "At 6 weeks [my daughter] had corrective surgery to push her clitoris inside her body more so that she'd look more like a girl." It is acceptable for a female to have a large and easily palpable clitoris as long as it is concealed. Gender is marked by the obviousness of an organ and not its existence, proving correct, on yet another level, those who describe gender as a "performance."[46]

Most parents of intersexed infants have never met anyone in their situation, and some complain that physicians are loath to link them up with other parents. One mother confided, "[The doctor] reacts like, 'Why would anyone want to discuss it with other people? I'm telling you everything you need to know and that's enough.'" One team of intersex managers writes, "Experience has taught us that parents who shared their grief with acquaintances came to regret that later on."[47] The message is that genital variations are shameful, and if parents need to confide, they should, according to the professionals, turn to professionals.

In spite of the outpouring of letters that one mother received in response to her appeal, neither she nor two other mothers who independently tried to start support groups for parents of intersexed children were successful. Although the mothers were contacted by some parents, none seemed interested in joining with others in the same situation. Physicians might regard this as verification of their opinion that parents do not require anything beyond the medical management. I suspect, though, that it verifies the mortification the parents experienced as a result of the management. They are ill prepared to give and receive support from similar others because the meanings of genitals and gender were never addressed. Physicians pride themselves in shielding parents from ticklish gender issues, but there is no protection from confronting gender in our culture. The confrontation is only delayed. As I showed, it emerges for the intersexed person years later.

The Everyday View

In chapter 3, I considered the medical standards for genitals and proposed that physicians have a very conservative sense of how much variability is tolerable. Not all parents, it seems, have as strict criteria for what constitutes normal genitals. Although the parents might tolerate some variability, they are not given the opportunity, as the medical management is hastily engineered. Would a sample of ordinary lay persons, not immediately caught up in the personal drama of their child's medical condition, find tolerable the mild and moderate forms of variant genitals that surgeons believe need to be corrected?[48]

My students and I began answering these questions by presenting 127 college students with a centimeter scale and asking them to estimate the ranges for a normal newborn clitoris and penis. As I mentioned in chapter 3, physicians specify .2 to .9 centimeters as appropriate for a neonate's clitoris and 2.5 to 4.5 centimeters as appropriate for a neonate's penis.[49] Not only is no overlap permitted between the male and female genitals, but they must be separated by neutral, gender unmarked territory. Fausto-Sterling refers to the distance between the largest allowable clitoris and the smallest allowable penis as "Phallic Netherland."[50]

College students, expecting larger clitorises and smaller penises than physicians permit, estimated that the range of newborn clitoral lengths was .9 to 1.9 centimeters and of newborn penile lengths was 2.1 to 3.6 centimeters. More importantly, the students did not imagine much of a gap between the largest clitoris and the smallest penis. In fact, 35 percent of the students allowed for some overlap between their estimated clitoral and penile lengths. Would people like these notice that an infant's genitals are the "wrong" size unless told so by a physician?[51]

Students were then given the physicians' standards for genital lengths, and women were asked to imagine having been born with a clitoris between 1.0 and 2.5 centimeters. Under what conditions would they have wanted it surgically reduced? Ninety-three

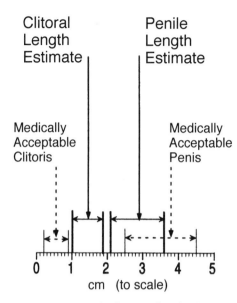

Figure 2. Ranges of college students' estimates of infant clitoral and penile lengths compared to medically acceptable ranges

percent would not have wanted their parents to agree to clitoral reduction if the condition were not life threatening and if it resulted in the loss of orgasm or pleasurable sensitivity. Over half of the women would not have wanted surgery even if the condition were unattractive and made them feel uncomfortable. This was particularly true of the lesbian and bisexual women in the sample. Twelve percent of the women would not have wanted a clitoral reduction under any circumstance.

Women predicted that having a large clitoris would not have had much of an impact on their peer relations and almost no impact on their relations with their parents. When given a choice as to when surgery should occur, almost half would have wanted to be able to make their own decision when they were old enough. Finally, they were more likely to want surgery to reduce a large nose, large ears, or large breasts than surgery to reduce a large clitoris.

All these findings are understandable inasmuch as the women rated pleasurable genital sensation and the ability to have an orgasm as being "very important" to the average woman, and the size of the clitoris as being not even "somewhat important." With a minimum of medical knowledge, the average college woman seems to suspect that surgery on her clitoris is likely to compromise the genital functions she values.

They were also asked about the possibility of having a vagina surgically constructed in the event they had been born without one or with an abnormally small one. Given that three-fourths of them believe the average woman derives more sexual pleasure from clitoral stimulation than from vaginal penetration, the findings are not surprising, and in many respects, mirror those on clitoral reduction.

Most of them would not have wanted vaginal surgery even if the condition made them feel uncomfortable or limited their ability to have sexual intercourse. Although the lesbian and bisexual women were more likely than the others to reject vaginal surgery, almost half of the females whose sexual partners are male would not have wanted a vaginal canal constructed even though they predicted that not having a vagina would have a major impact on their sexual relations. The percentage of women who say they would not have wanted vaginal surgery increased when they were presented with the possibility of complications and when they were told their vaginas would have to be dilated frequently over a long period of time. In general, the women rated vaginal length as not very important to the average woman and did not expect that not having a vagina would have had much of an impact on their relations with parents and peers or on their self-esteem.

Males were asked if they would have wanted surgery if they had been born with a penis whose urethral opening was off center— a mild form of hypospadias for which male infants are typically "corrected." A third of the men would not have wanted their parents to have agreed to surgery even if it kept the males from being able to urinate standing up, the common rationale for such surgery. Three-fourths would not have wanted the surgery if it resulted in the loss of pleasurable sensitivity. In general, they evaluated the risks of penile surgery to correct mild hypospadias similarly to how they evaluated hair-replacement surgery to correct baldness. Like the female students, those who would have wanted genital surgery wanted it to be delayed until they were adults and their bodies completely grown.

Presented with a difficult choice, whether to have been raised male with a micropenis that at birth measured between .9 and 2.5

centimeters or to have been reassigned to the female gender, over half of the men would have not wanted the reassignment. That percentage increases to almost all the men if the surgery was described as reducing pleasurable sensitivity or orgasmic capability. Contrary to beliefs about male sexuality, the college men in this study did not think that having a micropenis would have had a major impact on their sexual relations, peer or parental relations, or self-esteem.

An additional sample of sixty-three college students, asked to imagine that their daughter or son was born with nonstandard genitals, made more traditional choices. They opted for early surgery, much like real parents who are not apprised of alternatives. The reasons they gave included not wanting their child to feel out of place in society and wanting to prevent the trauma of later surgery. One student wrote, "The closer to birth the change is, the closer she is to having been born with it [a vagina]."

Although, in general, students elected early surgery for their hypothetical infants, there were response differences, depending on what genital condition the student had been presented with. They were most likely to want surgical correction for a daughter born without a vagina than for children born with other genital irregularities (a hypospadiac penis or a clitoris twice the average size).

As a comparison, some students were asked to imagine having an infant with a (nongenital) birthmark. We were interested in whether genital conditions, although not publicly visible (much like birthmarks on the stomach), are thought of as visible (much like facial birthmarks). Students who were asked to imagine their infant with a stomach birthmark or large clitoris were more likely than others to opt for either delaying surgery until after their daughter had gone through puberty or letting her make the surgical decision herself. Clitoral surgery, in particular, was evaluated less favorably when the students were informed about postsurgical complications and told they could have the option of postponing surgery to "see what happens." In chapter 6, I will develop the position suggested by these data—not all genital parts are conceptualized similarly.

Critics of this research will claim that college students have no idea what decisions they would have wanted made if their genitals (or their child's genitals) had been variant at birth. That criticism would carry more weight if physicians were basing their surgical decisions on good follow-up data instead of on their predictions about what it would be like to grow up with variant genitals or to raise a child with them. What evidence is there that the average physician's predictions are any more accurate than the average college student's predictions?[52] Should not all of these predictions be considered in the context of how successful the surgeries are? As I showed in chapter 4, their success is far from obvious and depends on what one thinks genitals are for. I begin the next chapter with that issue.

6

Rethinking

Genitals

and Gender

"Such [hermaphroditic] creatures seem to have been
formed merely to show us that this much-talked-of difference of sex is, after all, nothing inherent in the con-
stitution of things, and that individuals may be born,
live, and thrive, of both sexes or neither."

—Geo. H. Napheys, 1870

If genitals are not completely dimorphic, if
genital surgery to create dimorphism is problematic, and if people
under certain conditions are capable of accepting genital variability, then why is intersexuality managed in the way that it is?
Why are unusually sized and shaped genitals not accepted as reasonable markers of gender—gender either as we know it in the
two-option scheme or as we could know it in a new gender system? Why does the "solution" for variant genitals lie in knives
and not in words? We can begin to answer these questions by
considering two very different subjects: the criterion of heterosexuality and the history of cosmetic surgery.

There was a shift during the twentieth century from basing
gender-assignment decisions on whether the gonads have reproductive potential to how the genitals could best be used heterosexually. By giving a male gender assignment to a person with a

functioning penis and ovaries who is partnered with a woman, the physician "banished the specter of homosexuality."[1] Biologist Fausto-Sterling goes so far as to claim that successful heterosexuality is the main criterion by which gender assignments are made and genital surgery evaluated.[2] She reads between the lines of the requirement that a penis be capable of penetration to suggest that the criterion is: Can a child raised as a male become a successful heterosexual? She is correct to extend the criterion, because if it were penetration per se, then whether the male ultimately penetrated a woman's vagina or a man's anus would not be of concern, and yet researchers typically modify penetration with the word "vaginal." Given the values of gay male culture, one could even make the argument that the length of the ultimate phallus might be of greater concern to future male than female partners, but this is never addressed in the literature. Length of penis = penetrating ability = heterosexuality.[3]

The word "vagina" comes from the Latin word meaning "sheath"; the penis fits into the vagina like a sword.[4] That the vagina exists for the penis is confirmed by a drawing in a 1932 textbook that purports to be a "diagrammatic section in median plane of the female genital organs."[5] The figure, with no clitoris represented, shows a vagina with a penis in it. The figure is described as "the internal and more important part of the *female* sexual apparatus"[6] (my emphasis). The labia, too, have been described as though their function is as much for the man as for the woman: "The labia *majora* protect the deeper parts [of the female genitals], lead the male organ to them, and serve as buffers during coitus. [The *minora*] act as an irritant for the nerves of the male member at the same time that their own nerves are acted on."[7] These examples can cause us to ponder who the vagina and labia actually belong to.[8]

Many of the vaginoplasty follow-up studies for intersexed females include "marriage" as part of the proof of surgical success.[9] One group of surgeons suggests that "the right time for an introital operation is shortly before the woman intends to start having intercourse."[10] Should we conclude, then, that if the woman does not intend to have vaginal intercourse, or if her parents do not want to think about her having intercourse, then the vaginoplasty should be postponed indefinitely? One father reflected cultural beliefs about the vagina when he told me (laughingly) that he would not mind if vaginoplasty on his intersexed daughter were delayed until she was twenty-one. The mother concurred: "What with everything going on nowadays with sexual abuse of children," it was fine if her daughter did not have a vagina.

Reconstructive surgery for women with genital cancers is more often recommended to young, married, and sexually active women with healthy husbands, and the surgery is deemed successful if intercourse can be resumed. In a review of eleven follow-up studies of women with genital cancers who received vaginal reconstruction, the primary criterion for success in all but one was the capacity of the neovagina to accept a penis.[11] This criterion assumes that women of all ages focus on the capacity of their genitals for sexual intercourse as their primary attribute of femininity. The authors conclude that physicians believe that female sexuality equals heterosexual intercourse, that the goal of successful intercourse must be strived for at all costs, and that benefits will outweigh any costs.

One surgical oncologist believes that it is neither a male bias nor a physician bias to define normal sexual function as penile introduction into a vagina. Instead, he claims it is a female bias. "Women feel that it is expected of them in a normal marital relationship. . . . A sexual relationship is to be able to accept a male penis."[12]

Another physician, in discussing reconstructive surgery after cancer, asserts, "[They] end up with . . . a structure which has limited-to-no sensation if they're honest about it and . . . simply serves as a receptacle so they can have some kind of intercourse." Perhaps because of his assessment of the limitations of the surgery, he argues against making a new vagina for every woman, regardless of her circumstances and desires: "I don't know where [other physicians] get the data that suggest that just because you take it out, you gotta make one. People have amputations. A lot of people walk around with stumps. Not everybody gets a leg or cane." On one level, his reasoning is obvious, yet by comparing a vagina to a leg, he is treating the genital in a refreshingly unmarked way, disentangling it from category membership.

More commonly, surgeons believe that a woman needs a vagina: "If you can give a patient a functioning vagina, you've accomplished what you set out to accomplish. . . . Without a vagina a woman is not normal. It's like having a nose. You can breathe fine without a nose, but you look funny without a nose. [The women] don't feel normal. . . . I think it's very important, whether it's ever used." Should we interpret his answer about not needing to use the vagina as meaning that he does not use heterosexuality as a criterion for success? Or does his requirement of a vagina for complete femaleness reflect heterosexist cultural norms for a complete woman: the vagina should be there if it is ever needed.

If heterosexuality underlies the criterion for a successful vagina, then it is obvious that a woman needs a vagina in order to satisfy the man's penis. If, however, the belief in two genders grounds both heterosexuality and genital surgery decisions, then the relationship between sexual intercourse and genitals is reversed. The reason a woman needs a man's penis is so that she can have a vagina and thus be a woman.

Sexual intercourse between a postsurgical male-to-female transsexual and her male partner is described in one follow-up study as "contributing in keeping her vagina open," thereby contributing to a "successful surgical outcome."[13] A specific sexual act serves to create and maintain a particular anatomy, rather than the anatomy being created and maintained so that the activity can take place. This is a new take on "anatomy is destiny." If you are destined to have the anatomy, does it matter how you get that anatomy? Being a woman means having a vagina, at any cost, and if a woman needs to function heterosexually in order to have that vagina, then a penis is as good as a plastic dilator.

One method of vaginoplasty for women with genital cancer requires that women wear a vaginal mold for seven to ten days postoperatively; thereafter "intercourse . . . is encouraged as a means of retaining functional vaginal width and depth." (The reader will recall that the same kind of assertion is made about intersex surgery.) Nineteen of twenty vaginoplasties in one study were counted as successes even though six of the women never used the new vagina and six others died during the follow-up period. "Patients who died within a few months of surgery . . . are counted as successes if their *capacity* for vaginal intercourse was restored" (my emphasis). In another study, "satisfactory" outcome was defined as producing a "usable vagina." Note that the vagina need merely be usable, not actually used. One might quibble that this is just a preliminary assessment, based on cosmetics and presumable future use, but it is also clearly an outsider's perspective and neither the woman's nor her partner's.[14]

Given that the vagina need not be used, but only appear to be usable, how credible is this newly constructed genital? In describing

one procedure, a surgeon claims that "there's not any symmetry. . . .
[The vulva] amounts to being sort of two doughy mounds which
have a cleft . . . [but] sometimes there's no tissue left and that's
what you have to do in order to fill the hole and the fact that
there's a functional vagina into which a penis can be inserted is
sort of euphemistic. It doesn't have a whole lot in common with a
natural vagina." In essence, it is the *idea* of a vagina.[15]

The feminist perspective on the politics of health care treats
heterosexism, androcentrism, and phallocentrism as the underlying criteria for successful vaginoplasty. One intersexual holds this
view: "The establishment is trying to ensure that we'll all become
heteros—which I love to remind them I'm not." The evidence I
presented above encourages a reconsideration. Rather than seeing
a vulva and vagina as constructed for their sexual use, suppose
they are created fundamentally as a gender marker and need to be
only reasonable approximations, not necessarily mistaken for
"natural" ones. Even the intersexual quoted above supports this
when she says, "There is no care for whether or not I have perfectly functioning adult genitalia. . . . It's a kind of 'lookism.'"

If, according to the professional literature, a woman needs an
approximate vagina for a hypothetical penis, what does a man need
a penis for? One group of surgeons lists the following phallic requirements for males: "The presence of a sufficiently large phallus to function as a male urinary conduit, to offer a satisfactory
appearance when compared with peers [what is called the "locker
room factor"],[16] and to function satisfactorily for sexual activity."[17]
Assuming that the order is not arbitrary, the penis is, first of all,
for one's health, as a technical means for passing liquid waste out
of the body; secondarily for one's male friends to view in the locker
room and to use to validate one's masculinity; and lastly, for sexual
pleasure. The marking of maleness by the penis is so implicit that
it need not even be mentioned; gender attribution is penis attribution.[18] One consequence of this equation is that a female-to-male
transsexual, even if he is undeniably credited with the male gender based on social interaction, can lose that credibility if it is
discovered that he still has a vagina.[19]

If gender needs to be marked by a reasonably approximate genital, why then are some physicians willing to treat genital surgery
as optional for survivors of vulvar and vaginal cancer, when such
an option is not offered to intersexed infants (or more accurately,
their parents)? One possibility is that a woman with genital can-

cer has already lived as a woman with a vagina that was capable of receiving a penis, and her gender has already been marked. The vagina's removal does not unmark her, and she need not have the vagina recreated in order to validate her gender. I suspect the same is true of men who lose their penis through accidental trauma. They are still men, albeit with the presumption, by some, of diminished masculinity.

If the intersexed could prove that their gender did not need to be validated, would they, too, have the option of refusing genital surgery? How could one learn to validate gender differently? I will consider these questions further at the end of this chapter.

There is a long history of solving all kinds of bodily disappointments with surgery. Bernice Hausman, in a review of the early years of plastic surgery, describes the conflict from within medicine concerning the ethics of "aesthetic procedures."[20] In the first issue of *Plastic and Reconstructive Surgery*, in 1946, quacks were differentiated from responsible physicians, with the latter being entitled to provide legitimate services under the names "reconstructive or corrective surgery." Before long it was argued that plastic surgery could be provided in order to "improve the psychological functioning, even if there were no pressing physiological need."[21] Hausman analyzes speeches from presidential addresses at annual meetings of plastic surgeons that suggest that the surgeons became increasingly "unwilling to settle for the patients who would come to them due to accidents . . . or congenital deformities."[22]

Thus was born a subspecialty of plastic surgery called "cosmetic surgery," whose purpose is to make the body conform to the patient's ideal of herself or himself. Cosmetic surgeons have redefined the kinds of bodies in need of their services. One assumption underlying the practice of cosmetic surgery is that because society's standards of physical appearance cannot and should not be changed, plastic surgery can and should offer imperfect individuals a chance to look normal. Because of these surgical offerings, though, what is considered normal has changed, proving cosmetic surgery's original assumption wrong. Plastic surgeons "have shifted the boundaries of the categories 'normal' and 'abnormal' appearance such that the former has become smaller as the latter has grown."[23] The distinction between "normal" and "ideal" collapsed. Although plastic surgeons claimed to be describing the normal, in fact they were promoting the ideal.

Sociologists Diana Dull and Candace West discuss ways that cosmetic surgeons rationalize doing surgery that, by its own definition, is elective.[24] Surgeons describe elective surgery as a normal, natural pursuit to correct objectively flawed features. The body is reduced into parts. From this perspective, cosmetic procedures are neither luxuries nor investments but rather interventions that are needed. Dull and West note that the surgeons and patients they interviewed "alluded to technically normal features as 'flaws,' 'defects,' 'deformities,' and 'correctable problems of appearance.'" Once bodies are seen as "essentially in need of repair," then surgery is seen as a "moral imperative."[25]

Feminists have made it clear that the knife does not fall equally on men and women. The privileging of one gender—male—has resulted in the privileging of that gender's body. Because women's bodies are "underprivileged," they are more often the object of improvement campaigns. Kathryn Morgan writes about the language that plastic surgeons use to pathologize the ordinary female body: "problem areas," "ugly protrusions," "inadequate breasts," "unsightly concentrations of fat cells." The female body is "a potential, a kind of raw material to be exploited in terms of appearance, eroticism, nurturance, and fertility."[26] Cosmetic surgery, she argues, conceptualizes the female body as an object for others rather than as a serious, important object for use.

Hausman's analysis goes beyond critiques that analyze women's oppression as a product of the targeting of female bodies by the cosmetic-surgery industry. She suggests that gender itself is a product of plastic surgery. This proposition complements the argument I made in chapter 2 that gender is a product of the way intersexuality is managed. In discussing the emergence of transsexualism, she argues that "it is not possible to understand how the gender system impacts the development of technologies unless we also examine how technical practices [i.e., plastic surgery] affect the gender system."[27] Women (and to some extent men) have collaborated with surgeons to attain the best possible body for their gender, and transsexuals have contracted with surgeons to attain the best-gendered body for their mind. Given these manufactured interests and the need to enforce gender, one can begin to understand why there has been a surgical solution to variant (or missing) genitals for intersexed children.[28]

Genital Cosmetic Surgery

A nationally syndicated sexual advice column printed the following letter:

> I am a young woman who has had few sexual encounters. I am convinced that my vulva is unattractive and sloppy. Is it extremely unusual for a clitoris and inner labia to protrude from the outer labia? Are you aware of any plastic surgeons who specialize in correcting this abnormality?

This letter reflects more than a wish for a surgical solution from a woman who knows that there are surgical solutions to problem body parts. It indicates a lack of knowledge of other women's genitals and a shame about her own. The advisor/columnist concurs: "You could consult a gynecological surgeon, but you'd be best served by finding . . . a picture book of various vulva in all their spectacular array and identifying yours among the normal variation."[29]

In a later issue of the column, a reader offered his reaction to the original letter:

> I took an informal poll of the guys where I work. I could not find one male who was NOT extremely aroused by the physical conditions she described. Those of us who have only seen this in photographs were quite envious of the ones who were able to describe actual sexual encounters with these highly endowed females. This women [sic] doesn't have physical flaws, she has physical gifts![30]

How far a leap is it from arguing, as physicians do, that an intersexed child "need not grow up with the genitalia he or she was born with"[31] to arguing that none of us need do it? In the last twenty years we have seen the cosmetic surgeon's knife move from the nose to the breasts and thighs. What is to stop the knife from moving further down?[32]

If the young woman with unsatisfactory genitals does not accept the columnist's advice, she will probably find her way to a cosmetic surgeon. There is already a business in "repair" of labia minora. Medical journals report cases of women with what is referred to as "complaints of redundant labia," which means that the labia are too long, not that there are too many. Some redundant labia minora, are described as "extending over the perineum to the anal orifice," causing "mechanical difficulties, such as painful and difficult intercourse, pressure under tight clothing, and difficulty cleansing after elimination."[33] Hypertrophy of the labia does not indicate an underlying endocrine problem, nor is it related to any other physiologic deviation, yet "wing-like" labia are not considered a natural variation but something to be treated by excising the redundant skin.[34]

In some contemporary African and Middle Eastern cultures, all labia (not just long ones) are considered unsightly and unclean, and men reject for marriage "women who have not been 'done,'" that is, whose labia and clitoris have not been removed.[35] If the labia are not excised, it is believed that they will dangle between the legs and may threaten the penis. An 1884 medical text contains color drawings of what is referred to as the "Hottentot apron." The author writes, "In all the women of the Bushman in South Africa and in some of the Hottentot women, they [the labia minora] hang halfway down to the knees."[36] Similarly, an 1824 source reports the case of a "negress" with a clitoris four and a half inches long and one and a half inches in diameter and another with an enlarged clitoris that was twelve inches long and "resembled the neck of a goose." The author concludes that an enlarged clitoris appears to be a racial trait among the peoples of North Africa.[37] There is no indication that this is now or ever was true, but reading these old reports could have contemporary repercussions. Cheryl Chase reported to me that one African American intersexual woman who read anthropological accounts felt "that her body is some sort of atavistic throwback, apelike, related to chimpanzees." She got the message from these articles that women with large labia should be ashamed of them and could be helped by having them trimmed.[38]

Medical case reports of labia reduction contain a complicated set of messages for those interested in the meaning of variant genitals. The authors of one report in a recent medical journal admit that women do not normally raise the issue of labial size with physicians.[39] This reticence is interpreted not as satisfaction with their genitals but as ignorance about norms, coupled with embarrassment. The physician, having seen many more labia than the woman, is well aware of the variability. Yet he or she is advised by the authors to take seriously both those few women who voice concerns and the majority who do not verbalize them. The authors suggest that many women "may be silently troubled by the appearance of their vulva" and fail to share those concerns with physicians.[40] After an open discussion with the woman about her labia, *and a description of "the wide variation in normal-appearing labia"* (my emphasis), surgery, known as "aesthetic vaginal labioplasty," should be offered in selected cases.[41] Even when surgery is not deemed appropriate, "a candid discussion, education, and validation of their concerns" can be helpful.[42] But since most women, as the authors already asserted, do not express concerns, are the authors suggesting that a concern be planted? How long will it be before this germinating "concern" grows into a request for surgery?[43]

The authors of the case report discussed above present the hypothetical situation of a woman whose labia appear normal to the examiner but who still experiences distress—this is a psychiatric condition the authors call "dismorphobia." But they fail to address the opposite hypothetical case, when the patient has not voiced a concern (because she assumes her genitals are within the normal range), but the physician experiences distress. This second scenario is more consonant with the history of cosmetic surgery.[44] This medical report begins with a discussion of how cosmetic surgery on women is on the rise due to the increasing popularity of liposuction, breast augmentation, and "other methods of reshaping body contours," and the authors seem to regret that "external genitalia represent an area on which plastic surgery is performed infrequently."[45] When the report concludes with the comment that "it is incumbent upon physicians to be aware of patients' (often unexpressed) concern about the appearance of their external genitals," one is left wondering whose concerns are the issue.[46]

How do parents collaborate in the diagnosis and treatment of redundant labia? In one case report, the author describes the protuberant tissue of a seventeen-year-old female as causing irritation on walking and sitting, after voiding, and during menstrual periods. "Because of increasing discomfort, the patient *and her mother* were eager to have a corrective procedure performed."[47] These procedures are described as "most gratifying to the young girl *and her parents*"[48] (my emphases). When, one wonders, did the labia become a problem for the girl and/or her parents? What kind of conversations did the family have? If the labia were large at birth, had the parents spoken to the pediatrician about this? Was the whole family just waiting for growth to stop or for medical technology to find a solution for their (collective) problem? Some of the same questions posed about familial reaction to inter-sexuality are relevant here.

Taking note of the history of plastic surgery and the recruit-ment of customers from within the normal range (enterprising physicians not relying on the short supply of accidents or birth defects), it is conceivable that within a few years genital surgery will be as common and publicly acknowledged as cosmetic sur-geries on other body parts. One can imagine a woman in the not-too-distant future saying, "My self-esteem is tied up with the shape of my labia (or the size of my clitoris) and I'd just feel more femi-nine with more shapely labia (or a smaller clitoris)." Or, "For me, large clitorises are important. I'd like my clitoris to be lifted, and my prepuce redesigned." Or, "If movie stars can get clitoral im-plants why can't I?" Who will set the trend? Who will decide if the ideal minora are as "minor" as possible and the ideal majora as "major?" In *Taste of Latex*, a fetish sex magazine, a short item titled "Read my lips" presages one possible future:

> For those women who are always looking for another way to nip and tuck, we bring you the latest in cosmetic "enhance-ment" the labia trim. Yes, a surgeon will cut away any un-wanted pink tissue, and, if need be, reconstruct the labia. This procedure will set you back a few grand, and will put you out of commission for 3–6 weeks. What type of gal gets this op-eration? Strippers, nude models, porn starlets and any woman who feels her labia minora are not minora enough. What to call this procedure? A labia-ectomy? Genitoplasty? Lip-O-Suction? Who knows. Frankly, we don't see what all the flap is about.[49]

Given this context, it is not surprising to find genital surgery touted in some mainstream women's magazines and criticized by feminists. *Ms.* magazine reported on an article in a British maga-zine, *First for Women*, that promotes cosmetic genital surgery: vaginal tightening, liposuction of the pubic mound, vulvaplasty (labia trimming), and hymen reconstruction.[50] *Ms.* accuses the editors of *First* of concocting new, embarrassing problems for read-ers and capitalizing on their desire to please men. "Until you elimi-nate all flaws—including those pesky dangling labia—you won't deserve happiness, let alone a man."[51] In spite of the fact that the *First* article describes a number of cases of women with troublesome genitals who found relief in cosmetic surgery, the *Ms.* columnist doubts the veracity of the cases and quotes a surgeon in this country who doubts the demand. But history is full of examples of demand being created by technology and medical promotion; and the demand might be a well-kept secret, made by the rich who pay for their privacy. Like all fashions, it will inevitably filter down. One physician who does reconstructive surgery on women with genital cancers said that he has seen a few women who, for cosmetic reasons, wanted their labia minora made smaller.

Transsexuals, whose legitimacy has been in part created by the possibility of genital surgery, already think of it as at least partly cosmetic. In one sample of male-to-female transsexuals, "Over 1/3 had undergone second and third [genital] surgeries for the purpose of cosmetic improvement, indicating a possible interest in *beautifying* the genitals"[52] (my emphasis). Many surgeons claim to provide cosmetic clitorises for male-to-female transsexuals. These "skin tabs" reportedly do not provide erotic sensation and tend to disappear within two years. Clearly, surgeons are fulfilling the transsexuals' interest, which has gone beyond "correction."

Given the cosmetic industry's disproportionate focus on women (and women's collusion in this attention), it is not surprising that it is the female genitals that are seen as in need of improvement. But alteration of the male genitals is gaining respectability. Sexologist Leonore Tiefer analyzes the medicalization and marketing of the "better penis."[53] Men have fat injected into their penises and ligaments released in order to make those penises bigger and ostensibly to make them function more successfully. "Medicine is becoming the phallus' best friend."[54] In creating bigger and better penises, not only is phallocentrism served, but market opportunities blossom for underemployed urologists. From 1970 to 1990, the number of surgeons in the United States increased from 58,000 to more than 110,000. Tiefer suggests that this expansion created competition within and between medical subspecialties, including urology.[55]

Janice Irvine argues that interventions to enhance male sexuality have unlimited market potential (e.g., penile and testicle implants, hydraulic pumps, and intrapenile injections of smooth-muscle relaxants). Books, pamphlets, and tapes that describe and advise on ways to enlarge penises and scrotal sacs advertise extensively.[56]

Another potential cluster of male customers are members of

the "decircumcision" movement, men who (having been circumcised as infants) want their foreskins restored. They debate the pros and cons of surgical and nonsurgical techniques for stretching the foreskin. Although outlawing circumcision (which they want) would take some minimal work away from the surgeons, demands for restoration could prove lucrative. Circumcision, apart from religious ritual, is a procedure that undeniably ebbs and flows with fashion. Perhaps in the near future urologists will advertise (to the public and within the medical community) their skills in foreskin restoration. It is a short jump from suggesting that one's foreskin can be restored to implying that it should be, all under the auspices of supposedly giving men what they need for their psychological health.

At first consideration, elective genital surgery is open to the same analysis as any other type of cosmetic surgery. It is another example of surgeons gaining revenue and prestige by setting artificial ideals that create another burden for the genders, especially women. As with surgery on other body parts, genital cosmetic surgery ultimately reduces variability by setting narrower ranges for what is considered acceptable. Designating more constricted standards for genitals might (as I will discuss below) make genital surgery on intersexed infants even more likely.

What underlies both adult and infant genital surgery is that the genitals are taken very seriously. What I have been moving toward in this analysis is the opposite proposition—that genitals be taken *less* seriously—because it is in that position that relief from gender might be found.

The obvious tactic in fighting gender tyranny is to refuse cosmetic surgeries of all kinds. In a 1991 article, "Women and the Knife," Kathryn Morgan suggests two feminist responses to cosmetic surgery: refusing it and demanding it.[57] The consequences of refusing to alter the body in accordance with gender ideals are obvious. A world populated with flat-chested, hairy women with penis-sized clitorises and large-breasted, hairless men with micropenises would be a world of blended gender, and eventually, blended gender is no gender.[58]

It is less obvious how the tactic of demanding cosmetic surgery would work toward ending gender. Morgan suggests that women appropriate cosmetic surgery for parody and protest, making themselves deliberately ugly by having wrinkles sewn and carved into their skin, implanting freeze-dried fat cells into their thighs, and the like. She refers to these as "performative forms of revolt" and admits that this suggestion might offend, anger, or shock even feminist readers.[59] What if we demand cosmetic surgery for a different end, not to make ourselves deviant from an attractiveness standard but deviant from a gender standard? What if we demand surgery on our genitals? The recent popularity, among some groups, of labia and penis/scrotum piercing could be thought of as a tentative beginning. Although popular interventions, even when widespread, do not have the authority that medical ones have, ornamentation of the genitals is a first step in the direction of treating the genitals themselves as ornaments.

Unlike endocrinology, which "is at least nominally dedicated to describing human physiology," plastic surgery's purpose "is not to describe the body but to reconfigure it," and because of this, plastic surgery is "highly subject to ideological appropriation."[60] It is time to consider appropriating it for different ends. This consideration, however, clashes with the argument against unnecessary genital surgery unless we are prepared to accept that there is a difference between deciding to alter the genitals oneself and having a physician or parent make that decision. The fundamental difference lies in the intent. Institutionalized mutilations occur because the genitals are taken too seriously. It is not that the material genitals are respected but that the idea of genitals is. In wresting control of the "cutting," the idea of genitals is trivialized, and their meaning is degraded through the controlled trivialization of particular genitals. If we want people to respect particular bodies, they need to be taught to lose respect for ideal ones.

If genitals become as commonly correctable as noses, there might be no limit to who requests these changes. Treating the genitals as something to request is a step on the road to denaturalizing and destabilizing them and ultimately gender itself. Morgan alludes to this possibility when she imagines a day when before-and-after make-over displays for penises are advertised with the promotion, "The penis you were always meant to have."[61] Could anyone have them, even putative women? Is that a threat to those in control of the genital marketplace? A newspaper advertisement publicizing a "totally natural" penile enlargement and lengthening technique is framed (in triple-size letters) by the words "MEN ONLY." What is striking is not that penises are being enlarged and lengthened (at the same time that clitorises and labia minora are being reduced), but that the advertisement restricts the clientele to men. While it might be meant to deter female-to-male trans-sexuals, it might also be meant to caution women to squelch their desires for enlarged clitorises, a.k.a. penises.

It should be obvious by this point that there is "in nature" a range of genital formations and that various technological efforts have been marshaled by the medical profession to reduce variability within each gender and to increase differences between the two genders. As adults exercise their right to reshape their genitals and their gender, what might be the repercussions for those infants whose genitals are considered "misshapen" by physicians? Will broader standards for genitals be adopted and more infants excused from surgery, or might the opposite occur? Promoting elective genital surgery could lead to less tolerance for variability, rather than more.

The analogy to noses is obvious. People electing to alter theirs choose the small upturned one, characteristic of the privileged class, rather than a variety of "ethnic" ones. Given that pattern, what will happen if it becomes fashionable to alter one's genitals? Will this mean that everyone—female and male—will want large phalluses like the privileged gender, or will it mean that males, evoking their privilege, will restrict large phalluses to males and demand that more females have their clitorises reduced? Will women start to feel inadequate about yet another body part, in this case a body part that had been off limits, by virtue of our culture's puritanical silence about things "down there"? All of this is worth pondering as we play with the idea of usurping control of genital surgery to undercut gender.

Gender Theory Confronts Gender Practices

While gender scholars theorize gender, others practice it. Although we gender scholars immerse ourselves in the medical literature, taking it very seriously as a guide to how the culture operates, physicians do not usually address the theoretical. Their professional organizations do not need to take a position on inter-sex, for that would be to admit that intersex has analytic status and is grist for controversy.[62] From the physicians' point of view, surgical techniques are controversial, but the existence of inter-sex and the notion to treat it are not. We are not yet at a moment in history (unlike in the nineteenth century) when intersexuality is creating "conceptual, moral and practical messes."[63] If intersexuals have their way, though, that mess is in the making. Insofar as data from adult intersexuals are even acknowledged, they are dismissed as being "only anecdotal," even though physicians' own beliefs about the danger of not doing early surgery are based on those few single-case anecdotes of parental mismanagement sprinkled through the medical literature.

One prominent endocrinologist who has made many neonatal gender decisions, in responding to some of the new views of intersexuality from gender theorists, expressed concern that the material would not be very helpful to intersexuals because "it [does not] offer viable alternatives."[64] By implication, what the medical profession offers, from his point of view, is a viable alternative.

Heino Meyer-Bahlburg, a psychologist who works with intersexed children and their parents in a major developmental psychoendocrinology program, voices sympathy with the campaign for better follow-up data and more judicious use of surgery that is being led by the Intersex Society of North America (ISNA). He sees, however, a chasm between what gender theorists are arguing and what practitioners need to be concerned with, given the constraints of their practical job demands.[65] He believes that "destabilizing gender introduces more selection bias in [the] data and arguments than people such as myself can afford, since we are trying to establish associations and determinants in the context of what *is* rather than what *should be*"[66] (his emphasis). He ignores that what *is* constitutes a matter for reasoned debate and can be renegotiated through the authority of the medical profession. Professionals need to see themselves not only as constrained by real world demands but as creators of that world. It is the obligation of gender theorists to reiterate that message continually.

Intersexuals in the political vanguard, like transsexuals in the past, have turned to gender theorists not because we have tremendous influence on the medical profession but for an articulation of the grounds of gender's authority.[67] I have shown that the medical community through its practices has constructed a particularly powerful view of intersexuality. Intersexuals, through their discourse and politicking, have constructed another view. Gender theorists are in the position of being able to demonstrate that intersex need not be constructed at all, and this is one pathway toward arguing that gender need not be.

Fausto-Sterling, who conceptualized five categories of gender, the two standard ones and three intersexed ones (true hermaphrodites, female pseudohermaphrodites, and male pseudohermaphrodites), writes that her medical colleagues are horrified that she gives credibility to intersex gender categories. They ask her, "How could I possibly consider using a poor intersexual child as a battering ram to assault the fortress of sex inequality?"[68]

John Money mocks gender theorists who have gone to the extreme of proposing that there are five sexes. "It simply does not make sense to talk of a third sex, or of a fourth or fifth, when the phylogenetic scheme of things is two sexes. . . . To advocate medical nonintervention is irresponsible. It runs counter to everything this book stands for, which is to enhance health and well-being to the greatest extent possible."[69] The Catholic Church concurs. The Catholic League for Religious and Civil Rights, in its opposition to the progressive element at the Fourth United Nations Conference on Women, referred to discussions of five genders (without crediting Fausto-Sterling) as "maddening," given that "every sane person knows there are but two sexes, both of which are rooted in nature."[70]

The most frequent question I am asked is whether I am seriously suggesting that parents raise children whose genitals completely contradict their gender. This question implies, first of all, that gender theory is ultimately impractical and, secondly, that there have not been any fundamental changes in the way gender is practiced. In this section, I will discuss some ways gender *has* evolved, and in the last section, I will show how an alternative way of treating intersexed infants might evolve.

We might not expect surgeons to lead the (r)evolution by handing over control of their knives in the service of gender, but there are people who already function as transformers of gender categories. The transgender community, which emerged during the 1980s, is described by anthropologist Anne Bolin as composed of individuals who are challenging the obligatory two-gender system by blending public features of maleness and femaleness and/or taking bits and pieces of surgical options without "going all the way."[71] "The guiding principle of this movement is that people should be free to change, either temporarily or permanently, the sex type to which they were assigned since infancy."[72] While physicians practice gender on others, transgenderists, only sometimes with the help of physicians, practice it on themselves.

Some of those who are "transgender" disrupt gender by refusing to provide the kind of cues that would accommodate either a male or female gender attribution and by treating biological signs of gender (including genitals) as bodily ornaments—neither more nor less elective than a face lift.[73] Transgenderists, who may be transvestites, transsexuals, or gay, are arguing for the inclusion of intersexuals. In the words of one transsexual activist, "I've been waiting for years for you to show up. It's clear that transsexuals are not going to get our rights until intersexuals do." Riki Anne Wilchins, founder of Transexual Menace, said that she awaits the moment when ISNA members "start to become Menace-ing. And we will be right at their sides."[74]

In the first years of The Androgen Insensitivity Support Group, members disavowed any alliance between their intersexuality and the transgender community ("We do not want to be involved in the gender dysphoria, cross-dressing, transsexual arena").[75] More recently, however, they have begun to see connections that members of ISNA, such as Morgan Holmes, espouse. She, for example, views intersexed genitals, bisexual identity, and sexual behavior as conveniently related and bemoans the amputation of her clitoris, partly because a large phallus (in addition to a vagina) would have given her the mechanical versatility to accompany her bisexual-intersexual identity.[76] Admittedly, most new parents are unlikely to find Holmes's argument a persuasive reason not to tamper with their infant's genitals.[77]

One reason intersexuals are being embraced as the best representatives of transgender is because they have "altered physical characteristics, as well as altered mental or gender characteristics." They have what is referred to as a transgender "marker in their blood."[78] This argument can be seen as part of the project to ground transgender membership in biology, mirroring the argument proffered by some in the gay movement that an essentialist view of homosexuality or gender dysphoria will impel greater tolerance. As many persuasive writers have pointed out, this argument is not convincing. "Grounding difference in biology does not stem bigotry."[79] In addition, because revolutionary disruptions need to be public events, it is the act of announcing that one's body is chaotic (with respect to gender) that creates gender disruption, not the existence of concealed markers themselves. This option is available to anyone, not just intersexuals.

In spite of the widespread acceptance within medicine of a

single philosophy of intersex management, there are intimations of a different doctrine. At the 1995 International Congress on Gender, Cross-Dressing, and Sexual Issues, Walter Bockting, a psychologist, indicated that the Human Sexuality Program at the University of Minnesota allows transgendered people to express their chosen gender without having to undergo genital surgery. Based on what the psychologists are learning from their transsexual clients, who are not forced into rigid, stereotyped roles, Bockting would oppose surgery on intersexed children. Bockting airs his views at forums where human sexuality professionals are exposed to gender theories that might trickle down to more central players (endocrinologists and surgeons) within the medical community.

Members of the Androgen Insensitivity Syndrome Support Group have had some success in getting prominent endocrinologists to consider the organization's recommendations about a different management philosophy based on a more compassionate understanding of their patients and a more radical formulation of gender. One physician described their literature, which was critical of the medical management of intersexuality, as "remarkabl[y] illuminating." Even after expressing some qualms about accepting a third gender (which AISSG does not advocate), he ends with: "What is certainly gratifying about these writings is the trend towards fully [sic] and more open discussion of the complex issues involved in abnormal genital development."[80]

A change in attitudes about intersexuality will need to occur within a cultural context where other kinds of gender "contradictions" are legitimated. Consider the following case report: A happily married heterosexual man requested estrogen treatment to enlarge his breasts because, as he told physicians, stimulation of his nipples was erotic and he wanted to increase his pleasure. His wife was supportive of the request. The clinicians, who prescribed the hormone treatment in spite of the fact that they did not think he evidenced any gender dysphoria, concluded that "the sexual significance of his breasts was more important for [him] than their morphological aspects."[81] The man received the treatment, grew breasts, and at the one-year follow-up interview reported being satisfied with his body and his life. What is astonishing about this case is that the Dutch physicians were able to treat the breasts as not necessarily a gender cue. Might this ever be possible for genitals, and what would that mean about gender theory and practice?

For some people, a different gender/genital matching system is not somewhere in the distant future. Most female-to-male transsexuals, especially younger ones, do not have their vaginas sewn up but keep them, along with their two-and-a-half-inch testosterone-enlarged clitorises—all the sexual equipment possible. Their success in attracting female lovers suggests that there is a market for these new formulations.[82]

ISNA occasionally gets letters from people interested in meeting hermaphrodites: "As a straight male, the thought of a woman with a penis has always been a turn-on for me. Do you know of any organizations that cater to hermaphrodites on the East Coast? . . . Thank you in advance."[83] Because the hermaphrodite's "mismatch" is inborn, partnering with one might carry more status than partnering with a "she-male" or "he-female"—someone whose body "contradiction" (e.g., penis and breasts or vagina and mustache) is hormonally induced. Sexual attraction to intersexed forms (both congenital and constructed) deserves a complete analysis that would reveal the relative importance for eroticism of genitals—what some people still refer to as "sex"—and gender. I believe that gender—the presentation of agreed-upon social emblems—will carry a greater weight than can be determined when genitals and gender conventionally coincide. One can imagine that just as a heterosexual woman today can legitimately claim not to be attracted to men with excessive body hair, in a newly configured system she could claim not to be attracted to men with penises or to *be* attracted to men with breasts and a vagina. What then would heterosexual mean? In what sense could a woman with a vagina who is sexually gratified by being penetrated by a "woman" with a large clitoris (that looks and functions like a penis) be said to be a lesbian? If gendered bodies fall into disarray, sexual orientation will follow. Defining sexual orientation according to attraction to people with the same or different genitals, as is done now, will no longer make sense, nor will intersexuality.[84]

The Future of Intersex

Physicians see themselves as creating technology, not culture. A well-known pediatric surgeon envisions a time when surgical intervention on infants will be obsolete. Her utopia, though, does not hinge on an acceptance of either irregular genitals or intersex categories. She ends a lengthy article that details a myriad of surgical techniques with this concluding statement: "We envision early in utero detection in pregnancies of families at risk and possible [prenatal] correction of defects. . . . Better still, detection of carriers may reduce the incidence of such anomalies."[85]

Until such a future, can we at least count on physicians doing less cutting and more talking? Pediatric "teams" who claim they spend hours educating parents focus their pedagogy on the physiology of the intersex condition, not on reinterpreting the meaning of the genitals.[86] Typical is the pediatric surgeon who has operated on intersexed infants for twenty years and yet admits he does not have a consistent program of counseling, even after surgery.[87] One psychoendocrinologist whose job it is to speak with parents of intersexed children and who probably does more counseling of this sort than anyone else revealed in an interview that she believes that she does "the barest minimum" and admits that "there's no funding for this kind of thing."

What exactly is the nature of "this kind of thing"? Is "this kind of thing" different from other "kinds of things" that parents might need to face in regard to their atypical children? What "kind of things" might children be asked their opinion about? Where can one find models for how to approach intersex surgery?

A group of plastic surgeons at a hospital in Leeds, UK, have reported on a mandatory counseling program they developed for helping families reach a decision about reconstructive surgery for children. Parents are encouraged to identify their feelings for and against surgery, and children are given the opportunity to communicate their feelings about surgery in individual sessions away from parents. The justification for this level of counseling reflects the physicians' attitude about how necessary the surgery is, the probability of success, and the psychological needs of families and children. This management style is in striking contrast to what I have presented thus far. Physicians from this department of plastic surgery show their sensitivity when they state:

> In order to reach a stable decision about whether to proceed with surgery, [the parents] must deal with complex and unfamiliar technical issues and uncertainty about outcome. In addition, their emotional state may be dominated by unresolved emotional responses to the anomaly and is certainly influenced by their aspirations for their child. Thus it is difficult to appraise the issues calmly and to weigh alternatives,

and they often express the fear that their children will later criticize them for the decision they have taken. They lack confidence that they will still be valued by their child, whatever decision they make.[88]

Are these physicians unusually enlightened about the reasonable possibility of not "correcting" intersexed genitals? No. The physicians in Leeds are discussing the decision to reconstruct absent or deficient fingers on a child's hand by transferring a toe from the foot to the hand.

It is instructive to compare hand surgery with genital surgery because, although many of the issues are the same, the fact that the hand carries no gender baggage permits us to speculate about whatever differences in management are revealed. There is no question that both conditions (absence of digits and intersex) create in parents anxiety about surgery and about how their children will fare in life. In both cases, regardless of what decision parents make, they believe they have their children's best interest at heart.

For both kinds of surgery there are appearance/function considerations, and in some sense a trade-off. For children with no digits at all, there is a feeling by some families that the hand looks "neat," and, although there is a possibility of greater function with surgery, the postoperative appearance may be abnormal. For children with a less severe deficit, transferred toes might result in a better appearance, but improvement in function is less obvious. Genital surgery, as I have described it in an earlier chapter, trades function for appearance, without always achieving the desired appearance. The fact that appearance is so important for a body part that is almost always hidden (compared to a hand) is further evidence that more is at stake here than the body part itself.

The matter-of-fact way that counseling is handled in the case of missing digits suggests how intersex might be handled if gender meaning were stripped away. One illuminating exercise is to take quotations from parents of children with missing digits who decided against surgery and imagine (with the appropriate substitution) parents of intersexed children saying them:

Real quote: We felt that we didn't actually need fingers or toes in place of fingers to satisfy us.
Substitute: We felt that we didn't actually need a vagina to satisfy us.
Real quote: The teacher says she dresses herself very well and most of the other children can't dress themselves as well.

Substitute: The teacher says that he urinates very well on his own and that other children are still being potty trained.

Because the sense of emergency that accompanies intersex management is absent from the hand condition, parents deliberating about toe transfer have the luxury of time to evaluate information and to interrogate their feelings. There is also time to consult the children.[89] In contrast, gender is so fragile that it can barely go a day without being properly marked.

Since surgeons who operate on the hand are not constrained by gender ideology, they are free to consider some dangers of early surgery. In one study, an assessment of fourteen children (six months to thirteen years old at the time of surgery) led the researchers to conclude that young children who underwent toe transfer did not do well. They were more likely to contract infection in the hospital and were more difficult to manage on the ward. In addition, the authors referred readers to "a wide literature on the effects of hospitalization on children," suggesting that "the younger child [is] . . . more likely to misunderstand [the surgery's] purpose and perceive it as punishment." In stunning contrast to surgeons who operate on intersexed children, these surgeons admitted that "decisions had traditionally been taken about major reconstructive surgery with little knowledge about the effect this surgery had on the general well-being of the child." For example, not all children in their sample profited, despite acceptable technical outcomes and despite being more accepted by their parents. The authors draw an analogy to the use of plastic surgery to make children with Down's syndrome appear more "normal." "The reconstructive surgery is of more benefit to the parent than the child."[90]

Some parents of children with missing digits decided against surgery. They were resistant to the idea of mutilating one part of their child's body (the foot) in order to try to normalize another part (the hand). Parents who ultimately elected hand surgery for their children provide rationales that seem based on a thoughtful weighing of pros and cons. "I had feelings that she would get so far . . . but her hand would hold her back. But if [the surgery] is a success, then I don't think there will be anything she won't be able to manage."[91]

Frequently, parents of younger children described their concerns about making such a major decision as finger replacement on behalf of their child. In contrast, parents of intersexed children, who are cautioned to make decisions swiftly and without consulting support groups, rarely describe themselves as having made decisions. They may be in agony about their child, but they do not describe themselves as agonizing about what decision to make.[92]

Because of gender anxiety, genital regularity, unlike hand regularity, is an imperative thrust upon the parents. For this reason, it is not surprising that adult intersexuals have had such a difficult time getting their parents to accept complicity in the damage done to them or even to talk with them about why surgery was done. From the parents' point of view, what else could they have done?

There are many ways to make parents comfortable with their children. One way, the one currently preferred by intersex surgeons, is to use surgery to make the child look normal to the parents. Another is to use language to achieve this same purpose.[93]

What would it take for larger-than-typical clitorises, absent vaginas, smaller-than-typical penises, off-center urinary openings, and irregularly shaped scrota and labia to become acceptable markers of gender? Where would such a genital reconceptualization start and how would it impact on ideas about gender? In other words, how can what we mean by a female or a male be given more latitude? It could begin in the delivery room with a new script.

A psychiatrist who works in the field of intersexuality and recognizes that obstetricians often mishandle births of intersexed infants, proposes that a more sensitive approach is needed. She suggests this conversational strategy be followed "step-by-step and repeated": "Mother, you have a healthy baby, congratulations. Nature is unclear about your baby's external genitals or private parts. Let me show you (on baby). This means I must call Dr. X to see your baby." When the mother inevitably asks whether she has given birth to a boy or a girl, the sensitive physician is told to reassure her with the following words: "I cannot yet say. We will have to do some tests. It is not your fault, mother. These are rare conditions but quite well known. We will stand by you and your baby."[94]

Granted, this is an improvement over some of the mishandlings recounted in earlier chapters, but what should the physician say after the diagnosis has been made? Imagine this script for a physician who is explaining the birth of a girl whose clitoris has been affected by congenital adrenal hyperplasia:

You have a beautiful baby girl. The size of her clitoris and her *what should be said* fused labia provided us with a clue to an underlying medical problem that we might need to treat. Although her clitoris is on the large size, it's definitely a clitoris. Who knows what it'll look like as she grows! Some parents don't have a realistic sense of what a baby's genitals look like. You probably haven't seen that many, but I have. I'll consult an endocrinologist, but we won't need a surgeon since there's nothing we need to do about the clitoris. The important thing about the clitoris is how it functions, not how it looks. She's lucky. Her sexual partners will find it easy to locate her clitoris. She doesn't have a complete vagina now and she can decide whether she wants one constructed when she's older. Surgical techniques will be more advanced then and her grown body will tolerate the surgery better, if she chooses to have it.

The scenario I have invented maintains the two-gender system (since I cannot imagine a physician in the near future announcing: "Congratulations. You have an intersexed child"), but the criteria for genital normalcy is expanded, and a treatment (r)evolution begins.[95]

Even physicians who manage intersexuality in the traditional way reveal that it might be possible to see and name things otherwise: "Detailed examination [of a two-day-old infant's genitals] showed a structure . . . that *could be perceived as either a clitoris or a micropenis*"[96] (my emphasis). If the determination is to assign the infant to the female gender, based on internal reproductive structure (a return to nineteenth-century criteria), the genital would be called a clitoris. If the determination is to assign the infant to the male gender, the genital would be called a penis. In neither case would surgery be required; rhetoric would be.[97]

I propose two very different options for talking about what is now known as "intersexuality." One would be to confront intersexuality directly. Physicians would not be so quick to normalize the condition for parents but would help them acknowledge and deal with having an intersexed child and with prejudices about gender. In support groups conducted by adult intersexuals like those belonging to the Intersex Society of North America (ISNA), parents would be encouraged to explore their often unstated concerns:

Will my intersexed daughter be a lesbian if she has a large clitoris or XY chromosomes? Will my intersexed son be a real man if he has a small penis? What does it mean to have a child who is legitimately different from other children? If one looks, one can find some examples of parents ready to hear a new philosophy. There are the parents of a young girl who, when told about her XY chromosomal pattern, her absent vagina, and her diagnosis of androgen-insensitivity syndrome (AIS), responded: "Wow—how interesting! She's really special. Let's see what we can find out about this."[98] In a sample of boys and men with micropenises, those able to make the best adjustments had parents who thought the appearance of the penis was satisfactory and conveyed this to their sons.[99]

The medical literature, which is sprinkled with words like "trauma" and "tragedy" and cautionary tales of parents failing to abide by medical recommendations, is silent on "the wide variety of (often positive) responses to what one might see as a death sentence."[100] Obviously, in order for physicians to adopt a new stance, they would need to examine their own gender-related assumptions in the context of a major cultural shift in gender beliefs.

[The second way of talking differently about intersexuality would involve not seeing it.] By this I do not mean that physicians would shelter parents from intersexuality while believing in it themselves. This is how the situation is currently normalized. Rather, I mean that physicians would refuse to give intersexuality credibility, even for themselves. By bracketing the existence of intersexuality, they would be left with only genitals that might not even be noteworthy beyond their initial signal of an underlying medical condition. That it is possible to ignore or reinterpret conventional signs of intersexuality is evidenced by those men with diagnosable but "uncorrected" hypospadias and their sexual partners who were unaware of any penile "deformity."[101]

This second way of managing atypical genitals actually builds upon current medical practices. As I discussed in chapter 2, physicians know that they have to be careful about the language they use with parents. For example, they refrain from using the terms "hermaphrodite" or "intersex" because the meanings of those terms are so emotionally loaded. To talk in a new way about intersexuality would involve being even more mindful about language. Instead of referring to a girl's clitoris as "masculinized," or her chromosomes as "male," the girl would be described as having a clitoris larger than most, or labia more fused than most, or having XY chromosomes.[102] The doctor would convey expertise by telling parents, "That's not a penis on your daughter. It doesn't have a urethral tube or meatus." Given this script, it is not guaranteed that parents would always decide against surgical alteration, but they could at least make a more measured decision if they were led to see that what was being discussed was a cosmetic issue and not a gender one. Cosmetic issues are issues that lay persons can reasonably have an opinion about and disagree with surgeons about, but gender issues are not, or at least not yet.

Genital variability can continue to be seen as a condition to be remedied or in a new way—as an expansion of what is meant by female and male. Whether the meaning one imparts to genital variability reifies gender or trivializes it has important implications for gender and intersex management. We need to consider different possibilities about how to manage intersexuality, including the possibility of not managing it at all.

The future of intersex is in some sense the future of gender. In whose hands is this future? The parents of intersexed infants have the legal responsibility, but they take their cues from the medical professionals, whose status permits them to define the "real" view of intersexuality, relegating other views, like the political intersexuals', to a fringe perspective.[103] Self-help groups could provide parents with an alternative interpretation of their situation, thus altering their relationship to the medical community and to intersexuality. Viewing their child's "condition" in some of the ways I have been proposing will give parents the strength to authorize as little surgery and as much honesty as necessary. Through more-honest discussions of gender, parents may find some common ground with political intersexuals within the transgender movement, a force that has the potential for bending (if not breaking) the gender system.

Any revolution in thinking about gender hinges on understanding that there is no one best way to be a male or a female or any other gender possibility—not even in terms of what is between your legs. Physicians who pat themselves on the back because of their relaxed attitudes about gender roles ("It's OK that your AIS daughter wants to wear pants and play with trucks; she's still a girl")[104] convey, by their recommendations for genital surgery, that gender is not something one can be completely relaxed about. Until the unease about gender is satisfactorily analyzed by scholars and addressed by practitioners, the very practical suggestions I have made for handling intersexuality will seem preposterous.

Treating genital formations as innate but malleable, much like hair, would be to take them and gender less seriously. In the acceptance of genital variability and gender variability lies the subversion of both genitals and gender. Dichotomized, idealized, and created by surgeons, *genitals mean gender*. A belief in two genders encourages talk about "female genitals" and "male genitals" as homogenous types, regardless of how much variability there is within a category.[105] Similarly, the idea of "intersexed" masks the fact that "intersexed genitals" vary from each other as much as they vary from the more idealized forms.

Although it is unlikely that the nontransgender public will embrace an intersexed gender in the near future, as I have shown, people are capable of accepting more genital variation. Accepting more genital variation will maintain, at least temporarily, the two-gender system, but it will begin to unlock gender and genitals. Ultimately, the power of genitals to mark gender will be weakened, and the power of gender to define lives will be blunted.

By subverting genital primacy, gender will be removed from the biological body and placed in the social-interactional one. Even if there are still two genders, male and female, how you "do" male or female, including how you "do" genitals, would be open to interpretation.[106] Physicians teach parents of intersexed infants that the fetus is bipotential, but they talk about gender as being "finished" at sixteen or twenty weeks, just because the genitals are. Gender need not be thought of as finished, not for people who identify as intersexed, nor for any of us. Once we dispense with "sex" and acknowledge gender as located in the social-interactional body, it will be easier to treat it as a work-in-progress.

This is assuming, though, that gender is something worth working on. It may not be. If intersexuality imparts any lesson, it is that gender is a responsibility and a burden—for those being categorized and those doing the categorizing. We rightfully complain about gender oppression in all its social and political manifestations, but we have not seriously grappled with the fact that we afflict ourselves with a need to locate a bodily basis for assertions about gender. We must use whatever means we have to give up on gender. The problems of intersexuality will vanish and we will, in this way, compensate intersexuals for all the lessons they have provided.

Notes

1 Introduction

1. By "social construction," we mean that beliefs about the world create the reality of that world, as opposed to the position that the world reveals what is really there. Suzanne Kessler and Wendy McKenna, *Gender: An Ethnomethodological Approach* (New York: Wiley-Interscience, 1978; Chicago: University of Chicago Press, 1985).
2. See, for example: Holly Devor, *FTM: Female-to-Male Transsexuals in Society* (Bloomington: Indiana University Press, 1997).
3. See, for example: Morris Kaplan's chapter, "Psychoanalyzing the 'Third Sex,'" in his book *Sexual Justice* (New York: Routledge, 1997).
4. John Money and Anke A. Ehrhardt, *Man & Woman, Boy & Girl* (Baltimore: The Johns Hopkins University Press, 1972).
5. Milton Diamond, "Sexual Identity, Monozygotic Twins Reared in Discordant Sex Roles and a BBC Follow-Up," *Archives of Sexual Behavior* 11, no. 2 (1982):181–1987.
6. Milton Diamond and Keith Sigmundson, "Sex Reassignment at Birth: Long-term Review and Clinical Applications," *Archives of Pediatric and Adolescent Medicine* 151 (May 1997):298–304.
7. Kenneth J. Zucker, "Commentary On Diamond's Prenatal Predisposition and the Clinical Management of Some Pediatric Conditions," *Sex and Marital Treatment* 22, no. 3 (1996):148–160.
8. In a 1973 collection of readings, the editor (who coauthored a paper with Money) introduces Money's chapter on femininity and masculinity with, "John Money should receive the acclaim in the study of sexism that Kinsey or Masters and Johnson have received in the study of sexuality." (Clarice Stasz Stoll, ed., *Sexism: Scientific Debates* [Reading, Mass.: Addison-Wesley Publishing Company, 1973], 13). For the media's recent reinterpretation, see: Natalie Angier, "Sexual Identity Not Pliable After All, Report Says," *New York Times*, 14 March 1997, pp. A1 and A18.
9. In addition to Kessler and McKenna, see Holly Devor, *Gender Blending: Confronting the Limits of Duality* (Bloomington: Indiana University Press, 1989), and Judith Butler, *Gender Trouble: Feminism and the Subversion of Identity* (New York: Routledge, 1990).
10. Morgan Holmes, "Re-membering a Queer Body," *Undercurrents* (May 1994):11–14.
11. This discussion of genital meanings was originally presented at a plenary symposium titled "Genitals, Identity, and Gender" at The Society for the Scientific Study of Sexuality, San Francisco, November 1995, and later published in Suzanne J. Kessler, "Meanings of Genital Variability," *Chrysalis: The Journal of Transgressive Gender Identities* 2, no. 4 (fall/winter 1998):33–38.

12. A popularized version of Money and Ehrhardt's *Man & Woman, Boy & Girl* is John Money and Patricia Tucker's *Sexual Signatures: On Being a Man or a Woman* (Boston: Little Brown and Co., 1975). With few exceptions (see Julia Epstein, "Either/Or—Neither/Both: Sexual Ambiguity and the Ideology of Gender," *Genders* 7 [spring 1990]: 99–142; Deborah Findlay, "Discovering Sex: Medical Science, Feminism, and Intersexuality," *The Canadian Review of Sociology and Anthropology* 32 [February 1995]: 25–52; and material written by self-identified intersexuals), the intersex literature is not analytic.

2 The Medical Construction of Gender

1. For historical reviews of the intersexed person in ancient Greece and Rome, see Leslie Fiedler, *Freaks: Myths and Images of the Second Self* (New York: Simon and Schuster, 1978); and Vern Bullough, *Sexual Variance in Society and History* (New York: John Wiley and Sons, 1976). For the Middle Ages and Renaissance, see Michel Foucault, *History of Sexuality* (New York: Pantheon Books, 1980). For the eighteenth and nineteenth centuries, see Michel Foucault, *Herculine Barbin* (New York: Pantheon Books, 1978); and Alice Domurat Dreger, *Hermaphrodites and the Medical Invention of Sex* (Cambridge: Harvard University Press, 1998). For the early twentieth century, see Havelock Ellis, *Studies in the Psychology of Sex* (New York: Random House, 1942).

2. Traditionally, the term "gender" has designated psychological, social, and cultural aspects of maleness and femaleness, and the term "sex" has specified the biological and presumably more objective components. Twenty years ago, Wendy McKenna and I introduced the argument that "gender" should be used exclusively to refer to anything related to the categories "female" and "male," replacing the term "sex," which would be restricted to reproductive and "lovemaking" activities (Kessler and McKenna). Our reasoning was (and still is) that this would emphasize the socially constructed, overlapping nature of all category distinctions, even the biological ones. We wrote about gender chromosomes and gender hormones even though, at the time, doing so seemed awkward. I continue this practice here, but I follow the convention of referring to people with mixed biological gender cues as "intersexed" or "intersexuals" rather than as "intergendered" or "intergenderals." The latter is more consistent with my position, but I want to reflect both medical and vernacular usage without using quotation marks each time.

3. See, for example: M. Bolkenius, R. Daum, and E. Heinrich, "Paediatric Surgical Principles in the Management of Children with Intersex," *Progress in Pediatric Surgery* 17 (1984):33–38; Kenneth I. Glassberg, "Gender Assignment in Newborn Male Pseudohermaphrodites," *Urologic Clinics of North America* 7 (June 1980):409–421; and Peter A. Lee et al., "Micropenis. I. Criteria, Etiologies and Classification," *The Johns Hopkins Medical Journal* 146 (1980):156–163.

4. It is difficult to get accurate statistics on the frequency of intersexuality. Chromosomal abnormalities (like XOXX or XXXY) are registered, but those conditions do not always imply ambiguous genitals, and most cases of ambiguous genitals do not involve chromosomal abnormalities. None of the physicians interviewed would venture a guess on frequency rates, but all claimed that intersexuality is rare. One physician suggested that the average obstetrician may see only two cases in twenty years. Another estimated that a specialist may see only one a year or possibly as many as five a year. A reporter who interviewed physicians at Johns Hopkins Medical Center wrote that they treat, at most, ten new patients a year (Melissa Hendricks, "Is It a Boy or a Girl?" *Johns Hopkins Magazine* 45, no. 5 [November 1993]: 10–16). The numbers are considerably greater if one adopts a broader definition of intersexuality to include all "sex chromosome" deviations and any genitals that do not look, according to the culturally informed view of the moment, "normal" enough. A urologist at a Mt. Sinai School of Medicine symposium on Pediatric Plastic and Reconstructive Surgery (New York City, 16 May 1996) claimed that one of every three hundred male births involves some kind of genital abnormality. A meticulous analysis of the medical literature from 1955 to 1997 led Anne Fausto-Sterling and her students to conclude that the frequency of intersexuality may be as high as 2 percent of live births, and that between .1 and .2 percent of newborns undergo some sort of genital surgery (Melanie Blackless et al., "How Sexually Dimorphic Are We?" unpublished manuscript, 1997). The Intersex Society of North America (ISNA) estimates that about five intersex surgeries are performed in the United States each day.

5. Although the interviews in this chapter were conducted more than ten years ago, interviews with physicians conducted in the mid- to late-1990s and interviews conducted with parents of intersexed children during that same time period (both reported on in later chapters) indicate that little has changed in the medical management of intersexuality. This lack of change is also evident in current medical management literature. See, for example, F.M.E. Slijper et al., "Neonates with Abnormal Genital Development Assigned the Female Sex: Parent Counseling," *Journal of Sex Education and Therapy* 20, no. 1 (1994):9–17; and M. Rohatgi, "Intersex Disorders: An Approach to Surgical Management," *Indian Journal of Pediatrics* 59 (1992):523–530.

6. Mariano Castro-Magana, Moris Angulo, and Platon J. Collipp, "Management of the Child with Ambiguous Genitalia," *Medical Aspects of Human Sexuality* 18, no. 4 (April 1984):172–188.

7. For example, infants whose intersexuality is caused by congenital adrenal hyperplasia can develop severe electrolyte disturbances unless the condition is controlled by cortisone treatments. Intersexed infants whose condition is caused by androgen insensitivity are in danger of eventual malignant degeneration of the testes unless these are removed. For a complete catalogue of clinical syndromes related to the intersexed condition, see Arye Lev-Ran, "Sex Reversal as Re-

lated to Clinical Syndromes in Human Beings," in *Handbook of Sexology II: Genetics, Hormones and Behavior*, ed. John Money and H. Musaph (New York: Elsevier, 1978), 157–173.

8. Much of the surgical experimentation in this area has been accomplished by urologists who are trying to create penises for female-to-male transsexuals. Although there have been some advancements in recent years in the ability to create a "reasonable-looking" penis from tissue taken elsewhere on the body, the complicated requirements of the organ (requiring both urinary and sexual functioning) have posed surgical problems. It may be, however, that the concerns of the urologists are not identical to the concerns of the patients. While data are not yet available from the intersexed, we know that female-to-male transsexuals place greater emphasis on the "public" requirements of the penis (for example, being able to look normal while standing at the urinal or wearing a bathing suit) than on its functional requirements (for example, being able to achieve an erection) (Kessler and McKenna, 128–132). As surgical techniques improve, female-to-male transsexuals (and intersexed males) might increase their demands for organs that look and function better.

9. Historically, psychology has tended to blur the distinction between the two by equating a person's acceptance of her or his genitals with gender role and ignoring gender identity. For example, Freudian theory posited that if one had a penis and accepted its reality, then masculine gender role behavior would naturally follow (Sigmund Freud, "Some Psychical Consequences of the Anatomical Distinctions between the Sexes" [1925], in J. Strachy, trans. and ed., *The Complete Psychological Works* [New York: Norton, 1976], vol. 18).

10. Almost all of the published literature on intersexed infant case management has been written or cowritten by one researcher, John Money, professor of medical psychology and professor of pediatrics, emeritus, at Johns Hopkins University and Hospital, where he is director of the Psychohormonal Research Unit. Even the publications that are produced independently of Money reference him and reiterate his management philosophy. Although only one of the physicians interviewed has published with Money, they all essentially concur with his views and give the impression of a consensus that is rarely encountered in science. The one physician who raised some questions about Money's philosophy and the gender theory on which it is based has extensive experience with intersexuality in a nonindustrialized culture where the infant is managed differently with no apparent harm to gender development. Even though psychologists fiercely argue issues of gender identity and gender role development, doctors who treat intersexed infants seem untouched by these debates. There are still, in the late 1990s, few renegade voices from within the medical establishment. Why Money has been so single-handedly influential in promoting his ideas about gender is a question worthy of a separate substantial analysis. His management philosophy is conveyed in the following sources: John Money, J. G. Hampson, and J. L. Hampson, "Hermaphroditism: Recommendations

Concerning Assignment of Sex, Change of Sex, and Psychologic Management," *Bulletin of The Johns Hopkins Hospital* 97 (1955):284–300; John Money, *Sex Errors of the Body: Dilemmas, Education, Counseling* (Baltimore: The Johns Hopkins University Press, 1968, reprint 1994); John Money, Reynolds Potter, and Clarice S. Stoll, "Sex Reannouncement in Hereditary Sex Deformity: Psychology and Sociology of Habilitation," *Social Science and Medicine* 3 (1969):207–216; Money and Ehrhardt; John Money "Psychologic Consideration of Sex Assignment in Intersexuality," *Clinics in Plastic Surgery* 1 (April 1974):215–222; John Money, "Psychological Counseling: Hermaphroditism," in *Endocrine and Genetic Diseases of Childhood and Adolescence*, ed. L. I. Gardner (Philadelphia: W. B. Saunders, 1975):609–618; John Money, Tom Mazur, Charles Abrams, and Bernard F. Norman, "Micropenis, Family Mental Health, and Neonatal Management: A Report on Fourteen Patients Reared as Girls," *Journal of Preventive Psychiatry* 1, no. 1 (1981):17–27; and John Money, "Birth Defect of the Sex Organs: Telling the Parents and the Patient," *British Journal of Sexual Medicine* 10 (March 1983):14.

11. Money and Ehrhardt, 152.
12. One exception is the case followed by Milton Diamond in "Sexual Identity, Monozygotic Twins Reared in Discordant Sex Roles and a BBC Follow-up" and, with Keith Sigmundson, in "Sex Reassignment at Birth: Long-term Review and Clinical Applications."
13. Money, "Psychologic Consideration of Sex Assignment in Intersexuality."
14. Castro-Magana, Angulo, and Collipp.
15. Victor Braren et al., "True Hermaphroditism: A Rational Approach to Diagnosis and Treatment," *Urology* 15 (June 1980):569–574.
16. Studies of nonintersexed newborns have shown that, from the moment of birth, parents respond to their infant based on her/his gender. Jeffrey Rubin, F. J. Provenzano, and Z. Luria, "The Eye of the Beholder: Parents' Views on Sex of Newborns," *American Journal of Orthopsychiatry* 44, no. 4 (1974):512–519.
17. Money, Mazur, Abrams, and Norman.
18. There is evidence from other kinds of sources that once a gender attribution is made, all further information buttresses that attribution, and only the most contradictory new information will cause the original gender attribution to be questioned. Kessler and McKenna.
19. Castro-Magana, Angulo, and Collipp.
20. Money, "Psychologic Consideration of Sex Assignment in Intersexuality."
21. Technically, the term "micropenis" should be reserved for an exceptionally small but well-formed structure; a small, malformed "penis" should be referred to as a "microphallus" (Peter A. Lee et al.).
22. Money, Mazur, Abrams, and Norman, 26. A different view is argued by another leading gender-identity theorist: "When a little boy (with an imperfect penis) knows he is a male, he creates a penis that functions symbolically the same as those of boys with normal penises"

(Robert J. Stoller, *Sex and Gender* [New York: J. Aronson, 1968], 1:49).

23. W. Ch. Hecker, "Operative Correction of Intersexual Genitals in Children," *Progress in Pediatric Surgery* 17 (1984):21–31.

24. This way of presenting advice fails to understand that parents are part of a larger system. A pediatric endocrinologist told biologist Anne Fausto-Sterling that parents, especially young ones, are not independent actors. They rely on the advice of grandparents and older siblings, who, according to the physician, are more hysterical and push for an early gender assignment before all the medical data are analyzed (private communication, summer 1996).

25. Elizabeth Bing and Esselyn Rudikoff, "Divergent Ways of Parental Coping with Hermaphrodite Children," *Medical Aspects of Human Sexuality* (December 1970):73–88.

26. These evasions must have many ramifications in everyday social interactions between parents, family and friends. How people "fill in" the uncertainty such that interactions remain relatively normal is an interesting question that warrants further study. One of the pediatric endocrinologists interviewed acknowledged that the published literature discusses intersex management only from the physicians' point of view. He asks, "How [do parents] experience what they're told; and what [do] they remember . . . and carry with them?" One published exception to this neglect of the parents' perspective is a case study comparing two different coping strategies. The first couple, although initially distressed, handled the traumatic event by regarding the abnormality as an act of God. The second couple, more educated and less religious, put their faith in medical science and expressed a need to fully understand the biochemistry of the defect. Bing and Rudikoff. See chapter 5 for further discussion of parental reactions.

27. Tom Mazur, "Ambiguous Genitalia: Detection and Counseling," *Pediatric Nursing* 9 (November/December 1983):417–431; and Money "Psychologic Consideration of Sex Assignment in Intersexuality," 218.

28. Money, Potter, and Stoll, 211.

29. The term "reassignment" is more commonly used to describe the gender changes of those who are cognizant of their earlier gender, e.g., transsexuals—people whose gender itself was a mistake.

30. Although Money and Ehrhardt's socialization theory is uncontested by the physicians who treat intersexuality and is presented to parents as a matter of fact, there is actually much debate among psychologists about the effect of prenatal hormones on brain structure and ultimately on gender role behavior and even on gender identity. The physicians interviewed agreed that the animal evidence for prenatal brain organization is compelling but that there is no evidence in humans that prenatal hormones have an inviolate or unilateral effect. If there is any effect of prenatal exposure to androgen, they believe it can easily be overcome and modified by psychosocial factors. It is this latter position, not the controversy in the field, that is communicated to the parents. For an argument favoring prenatally

organized gender differences in the brain, see Milton Diamond, "Human Sexual Development: Biological Foundations for Social Development," in *Human Sexuality in Four Perspectives*, ed. Frank A. Beach (Baltimore: The Johns Hopkins University Press, 1976), 22–61; for a critique of that position, see Ruth Bleier, *Science and Gender: A Critique of Biology and Its Theories on Women* (New York: Pergamon Press, 1984).

31. Money, "Psychological Counseling: Hermaphroditism," 610.
32. Money, Mazur, Abrams, and Norman, 18.
33. P. Donahoe, "Clinical Management of Intersex Abnormalities," *Current Problems in Surgery*, 28 (1991):519–579.
34. John Money, "Hermaphroditism and Pseudohermaphroditism," in *Gynecologic Endocrinology*, ed. Jay J. Gold (New York: Hoeber, 1968), 449–464, esp. 460.
35. Mojtaba Beheshti, Brian E. Hardy, Bernard M. Churchill, and Denis Daneman, "Gender Assignment in Male Pseudohermaphrodite Children," *Urology* 22, no. 6 (December 1983):604–607. Of course, if the penis looked normal and the empty scrotum was overlooked, it might not be discovered until puberty that the male child was XX with a female internal structure.
36. Money, "Psychologic Consideration of Sex Assignment in Intersexuality," 216.
37. Weighing the probability of achieving a "perfect" penis against the probable trauma such procedures may entail is another social factor in decision making. According to an endocrinologist interviewed, if it seems that an XY infant with an inadequate penis would require as many as ten genital operations over a six-year period in order to have an adequate penis, the infant would be assigned the female gender. In this case, the endocrinologist's practical and compassionate concerns would override purely genital criteria.
38. Money, "Psychologic Consideration of Sex Assignment in Intersexuality," 217.
39. Castro-Magana, Angulo, and Collipp, 180.
40. It is unclear how much of this bias is the result of a general cultural devaluation of the female and how much is the result of physicians' belief in their ability to construct anatomically correct and functional female genitals.
41. John F. Oliven, *Sexual Hygiene and Pathology: A Manual for the Physician* (Philadelphia: J. B. Lippincott Co., 1955), 318.
42. Money, "Psychologic Consideration of Sex Assignment in Intersexuality," 215. Remnants of this anachronistic view can still be found, however, when doctors justify the removal of contradictory gonads on the grounds that they are typically sterile or at risk for malignancy (J. Dewhurst and D. B. Grant, "Intersex Problems," *Archives of Disease in Childhood* 59 (July-December 1984):1191–1194). Presumably, if the gonads were functional and healthy, their removal would provide an ethical dilemma for at least some medical professionals.
43. Although one set of authors argued that the views of the parents on

the most appropriate gender for their child must be taken into account (Dewhurst and Grant, 1192), the physicians interviewed here denied direct knowledge of this kind of participation. They claimed that they personally had encountered few, if any, cases of parents who insisted on their child being assigned a particular gender. Yet each had heard about cases where a family's ethnicity or religious background biased them toward males. None of the physicians recalled whether this preference for male offspring meant the parents wanted a male regardless of the "inadequacy" of the penis, or whether it meant that the parents would have greater difficulty with a less-than-perfect-male than with a "normal" female.

44. Money, "Psychological Counseling: Hermaphroditism," 613.
45. As with the literature on infancy, most of the published material on adolescents is on surgical and hormonal management rather than on social management. See, for example, Joel J. Roslyn, Eric W. Fonkalsrud, and Barbara Lippe, "Intersex Disorders in Adolescents and Adults," *The American Journal of Surgery* 146 (July 1983):138–144.
46. Mazur, 421.
47. Dewhurst and Grant, 1193.
48. Mazur, 422.
49. Ibid.
50. For an extended discussion of different ways of conceptualizing what is natural, see Richard W. Smith, "What kind of sex is natural?" in *The Frontiers of Sex Research*, ed. Vern Bullough (Buffalo: Prometheus, 1979), 103–111.
51. This supports sociologist Harold Garfinkel's argument that we treat routine events as our *due* as social members and that we treat gender, like all normal forms, as a moral imperative. It is no wonder, then, that physicians conceptualize what they are doing as natural and unquestionably "right." Harold Garfinkel, *Studies in Ethnomethodology* (Englewood Cliffs, N.J.: Prentice Hall, 1967).
52. Sherry B. Ortner, "Is Female to Male as Nature is to Culture?" in *Woman, Culture, and Society*, ed. Michelle Zimbalist Rosaldo and Louise Lamphere (Stanford, Calif.: Stanford University Press, 1974), 67–87.
53. Money, "Psychological Counseling: Hermaphroditism," 618.

3 *Defining and Producing Genitals*

1. There are grading schemes for describing phenotypic features of external genitals: for example, the Prader stage classification for congenital adrenal hyperplasia (referred to in Ursula Kuhnle, Monika Bullinger, and H. P. Schwarz, "The Quality of Life in Adult Female Patients with Congenital Adrenal Hyperplasia: A comprehensive study of the impact of genital malformations and chronic disease on female patients' life," *European Journal of Pediatrics* 154 [1995]: 708–716) and a comparable system developed by Quigley and French for androgen-insensitivity syndrome (Charmian Quigley and Frank

French, "Androgen Receptor Defects: Historical, Clinical and Molecular Perspectives," *Endocrine Reviews* 16, no. 3 [1995]: 271–321). These kinds of systems, though, are used to grade levels of intersex severity *after* the physician has already determined, through commonsense reasoning, that this is a case of genital "ambiguity." The scales are not used in the delivery room.

2. Jared Diamond, "Turning A Man," *Discover* 13, no. 6 (June 1992):74.
3. John K. Lattimer, "Relocation and Recession of the Enlarged Clitoris with Preservation of the Glans: An Alternative to Amputation," *The Journal of Urology* 81, no. 1 (1961):113.
4. Judson G. Randolph and Wellington Hung, "Reduction Clitoroplasty in Females with Hypertrophied Clitoris," *Journal of Pediatric Surgery* 5, no. 2 (April 1970):224.
5. See, for example: William A. Schonfeld and Gilbert W. Beebe, "Normal Growth and Variation in the Male Genitalia from Birth to Maturity," *The Journal of Urology* 48 (1942):759–777.
6. Surgeons are taught as part of their general training to distinguish degrees of urgency, from those conditions requiring immediate attention to those where surgery is elective (C. I. Clark and S. Snooks, "Objectives of Basic Surgical Training," *British Journal of Hospital Medicine* 50 [1993]: 477–479). It seems as if, once intersex becomes the topic, those distinctions become obscure.
7. Barbara C. McGillivray, "The Newborn with Ambiguous Genitalia," *Seminars in Perinatology* 16, no. 6 (1992):365. See also Domeena C. Renshaw, "Sexual Birth Defects: Telling The Parents," *Resident And Staff Physician* 39, no. 2 (February 1993):87–89.
8. Ellen K. Feder, "Disciplining the Family: The Case of Gender Identity Disorder," *Philosophical Studies* 85 (1997):200.
9. Reported in Donna Alvarado, "Intersex," *San Jose Mercury News*, 10 July 1994, p. 1.
10. Reported in Sarah Horowitz, "The Middle Sex," *SF Weekly* 13, no. 5 (1 February 1995):12.
11. Robert E. Gross, Judson Randolph, and John F. Crigler Jr., "Clitorectomy for sexual abnormalities: Indications and technique," *Surgery* (February 1966):300. The authors of this report also refer to girls in need of clitoral surgery as having "grossly enlarged" clitorises (ibid., 301).
12. Judson Randolph, Wellington Hung, and Mary Colaianni Rathlev, "Clitoroplasty for Females Born with Ambiguous Genitalia: A Long-Term Study of 37 patients," *Journal of Pediatric Surgery* 16, no. 6 (December 1981):882, 883, 885, 886, and 887.
13. Kurt Newman, Judson Randolph, and Kathryn Anderson, "The Surgical Management of Infants and Children With Ambiguous Genitalia," *Ann. Surg.* 215, no. 6 (June 1992):651.
14. Stanley J. Kogan, Paul Smey, and Selwyn B. Levitt, "Subtunical Total Reduction Clitoroplasty: A Safe Modification of Existing Techniques," *The Journal of Urology* 130 (October 1983):748.
15. Randolph and Hung, "Reduction Clitoroplasty in Females with Hypertrophied Clitoris," 230.

16. Lawrence E. Allen, B. E. Hardy, and B. M. Churchill, "The Surgical Management of the Enlarged Clitoris," *The Journal of Urology* 128 (August 1982):352.
17. Julia Epstein makes a similar point about how emotionally charged the language of intersexuality is in her excellent historical analysis "Either/Or—Neither/Both."
18. Private communication from Cheryl Chase, 3 December 1994.
19. Randolph and Hung, "Reduction Clitoroplasty in Females with Hypertrophied Clitoris," 230.
20. Frank Hinman Jr., "Microphallus: Characteristics and Choice of Treatment from a Study of 20 Cases," *The Journal of Urology* 107 (March 1972):499.
21. Newman, Randolph, and Anderson, 650.
22. Ibid., 650.
23. Ibid., 645.
24. Ibid.
25. Robert D. Guthrie, David W. Smith, and C. Benjamin Graham, "Testosterone treatment for micropenis during early childhood," *The Journal of Pediatrics* 83, no. 2 (1973):250.
26. Jared Diamond, 71.
27. The examples in this section refer to the *need* for clitoral reduction. There are also references in both the intersex literature and genital cancer literature to women *needing* to have vaginas created (Examples are cited in Kathleen V. Cairns and Mary Valentich, "Vaginal Reconstruction in Gynecologic Cancer: A Feminist Perspective," *The Journal of Sex Research* 22, no. 3 [August 1986]: 333–346). The connection between the requirements of the vagina and penis is obvious. Flaccid penises and micropenises are presumably in need of medicalization because the vagina "demands" to be filled. I will have more to say in the next chapter about how well the artificially constructed vagina meets the "demands" of the penis.
28. Lattimer, "Relocation and Recession," 113.
29. H. Kumar, J. H. Kiefer, I. E. Rosenthal, and S. S. Clark, "Clitoroplasty: Experience During a 19–Year Period," *The Journal of Urology* 111, no. 1 (January 1974):81.
30. Gross, Randolph, and Crigler, 307.
31. Allen, Hardy, and Churchill, 351.
32. A. P. van Seters and A. K. Slob, "Mutually Gratifying Heterosexual Relationship with Micropenis of Husband," *Journal of Sex & Marital Therapy* 14, no. 2 (1988):98–107; and Justine M. Reilly and C.R.J. Woodhouse, "Small Penis and the Male Sexual Role," *The Journal of Urology* 142 (August 1989):569–571. Leonore Tiefer discusses a study of men whose erections were not adequate for vaginal intercourse yet who reported high levels of sexual activity. "These men would seem to have sexual activity scripts and masculinity constructions which don't require long-lasting, rigid erections." Wives of men with erection problems worry that their pleasurable sexual lives will be endangered by penile injections and implants. Tiefer quotes: "He'll want to use it all the time, and what will that do for me?" Her argu-

ment is that "in the world of medicalization, . . . deviations (from a universal erection) are abnormal and need treatment." This belief is sustained in spite of data showing that the treatment is far from successful. Forty-three percent of penile implants malfunction and require reoperation. Leonore Tiefer, "The Medicalization of Impotence—Normalizing Phallocentrism," *Gender & Society* 8, no. 3 (September 1994):371.

33. This *need* is considered so indisputable, emanating from nature and not from anyone's personal motivation, that physicians have been known to donate their services to provide the correction. One intersexual described to me how she was supposed to feel grateful to "some hot-shot technician" who removed her clitoris gratis.

34. Bernice L. Hausman, *Changing Sex: Transsexualism, Technology, and the Idea of Gender* (Durham and London: Duke University Press, 1995); and Anne Fausto-Sterling, *Body-Building: How Biologists Construct Sexuality* (New York: Harper-Collins, forthcoming).

35. Suzanne J. Kessler, "Creating Good-looking Genitals in the Service of Gender," paper presented at the City University of New York (CUNY) Center for Lesbian and Gay Studies (CLAGS) in May 1994 and later published in *A Queer World: The Center for Lesbian and Gay Studies Reader*, ed. Martin Duberman (New York: New York University Press, 1997), 153–173.

36. Jim Bigelow, *The Joy of Uncircumcising!* (Aptos, Calif.: Hourglass Book Publishing, 1995), 33.

37. Thomas W. Filardo, "Use of 'Normal' to Describe Penile Appearance After Circumcision," *American Family Physician* 53, no. 8 (June 1996):2440.

38. In spite of the female genitals being at least as complex as the male genitals, specifications of the former have historically been limited. For example, a 1916 medical text devotes forty-three pages to a discussion of the anatomy and physiology of the male sexual organ but only ten to the female (Winfield Scott Hall, *Sexual Knowledge* [Philadelphia: The John C. Winston Co., 1916]). Sarah Hrdy, in her review of Roger Short's comprehensive analysis of sexual selection and genital selection in humans and great apes, points out that he allocates twenty sections of the paper to the male genitals with scarcely a mention of female genitals (Sarah Hrdy, *The Woman That Never Evolved* [Cambridge, Mass.: Harvard University Press, 1981]). The most recent edition of *Dorland's Illustrated Medical Dictionary* (28th ed. [Philadelphia: W. B. Saunders, 1997], 341 and 1253) uses nine lines to define the penis but only three for the clitoris. One of the lines defining the clitoris reads: "Homologous with the penis in the male," and one of the lines defining the penis reads: "Homologous with the clitoris in the female," the latter being absent from the twenty-third edition of the dictionary, published forty years earlier. Insofar as dictionaries reflect changes in the culture, an incipient symmetry between "female" and "male" genitals is confirmation that genital features can be recast over time, giving hope to those of us trying to reconceptualize intersexed genitals.

39. Kenneth W. Feldman and David W. Smith, "Fetal Phallic Growth and Penile Standards for Newborn Male Infants," *The Journal of Pediatrics* 86, no. 3 (March 1975):395–398.
40. E. Flateau, "Penile size in the newborn infant," Letters to the Editor, *The Journal of Pediatrics* 87, no. 4 (October 1995):663–664; Schonfeld and Beebe.
41. Peter A. Lee et al.
42. Hinman; Flateau.
43. Flateau, 664. John Money and colleagues discuss the discrepancy in data on norms for adult penile length. John Money, Gregory K. Lehne, and Frantz Pierre-Jerome, "Micropenis: Adult Follow-Up and Comparison of Size against New Norms," *Journal of Sex & Marital Therapy* 10, no. 2 (1984):105–114. Although there are published standards for infant and adult stretched penises, norms for adult erect penises are more difficult to locate in the medical literature. Sex researcher Leonore Tiefer claims that "the assumption that everyone knows what a normal erection is is central to the universalization and reification that supports both medicalization and phallocentrism. . . . The symbolic need for a universal phallus has prevented examination of the range of real erections" (Tiefer, "The Medicalization of Impotence," 365). On the other hand, organizations whose members are extremely interested in penile size publish norms, have standards for membership, and give advice on how to reliably measure the adult penis (*Measuring Up*, a magazine published by The Hung Jury, a social organization for men with penises at least eight inches long, as measured erect from the base). In the words of one researcher: "The true physiological length of the penis is its erect length" (Schonfeld and Beebe, 761).
44. Reilly and Woodhouse, 549; Peter A. Lee et al.
45. Donahoe.
46. Money, Lehne, and Pierre-Jerome.
47. James Green, "Getting Real about FTM Surgery," *Chrysalis: The Journal of Transgressive Gender Identities* 2, no. 2 (1995):27–32.
48. Jan Fichtner, D. Filipas, A. M. Mottrie, G. E. Voges, and R. Hohenfellner, "Analysis of Meatal Location in 500 Men: Wide Variation Questions Need For Meatal Advancement In All Pediatric Anterior Hypospadias Cases," *The Journal of Urology* 154 (August 1995):833–834.
49. Money and Ehrhardt, 286.
50. Steven Y. C. Tong, Karen Donaldson, and John M. Hutson, "When Is Hypospadias Not Hypospadias?" *MJA* 164 (5 February 1996):153–154.
51. Gross, Randolph, and Crigler, 307.
52. The average adult clitoris, including the glans, body, and crura, is about an inch long. Although the growth of the clitoris does not receive the same degree of cultural attention as the growth of the penis, the clitoris, like all the female's other body parts, grows throughout her life. There are moderate increases through puberty. Kumud Sane and Ora Hirsch Pescovitz, "The Clitoral Index: A determination of clitoral size in normal girls and in girls with abnor-

mal sexual development," *The Journal of Pediatrics* 120 (2 Pt 1) (February 1992):264–266.In geriatric patients, the average clitoral index is about thirty millimeters and may exceed eighty millimeters. John W. Huffman, "Some Facts about the Clitoris," *Post Graduate Medicine* 60, no. 5 (November 1976):245–247.

53. Hall.

54. Ellen Hyun-Ju Lee, "Producing Sex: An Interdisciplinary Perspective on Sex Assignment Decisions for Intersexuals," unpublished senior thesis, Brown University, April 1994.

55. Sharon E. Oberfeld et al., "Clitoral Size in Full-Term Infants," *American Journal of Perinatology* 6, no. 4 (October 1989):453–454.

56. Sane and Pescovitz; Huffman.

57. Sane and Pescovitz.

58. A. Sotiropoulos et al., "Long-Term Assessment of Genital Reconstruction in Female Pseudohermaphrodites," *The Journal of Urology* 115 (May 1976):599–601.

59. This is particularly true in literature directed to the lay person. See, for example, M. J. Exner, *The Sexual Side of Marriage* (New York: W. W. Norton and Co., 1932).

60. Ellen Hyun-Ju Lee, 59.

61. Ibid., 32.

62. Huffman, 245.

63. The hymen, like the labia, is described in its variability, with a focus on individual differences of thickness and completeness. It is also interesting to note that the hymen is the only part of the female genitals described as tough. Kenneth M. Walker, *Preparation for Marriage* (New York: W. W. Norton, 1933); and Henry J. Garriques, *A Textbook of the Diseases of Women* (Philadelphia: W. B. Saunders, 1894).

64. Garriques, 37.

65. Hinman. The same could be said about adult genitals: "Extremely fleshy women may be so plump that the clitoris cannot be seen within the inner lips" (L. T. Woodward, *Sophisticated Sex Techniques in Marriage* [New York: Lancer Books, 1968]).

66. Guthrie, Smith, and Graham, 251.

67. Kessler and McKenna.

68. Chandler Burr, "Homosexuality and Biology," *The Atlantic Monthly* (March 1993):59.

69. "Is Early Vaginal Reconstruction Wrong for Some Intersex Girls?" *Urology Times* (February 1997):12.

70. John H. Holzaepfel, *Marriage Manual,* pamphlet, 1959; Hall.

71. Robert Crooks and Karla Baur, *Our Sexuality*, 6th ed (Pacific Grove, Calif.: Brooks/Cole Publishing, 1996).

72. Interview conducted spring 1994. It is confirmed by women who have received labioplasty that, although passable outer labia can be produced, normal-looking inner labia cannot, and that within a few years the newly fashioned labia minora merge back into the vulva area. A clinical sexologist who has seen the labia of many male-to-female transsexuals claims that they "look like a remodeling job"

(*Hermaphrodites with Attitude,* newsletter of the Intersex Society of North America [fall/winter 1995–96]: 15).

73. Alan Perlmutter and Claude Reitelman, "Surgical Management of Intersexuality," in *Campbell's Urology,* ed. Patrick Walsh (Philadelphia: W. B. Saunders, 1992), 1951–66.
74. Kumar et al.
75. Gross, Randolph, and Crigler, 307.
76. Randolph and Hung, "Reduction Clitoroplasty in Females with Hypertrophied Clitoris."
77. Kumar et al.
78. Randolph, Hung, and Rathlev, "Clitoroplasty for Females Born with Ambiguous Genitalia." In a 1993 personal letter to Cheryl Chase, the senior author wrote, "I came to the conclusion that sparing the clitoris would be more physiologic and more appropriate."
79. David T. Mininberg, "Phalloplasty in Congenital Adrenal Hyperplasia," *The Journal of Urology* 128 (August 1982):355–356.For a review of these techniques, see: Joseph E. Oesterling, John P. Gearhart, and Robert D. Jeffs, "A Unified Approach to Early Reconstructive Surgery of the Child With Ambiguous Genitalia," *The Journal of Urology* 138 (October 1987):1079–1084.
80. Reported in Hendricks.
81. Lattimer, "Relocation and Recession," 113.
82. Kumar et al.
83. Described in Mininberg, 355.
84. Randolph and Hung, "Reduction Clitoroplasty in Females with Hypertrophied Clitoris."
85. Perlmutter and Reitelman, 1957.
86. Private communication from Cheryl Chase, 29 January 1993.
87. Lattimer, "Relocation and Recession."
88. W. Hardy Hendren and Anthony Atala, "Repair of High Vagina in Girls With Severely Masculinized Anatomy From the Adrenogenital Syndrome," *Journal of Pediatric Surgery* 30, no. 1 (January 1995):91–94.
89. *ALIAS,* newsletter of the Androgen Insensitivity Support Group, 1, no. 4 (spring 1996).
90. See, for example: Slijper et al., "Evaluation of Psychosexual Development of Young Women with Congenital Adrenal Hyperplasia: A Pilot Study," *Journal of Sex Education and Therapy* 18, no. 2 (1992):200–207.
91. See, for example: Thom E. Lobe et al., "The Complications of Surgery For Changing Patterns Over Two Decades," *Journal of Pediatric Surgery* 22, no. 7 (July 1987):651–652.
92. Tom P.V.M. De Jong and Thomas M. L. Boemers, "Neonatal Management of Female Intersex by Clitorovaginoplasty," *The Journal of Urology* 154 (August 1995):832.
93. *ALIAS,* newsletter of the Androgen Insensitivity Support Group, 1, no. 4 (spring 1996).
94. Kuhnle, Bullinger, and Schwarz.

95. Sava Perovic, "Phalloplasty in Children and Adolescents Using the Extended Pedicle Island Groin Flap," *The Journal of Urology* 154 (August 1995):848–853.
96. Hinman.
97. Saul P. Greenfield, Barry T. Sadler, and Julian Wan, "Two-Stage Repair for Severe Hypospadias," *The Journal of Urology* 152 (1994):498.
98. Newman, Randolph, and Anderson, 651.
99. Edward Shlasko, lecture at Update in Pediatric Plastic and Reconstructive Surgery Symposium at The Mount Sinai Medical Center, 17 May 1996.
100. Hendren and Atala, 94.
101. Howard W. Jones and William Wallace Scott, *Hermaphroditism, Genital Anomalies, and Related Endocrine Disorders* (Baltimore: The Williams and Wilkins Co., 1958), 280.
102. Anonymous transsexual writing to TRANSGEN, an internet Usenet newsgroup.
103. Randolph, Hung, and Rathlev, "Clitoroplasty for Females Born with Ambiguous Genitalia," 884.
104. Marjorie Garber, "Spare Parts: The Surgical Construction of Gender," *Differences: A Journal of Feminist Cultural Studies* 1, no. 3 (fall 1989):149.
105. It is not uncommon for writers aware of the social construction of genital "normalcy" and the limitation of surgery to "normalize" the genitals—to put these kind of terms in quotation marks, as I have done throughout this chapter. I was struck, though, that in an article on the medical management of intersexuality, the authors (who would not be expected to share these views) put "normalizing" in quotation marks (Kenneth J. Zucker et al., "Psychosexual Development of Women with Congenital Adrenal Hyperplasia," *Hormones and Behavior* 30 [1996]: 302). I wrote to the senior author and asked him why quotation marks were used. He responded, "Statistically normal-looking external female genitalia may not be experienced as normal by some women." I will have more to say, in chapter 5, about the discrepancy between looks and experience.

4 *Evaluating Genital Surgery*

1. Randolph, Hung, and Rathlev, "Clitoroplasty for Females Born with Ambiguous Genitalia"; Newman, Randolph, and Anderson; Sotiropoulos et al.; Kumar et al.; Allen, Hardy, and Churchill; Hendren and Atala; Oesterling, Gearhart, and Jeffs; A. Pinter and G. Kosztolanyi, "Surgical Management of Neonates and Children with Ambiguous Genitalia," *University Children's Hospital of Pecs/Hungary* 30, no. 1 (1990):111–121; John P. Gearhart, Arthur Burnett, and Jeffrey H. Owen, "Measurement of Pudendal Evoked Potentials During Feminizing Genitoplasty: Technique and Applications," *The Journal of Urology* 153 (February 1995):486–487; John R. Wesley and Arnold G. Coran, "Intestinal Vaginoplasty for Congenital Absence

of the Vagina," *Journal of Pediatric Surgery* 27, no. 1 (July 1992):885–889; De Jong and Boemers; and J. Martinez-Mora et al., "Neovagina in Vaginal Agenesis: Surgical Methods and Long-Term Results," *Journal of Pediatric Surgery* 27, no. 1 (January 1992):10–14.

2. Randolph, Hung, and Rathlev, "Clitoroplasty for Females Born with Ambiguous Genitalia," 882.
3. Randolph and Hung, "Reduction Clitoroplasty in Females with Hypertrophied Clitoris," 229.
4. Kumar et al., 83.
5. Jared Diamond, 72.
6. Pinter and Kosztolanyi, 115.
7. Fausto-Sterling and Laurent similarly found, in their independent analysis of seven other reduction-clitoroplasty clinical reports, that the reports rarely state the criteria for success or consider psychological health; they tend instead to emphasize cosmetic criteria. Fausto-Sterling, *Body-Building*.
8. Randolph, Hung, and Rathlev, "Clitoroplasty for Females Born with Ambiguous Genitalia."
9. Newman, Randolph, and Anderson.
10. Randolph, Hung, and Rathlev, "Clitoroplasty for Females Born with Ambiguous Genitalia," 886.
11. Sotiropoulos et al., 599.
12. Allen, Hardy, and Churchill, 353.
13. Newman, Randolph, and Anderson, 652.
14. Oesterling, Gearhart, and Jeffs, 1081.
15. Hendren and Atala, 94.
16. F.M.E. Slijper et al., "Neonates with Abnormal Genital Development Assigned the Female Sex," 15.
17. See, for example: Pinter and Kosztolanyi, 115.
18. Randolph, Hung, and Rathlev, "Clitoroplasty for Females Born with Ambiguous Genitalia," 886.
19. Sotiropoulos et al.
20. Kumar et al., 83.
21. Mininberg, 355.
22. Randolph and Hung, "Reduction Clitoroplasty in Females with Hypertrophied Clitoris," 230.
23. Money, *Sex Errors of the Body*, 39–40.
24. Ibid., 42.
25. Private communication from Cheryl Chase, 29 January 1993.
26. Gearhart, Burnett, and Owen, "Measurement of Pudendal Evoked Potentials," 486.
27. Cheryl Chase, "Letter to the Editor Re: Measurement of Pudendal Evoked Potentials during Feminizing Genitoplasty: Technique and Applications," *The Journal of Urology* 156, no. 3 (1995):1139.
28. J. P. Gearhart, A. Burnett, and J. H. Owen, "Reply by Authors "Re: Measurement of Pudendal Evoked Potentials During Feminizing Genitoplasty: Technique and Applications," *The Journal of Urology* 153 (1995):1140.
29. To eliminate vulvar or vaginal cancer, some women might have a

complete pelvic exenteration (removal of the bladder, rectum, vagina, uterus, fallopian tubes, and ovaries, and perhaps a significant part of their vulvas) as well as construction of a new urinary tract, colon, bladder, and GI tract. Not all women with genital cancers, though, would be candidates for or would elect to have genital reconstruction. One physician interviewed estimated that only one woman in ten would elect it. Physician responses not from referenced literature are culled from interviews conducted in 1994. The three physicians quoted are affiliated with a major metropolitan teaching hospital in New York City. One is a plastic surgeon and the other two are gynecological oncologists who also do genital surgery.

30. Cairns and Valentich.

31. Just as this surgeon's "innovation" was a consequence of a woman's demand, women with breast cancer have influenced surgeons to perform (and find justification for) lumpectomies over mastectomies.

32. The size of the normal vagina, like the other genital parts I have considered in the previous chapter, is related to the conditions of measurement. It is interesting to note that while "natural born adult vaginas are between ten and twelve centimeters long (less than four inches to four and three-fourths inches), those created for transsexuals are bigger—nine to eighteen centimeters (three and a half inches to over seven inches)" (Sara Perovic, "Male to Female Surgery: A New Contribution to Operative Techniques," *Plastic and Reconstructive Surgery* 91, no. 4 [April 1993]: 708–709). One surgeon who does vaginal construction for male-to-female transsexuals quips, "What's the use of doing it if you don't wind up with a deep vagina?"

33. Rose M. Mulaikai, Claude J. Migeon, and John A. Rock, "Fertility Rates in Female Patients with Congenital Adrenal Hyperplasia Due to 21-Hydroxylase Deficiency," *The New England Journal of Medicine* 316, no. 4 (22 January 1987):179.

34. One sexually inactive woman in the sample is described as having an adequate vaginal opening, "but she is obese and has not secured a partner" (Hendren and Atala, 91). The girls in that study who had difficulty making "social adjustments" were those who were overweight. Any teenage girl or woman could have told the researchers that in the dating market vaginal size is less important than breast and hip size.

35. Findings regarding the sexual orientation of intersexuals are contradictory. In an early study, John Money and his colleagues claimed that 48 percent of their sample of intersex girls were lesbians. John Money, M. Schwartz, and V. G. Lewis, "Adult Erotosexual Status and Fetal Hormonal Masculinization and Demasculinization: 46,XX Congenital Virilizing Adrenal Hyperplasia and 46,XY Androgen-insensitivity Syndrome Compared," *Psychoneuroendocrinology* 9 (1984):9, 405–414. Recent research with more sophisticated methodology found that although thirty-one women with congenital adrenal hyperplasia (CAH) reported fewer heterosexual experiences than a control sample, they did not report more sexual experiences with women than the controls. Zucker et al., "Psychosexual Development

of Women with Congenital Adrenal Hyperplasia." It is my impression, based on evidence from adult intersexed women with whom I have been in contact, that lesbianism is more common among intersexed women than among women in general.
36. See, for example: Mulaikai, Migeon, and Rock.
37. *Hermaphrodites with Attitude* (winter 1994):5.
38. Interview conducted with a New York City clinician, spring 1996.
39. W.C.M. Weijmar Schultz et al., "Sexual Rehabilitation of Radical Vulvectomy Patients. A Pilot Study," *Journal of Psychosomatic Obstetrics and Gynecology* 5 (1986):124.
40. Kenneth D. Hatch, "Neovaginal Reconstruction," *CANCER* supplement 71, no. 4 (February 1993):1661.
41. Mulaikai, Migeon, and Rock, 181.
42. Allen, Hardy, and Churchill, 353.
43. Slijper et al., "Evaluation of Psychosexual Development of Young Women with Congenital Adrenal Hyperplasia," 201.
44. Sotiropoulos et al., 601.
45. Newman, Randolph, and Anderson, 650.
46. Hendren and Atala, 91.
47. Anonymous, "Once a Dark Secret," *British Medical Journal* 308 (February 1994):542.
48. Private communication with an intersexed woman, 18 December 1995.
49. *ALIAS*, newsletter of the Androgen Insensitivity Support Group, 1, no. 4 (spring 1996).
50. Randolph and Hung, "Reduction Clitoroplasty in Females with Hypertrophied Clitoris," 229.
51. Oesterling, Gearhart, and Jeffs, 1081.
52. See, for example: Sotiropoulos et al.
53. See, for example: Newman, Randolph, and Anderson; and De Jong and Boemers.
54. Fausto-Sterling, *Body-Building*.
55. Wesley and Coran, 885.
56. Allen, Hardy, and Churchill, 354.
57. These quotations are from letters written to a mother by other mothers whose daughters also have congenital adrenal hyperplasia. See chapter 5 for a description of how these letters were acquired.
58. Hendren and Atala, 94.
59. Mulaikai, Migeon, and Rock.
60. Slijper et al., "Evaluation of Psychosexual Development of Young Women with Congenital Adrenal Hyperplasia," 201.
61. *Hermaphrodites with Attitude*, spring 1995, 2.
62. Randolph, Hung, and Rathlev, "Clitoroplasty for Females Born with Ambiguous Genitalia," 885.
63. *Hermaphrodites with Attitude*, fall/winter 1995–1996, 14. The medical profession's self-critiques emerge only between the lines, as suggested by the following: "We have learned, in some instances bitterly, the absolute essentiality of a structured, regular, comprehensive pro-

gram from infancy . . . into adult life" (Newman, Randolph, and Anderson, 652).

64. Randolph, Hung, and Rathlev, "Clitoroplasty for Females Born with Ambiguous Genitalia," 885.

65. U. Patil and F. P. Hixson, "The Role of Tissue Expanders in Vaginoplasty for Congenital Malformations of the Vagina," *British Journal of Urology* 70 (1992):556.

66. Fausto-Sterling, *Body-Building.*

67. As mentioned earlier, vaginas reconstructed for women recovering from genital cancer are far from perfect. The new vagina needs artificial lubrication, produces an unpleasant odor and discharge, and requires daily douching. It is numb for the first three months and takes six to twelve months to reach a satisfactory vaginal size. There is also postcoital bleeding, disfigurement of the upper thighs, and painful intercourse, at least initially. For discussions, see: Cairns and Valentich; and Hatch.

68. Harold I. Lief and Lynn Hubschmann, "Orgasm in the Postoperative Transsexual," *Archives of Sexual Behavior* 22, no. 2 (1993):145–155.

69. Perovic, "Male to Female Surgery," 706.

70. June Martin, "The Incidence, Frequency and Rate of Genital Satisfaction of Sixty-Four Post-Operative Male-to-Female Transsexuals Reported to be Experienced During Various Sexual Behaviors: A Descriptive Study," Ph.D. dissertation, Institute for Advanced Study of Human Sexuality, San Francisco, 1988.

71. Usenet newsgroup TRANSGEN: Conversation between Victoria Heisner and Robin Mitchell, 18 July 1994.

72. Money, Lehne, and Pierre-Jerome, 109.

73. Ibid.

74. Cited in Hendricks, 10.

75. P. Frey and A. Bianchi, "One-Stage Preputial Pedicle Flap Repair for Hypospadias: Experience with 100 Patients," *Progress in Pediatric Surgery* 23 (1989):189.

76. Greenfield, Sadler, and Wan, 501.

77. John F. Stecker Jr. et al., "Hypospadias Cripples," Symposium on Hypospadias, *Urologic Clinics of North America* 8, no. 3 (October 1981):539–544; and Frey and Bianchi.

78. A. B. Belman, "Editorial Comment Re: One-Stage Repair of Hypospadias: Is There No Simple Method Universally Applicable To All Types of Hypospadias?" *The Journal of Urology* 152 (October 1994):1237.

79. Greenfield, Sadler, and Wan.

80. Mark A. M. Mureau et al., "Genital Perception of Children, Adolescents and Adults Operated on for Hypospadias: A Comparative Study," *The Journal of Sex Research* 32, no. 4 (winter 1995):289–298.

81. Richard Schlussel lecture at Update in Pediatric Plastic and Reconstructive Surgery, a symposium at The Mount Sinai Medical Center, New York, 17 May 1996.

82. Newman, Randolph, and Anderson, 651.

83. Schlussel.
84. Mureau et al., 290.
85. Private communication from Morgan Holmes, fall 1995.
86. J. L. Teague, D. R. Roth, and E. T. Gonzales, "Repair of Hypospadias Complications Using the Meatal Based Flap Urethroplasty," *The Journal of Urology* 151 (February 1994):470–472; Tomohiko Koyanagi et al., "One-Stage Repair of Hypospadias: Is There No Simple Method Universally Applicable to All Types of Hypospadias?" *The Journal of Urology* 152 (October 1994):1232–1237; Jeffrey A. Stock et al., "The Management of Proximal Hypospadias Using a 1–Stage Hypospadias Repair with a Preputial Free Graft for Neourethral Construction and a Preputial Pedicle Flap for Ventral Skin Coverage," *The Journal of Urology* 152 (December 1994):2335–2337; Frey and Bianchi; and Greenfield, Sadler, and Wan.
87. Frey and Bianchi, 189.
88. Mureau et al., 290.
89. Stecker et al.
90. Teague, Roth, and Gonzales; Koyanagi et al.
91. Frey and Bianchi.
92. Ibid.; Koyanagi et al.
93. John W. Duckett and Laurence S. Baskin, "Genitoplasty for Intersex Anomalies," *European Journal of Pediatrics* 152 (1993):80–84.
94. Frey and Bianchi.
95. The "natural" urethra is made of tissue that is able to resist the irritating effect of urine and the growth of bacteria. Skin tubes that are surgically created do not have these properties; consequently, the reconstructed penis is susceptible to many complications, making multiple surgeries standard. Those who argue against doing circumcisions on male infants, admittedly a much simpler penile surgical procedure, make some of the same points. They describe the foreskin as dense with nerve endings and a rich blood supply. "The result [of circumcision] to the glans . . . is that the natural mucous covering is traumatized and becomes to some degree scarified." Men who were circumcised later in life "complain that having intercourse with their circumcised glans is like having intercourse with their elbow." Bigelow, 22–23.
96. Mureau et al.
97. Ibid., 294.
98. Ibid., 297.
99. *Hermaphrodites with Attitude,* spring 1995.
100. Green, 27.
101. Devor, *FTM: Female-to-Male Transsexuals in Society.*
102. Private communication from Morgan Holmes, 13 December 1995.
103. Randolph, Hung, and Rathlev, "Clitoroplasty for Females Born with Ambiguous Genitalia," 882.
104. Allen, Hardy, and Churchill, 351.
105. Newman, Randolph, and Anderson, 644.
106. Gearhart, Burnett, and Owen, "Measurement of Pudendal Evoked Potentials During Feminizing Genitoplasty," 487.

107. Lobe et al., 652.
108. Hendren and Atala, 92.
109. Lattimer, "Relocation and Recession," 113.
110. Described in Hendricks.
111. Ibid., 16.
112. Schlussel.
113. Cited in private communication from Cheryl Chase, 7 January 1993.
114. Cheryl Chase, "'Corrective' Surgery Unnecessary: Reply to 'Is It a Boy or a Girl'?" *Johns Hopkins Magazine* 46, no. 1 (February 1994): 6–7.
115. Fausto-Sterling, private communication, 30 November 1995.

5 *Questioning Medical Management*

1. Toby, *Finding Our Own Ways*, self-published newsletter (1987):1.
2. Ibid., 3.
3. Natalie Angier, "New Debate over Surgery on Genitals," *New York Times*, 13 May 1997, pp. C1 and C6; Geoffrey Cowley, "Gender Limbo," *Newsweek*, 19 May 1997, 64–66.
4. *Hermaphrodites with Attitude*, 1, no. 1 (winter 1994).
5. For a discussion of how the social constructionist view of gender has become mainstream, at least among academics, see: Wendy McKenna and Suzanne Kessler, "Who Needs Gender Theory?" *Signs: Journal of Women in Culture and Society* (spring 1997):687–691.
6. Private communication, 25 October 1993.
7. H.R. 109; passed 30 September 1996.
8. Health insurance policies in the United States routinely cover intersex surgeries. A typical policy reads: "Charges for 'cosmetic treatment or surgery' will be covered only if they result from . . . a congenital disease or anomaly of a dependent child resulting in a *functional defect*" (my emphasis) (United States Life Insurance Company). Almost no policies cover "sexual transformations," a restriction aimed at transsexual surgery but one that could easily be applied to unnecessary genital surgery on anyone, even intersexed infants. If intersex surgery is reconceptualized as either not correcting a functional defect or as a "sex change," the insurance companies might respond by refusing to fund them.
9. See chapter 2, note 4.
10. Bigelow, 236.
11. Ibid.
12. Ibid., 4 and 2.
13. Ibid., 48.
14. Ibid., 220.
15. Ibid., 7.
16. Ibid., 49.
17. Chase describes in lucid detail the complexity of her "coming out" as an intersexual in "Affronting Reason," in *Looking Queer: Image and Identity in Lesbian, Bisexual, Gay, and Transgendered Communities*, ed. D. Atkins, (Binghamton, N.Y.: Haworth, forthcoming).

18. Alice Domurat Dreger, "Hermaphrodites in Love: The Truth of the Gonads," in *Science and Homosexualities*, ed. Vernon Rosario (New York: Routledge, 1996), 46–66.
19. In the course of my investigations, I have spoken directly to nineteen people with an intersex diagnosis and have had lengthy correspondences with a number of others. Those who are identified in the text (Cheryl Chase, Sherri Groveman, and Morgan Holmes) have written on the topic of intersexuality, have been publicly quoted, and have been identified as intersexuals in the press. The others I have elected to quote anonymously, even though some have identified themselves as intersexuals in *Hermaphrodites with Attitude* and *ALIAS*, intersex newsletters. All communications—face-to-face interviews, phone conversations, and correspondences—took place between January 1993 and September 1997.
20. Gender scholar Holly Devor prefers "intersexed" over "intersexual" (private communication, June 1997), which is consistent with her argument for using "transsexed" instead of the more common "transsexual." Holly Devor, "Female Gender Dysphoria in Context: Social Problems or Personal Problems," *Annual Review of Sex Research* 7 (1996):7. She reasons that the "sexual" morpheme in both "intersexual" and "transsexual" draws attention to questions of sexuality, which are incidental to both identities. As I indicated in chapter 2, were it not so cumbersome, "intergenderal" reflects my views more accurately than either "intersexed" or "intersexual."
21. Holmes, "Re-membering a Queer Body," 13.
22. One man with Klinefelter's syndrome wrote me that he thought few people who shared his condition think of themselves as intersexed. It may be that those whose "gender anomaly" is uncorrected or uncorrectable are less likely to identify as intersexuals than those who have had surgical interventions.
23. Gross, Randolph, and Crigler, 300.
24. Kessler and McKenna, 154.
25. For a discussion of spoiled identity, see: Erving Goffman, *Stigma: Notes on the Management of Spoiled Identity* (Englewood Cliffs, N.J.: Prentice Hall, 1963).
26. Endocrinologists and gynecologists who had attended The Royal Society of Medicine symposium on androgen-insensitivity syndrome (AIS) in 1995 wrote letters praising the presentations of representatives from AISSG and indicating how impressed they were with the organization's aims (*ALIAS* 1, no. 3 [winter 1995]). This contrasts with the cold shoulder that representatives of the Intersex Society of North America (ISNA) received at a Mt. Sinai School of Medicine conference on Pediatric Plastic and Reconstructive Surgery 16 May 1996.
27. Cited in: Horowitz, 12.
28. See note 36, below.
29. Kuhnle, Bullinger, and Schwarz.
30. Morgan Holmes, "Homophobia in Health Care: Abjection and the Treatment of Intersexuality," paper presented at the Learned Societies CSAA meetings, Montreal, June 1995.

31. Ibid., 16.
32. Ibid., 2.
33. Anne Fausto-Sterling, "The Five Sexes," *The Sciences* (March/April 1993):20–24; and Anne Fausto-Sterling, "How Many Sexes Are There?" *New York Times*, 12 March 1993.
34. Suzanne J. Kessler, letter in response to Anne Fausto-Sterling's "The Five Sexes," *The Sciences* (July/August 1993):3.
35. Holmes, "Homophobia in Health Care,"14.
36. Some data reported in this chapter are from direct interviews with parents of intersexed children, but most are from letters sent to Eileen Wells, a mother of an intersexed infant, when, in 1993, she solicited responses in a national women's magazine. She asked to hear from other parents who, like her, have children with a diagnosis of congenital adrenal hyperplasia. About one hundred people, mostly mothers, wrote to her, some more than once. I am indebted to her for giving me access to those letters, many of which I will draw upon in this chapter. All names of children are pseudonyms.
37. Heino F. L. Meyer-Bahlburg, "Gender Assignment from the Clinician's Perspective," paper presented at the annual meeting of The Society for the Scientific Study of Sex, November 1995.
38. Tom Majeski, "Surgery Changes Russian Child's Sex," *San Jose Mercury News*, 25 July 1994.
39. Allen, Hardy, and Churchill.
40. Newman, Randolph, and Anderson, 651.
41. Alvarado.
42. Randolph, Hung, and Rathlev, "Clitoroplasty for Females Born with Ambiguous Genitalia," 886.
43. Louis Gooren and Peggy T. Cohen-Kettenis, "Development of Male Gender Identity/Role and a Sexual Orientation Towards Women in a 46,XY Subject with an Incomplete Form of the Androgen Insensitivity Syndrome," *Archives of Sexual Behavior* 20, no. 5 (1991):461–462.
44. Fausto-Sterling and Laurent found seventy cases in the medical literature (post-1950) of people who grew up with obviously unusual genitals yet, with few exceptions, were able to adjust to those genitals and develop into functioning adults. Fausto-Sterling, *Body-Building*.
45. AISSG annual meeting, New York City, 7 September 1996. Some physicians believe that women with genital cancers feel "less of a woman" without a vagina and are "in need of vaginal reconstruction" (Cairns and Valentich, 340). However, the data suggest that, first of all, these women find satisfying alternative sexual activities, and, secondly, they "express far greater anxiety about their inability to fulfill family functions such as wage-earning and taking care of household chores" (L. W. Schover and M. Fife, "Sexual Counseling of Patients Undergoing Radical Surgery for Pelvic or Genital Cancer," *Journal of Psychosocial Oncology* 3 [1986]: 21–41). They also are far more worried about the cancer itself than about their ability to have intercourse (R. H. Corney et al., "Psychosocial Adjustment

Following Major Gynaecological Surgery for Carcinoma of the Cervix and Vulva," *Journal of Psychosomatic Research* 36, no. 6 [1992]: 564).
46. Butler.
47. Slijper et al., "Neonates with Abnormal Genital Development Assigned the Female Sex," 11.
48. There are two related questions: How much does the average person recognize and tolerate variations in others' genitals and how does the recognition of one's own variant genitals unfold? Cheryl Chase, in an autobiographical article ("Affronting Reason"), provides a moving description of the dawning recognition of her genital difference as a consequence of a childhood clitoridectomy.
49. Flateau.
50. Fausto-Sterling, *Body-Building*, 55.
51. In one study of "what women know about their sex organs," adult women were asked to draw their genitals (Lucille Hollander Blum, "Darkness in an Enlightened Era: Women's Drawings of their Sexual Organs," *Psychological Reports* 42 [1978]: 867–873). Although fewer than half of the drawings included the clitoris, of those women who drew the clitoris, more than half drew it in what the author calls "conspicuously exaggerated form." Although one could just attribute this to the women's ignorance about anatomy, it is intriguing to consider whether it indicates a broader acceptance of (or even wish for) larger clitorises than their own or those they have seen. The author offers a psychoanalytic interpretation of the crude, inaccurate drawings but has no comparison data—for example, women's drawings of a car.
52. One physician interviewed, who reconstructs vaginas for women with genital cancers, believes that having a vagina is very important to women: "It's a sense of feeling whole, even if it's not used." When questioned about the basis of his belief, he admitted not being aware of any psychological studies on the importance of a vagina to women, and in general seemed not to be fazed that his unsupported beliefs were the bedrock of his surgical decisions.

6 *Rethinking Genitals and Gender*

1. Hausman, 201.
2. Fausto-Sterling, *Body-Building*.
3. Citing evidence from pediatric surgeon Patricia Donahoe, one writer questions the heterosexual imperative of genital surgery and gender assignment of intersexuals based on infant phallic size: "Using newborn phallus length as an indication of penetrative ability is misguided, for 'phallus size at birth has not been reliably correlated with size and function at puberty'" (Ellen Hyun-Ju Lee, 26).
4. Helena Wright, *The Sex Factor in Marriage* (New York: The Vanguard Press, 1931).
5. August Forel and C. F. Marshall, *The Sexual Question* (Brooklyn, N.Y.: Physicians and Surgeons Book Co., 1906), 20.

6. Ibid., 55.
7. Garriques, 37.
8. Creating genitals in one gender for the purpose of the other is illustrated in a conversation between a genitally mutilated woman and her mutilator in Alice Walker's *Possessing the Secret of Joy* (New York: Pocket Star Books, 1992). The woman whose clitoris and labia were cut accuses the elder, "I felt I had been made into something other than myself." The elder replies, "You had been made into a woman. . . . It is only because a woman is *made* into a woman that a man *becomes* a man" (246; my emphasis).
9. Hendren and Atala; Allen, Hardy, and Churchill; Mulaikai, Migeon, and Rock.
10. Sotiropoulos et al., 601.
11. Cairns and Valentich.
12. Quotations from surgeons, unless otherwise referenced, are from interviews conducted for this book in 1994.
13. Cunnar Lindemalm, D. Korlin, and N. Uddenberg, "Long-term Follow-up of 'Sex Change' in 13 Male-to-Female Transsexuals," *Archives of Sexual Behavior* 15, no. 3 (1996):193.
14. All quotations in this paragraph were from studies cited in Cairns and Valentich, 336.
15. For the purpose of gender attribution, males and females do not need physical genitals. They need cultural genitals, those that *should* be there. The argument we made was that there were only cultural penises (Kessler and McKenna). It may be that cultural vaginas have emerged in the interim, but clearly the evidence I presented in previous chapters should leave no doubt that there are no cultural clitorises.
16. Reported in Hendricks, 14.
17. Newman, Randolph, and Anderson, 646.
18. Kessler and McKenna.
19. Holly Devor, private communication, June 1997.
20. Hausman, chap. 2.
21. Ibid., 52.
22. Ibid., 63.
23. Ibid., 61.
24. Diana Dull and Candace West, "Accounting for Cosmetic Surgery: The Accomplishment of Gender," *Social Problems* 38, no. 1 (February 1991):54–70.
25. Ibid., 66.
26. Kathryn Pauly Morgan, "Women and the Knife: Cosmetic Surgery and the Colonization of Women's Bodies," *Hypatia* 6, no. 3 (fall 1991):37.
27. Hausman, 70.
28. Surgical solutions for variant genitals need to be seen in the context of a cultural tide that is shrinking rather than expanding the range of what is considered normal for all parts of the body. Endocrinologists are prescribing a regimen of growth hormone for children who are deemed too short. Orthodontists are diagnosing denture abnormali-

ties and providing "necessary" corrections for virtually every middle-class child's teeth. "Imperfections [are] remediable today with the early help of a skilled surgeon" (Renshaw, 87).

29. Ask Isadora, "Ongoing Conversations," *The Westchester County Weekly*, 14 September 1995, p. 28.

30. Ask Isadora, "I Yam What I Yam," *The Westchester County Weekly*, 21 December 1995, p. 28.

31. Hendricks, 10.

32. One might expect resistance to genital surgeries to come from managed health care companies in the United States, which are less inclined than ever to pay for what is construed as elective surgeries.

33. William Chavis, John J. LaFerla, and Robert Niccolini, "Plastic Repair of Elongated, Hypertrophic Labia Minora," *The Journal of Reproductive Medicine* 34, no. 5 (1989):373.

34. Melvin H. Radman, "Hypertrophy of the Labia Minora," *Obstetrics and Gynecology* 48, no. 1 (July 1976):78–80.

35. J. Ruminjo, "Circumcision in Women," *East African Medical Journal* (September 1992):478.

36. Garriques, 37.

37. Woodward.

38. For discussions of the exhibition in nineteenth-century Europe (at fashionable Parisian parties) of Sarah Bartmann, the so-called "Hottentot Venus," whose elongated labia minora (which she modestly tried to hide) represented to Europeans the presumed deviant sexuality of the Africans rather than the range of "normal" genital variation, see: Patricia Hill Collins, *Black Feminist Thought: Knowledge, Consciousness, and the Politics of Empowerment* (New York: Routledge, 1991), and Anne Fausto-Sterling, "Gender, Race, and Nation: The Comparative Anatomy of 'Hottentot' Women in Europe, 1815–1817," in *Deviant Bodies: Critical Perspectives on Difference in Science and Popular Culture*, ed. Jennifer Terry and Jacqueline Urla (Bloomington: Indiana University Press, 1995), 19–48.

39. Chavis, LaFerla, and Niccolini.

40. Ibid., 373.

41. Ibid., 374.

42. Ibid.

43. Unspoken concern is also alluded to in the clitoroplasty literature for intersexed infants. One well-known surgeon chastises physicians who fail to reduce the size of the glans "drastically." He laments that this is often neglected, causing parents and patients much dissatisfaction, although "they are sometimes reluctant to speak out about it" (John K. Lattimer, "Editorial Comment on Stanley Kogan, et al's 'Subtunical Total Reduction Clitoroplasty: A Safe Modification of Existing Techniques,'" *The Journal of Urology* 130 [October 1983]: 748).

44. Dull and West; and Hausman.

45. Chavis, LaFerla, and Niccolini, 373.

46. Ibid., 374. The authors describe the success of the surgery in its en-

tirety: "The postoperative course was uncomplicated. The patient was exceedingly pleased with the resultant size and configuration of her labia. She has declined to have the area photographed, however."
47. Radman, 78.
48. Ibid.
49. "Read My Lips," *Taste of Latex* (9 November 1993):7.
50. Helen Rogan, "A Woman's Mag Masks Sleaze as Service," *Ms.* (September-October 1994):92–93.
51. Rogan, 93, cites a former editor of *First*.
52. Martin, 76.
53. Tiefer, "The Medicalization of Impotence."
54. Leonore Tiefer, "Might Premature Ejaculation Be Organic? The Perfect Penis Takes a Giant Step Forward," *Journal of Sex Education and Therapy* 20, no. 1 (1994):8.
55. Ibid.
56. Janice Irvine, *Disorders of Desire: Sex and Gender in Modern American Sexology* (Philadelphia: Temple University Press, 1990).
57. Morgan.
58. Holly Devor writes, "Were gender to become divided from sex, it would begin to lose its meaning" (*Gender Blending*, 154). The simple replacement of her word "sex" with the word "genitals" makes our arguments similar and makes it clear that there is no reason to retain the word "sex." (See chap. 2, n. 2.)
59. Morgan, 44.
60. Hausman, 49.
61. Morgan, 46.
62. The American Academy of Pediatrics, in response to members' of the Intersex Society of North America (ISNA) picketing of its annual meeting in 1996, issued to the press a "Position on Intersexuality" (American Academy of Pediatrics, Position on Intersexuality News Release, reprinted in *Chrysalis: The Journal of Transgressive Gender Identities* 2, no. 4 [fall 1997/winter 1998]: 3). This act, although it was intended to bolster the medical viewpoint that early genital surgery is necessary for the emotional and cognitive development of intersex/ed children, paradoxically undermines medical authority. ISNA, for the first time, forced a medical group to publicly acknowledge that intersexuality was something about which a view could be taken.
63. Dreger, "Hermaphrodites in Love."
64. Correspondence from D. B. Grant to a member of the Androgen-Insensitivity Support Group, 6 December 1995.
65. Meyer-Bahlburg.
66. Private communication from Heino Meyer-Bahlburg, 9 May 1994.
67. McKenna and Kessler, "Who Needs Gender Theory?"
68. Fausto-Sterling, *Body-Building*, 84. For her five-gender category system, see: Fausto-Sterling, "The Five Sexes"; Anne Fausto-Sterling, "How Many Sexes Are There?"
69. Money, *Sex Errors of the Body*.
70. Paid announcement published in *New York Times*, 3 September 1995.

71. Anne Bolin, "Transcending and Transgendering: Male-to-Female Transsexuals, Dichotomy and Diversity," in *Third Sex, Third Gender: Beyond Sexual Dimorphism in Culture and History*, ed. Gilbert Herdt, 447–485 (New York: Zone, 1994).
72. Martine Rothblatt, "Gender Manifesto," *Tapestry Journal* 71 (spring 1995):32.
73. Not all transgenderists treat the body, especially the genitals, in a cavalier fashion. One contributor to a 1997 Internet discussion posted "A Bill of Gender Rights," which proclaimed, "Given that each individual has the right to assume gender roles, it then follows that each individual has the right to change their [*sic*] body or alter its physiology so it better fits a gender role" (attributed to JoAnn Roberts, 1990). While giving people permission to cosmetically, chemically, or surgically change their bodies, including their genitals, the writer is still prescribing that the newly designed body match a gender role.
74. Private communication from Cheryl Chase, 8 July 1995.
75. Private communication from AISSG member, 18 December 1995.
76. Private communication from Morgan Holmes, November 1994.
77. The medical profession is careful to disentangle intersexuality from transgender concerns like sexual identity and gender role behavior. "Dr. Y," a surgeon, objects to any presumed link between homosexuality and intersexuality. "The most important thing about the handling of intersexuality is to not lay any labels on these kids" (Ellen Hyun-Ju Lee, 60).
78. Sheila Kirk, "It's Time for Your Medicine: Signs and Treatment for Intersexuality," *Tapestry Journal* 71 (spring 1995):11. For the historical roots of this view, see Dreger, "Hermaphrodites and the Medical Invention of Sex." The contradiction between the impulse of some transgenderists to claim a congenital foundation and the social constructionist bent of most intersexuals may deter the identification of some intersexuals with the aims of some transgenderists. In another sense, the aims of some transgenderists and intersexuals are at cross purposes. If intersexuals' demands about changing medical practices were met, this would result in *less* surgery and a monetary disadvantage to physicians. In contrast, the demands of transgenderists would result in *more* surgery and a monetary advantage to physicians.
79. Ruth Hubbard and Elijah Wald, *Exploding the Gene Myth* (Boston: Beacon Press, 1993), 95.
80. Correspondence from Ieuan A. Hughes to a member of AISSG, 2 January 1996.
81. J. Kremer and H. P. den Daas, "Case Report: A Man with Breast Dysphoria," *Archives of Sexual Behavior* 19, no. 2 (1990):181.
82. Cherry Smyth, "How Shall I Address You? *On Our Backs* (Jan./Feb. 1995):19–23; and Devor, *FTM: Female-to-Male Transsexuals in Society*. The attraction to intersexed bodies is far more common than what would be revealed in counting partners of the intersexed, as is evident in the abundant pornography available featuring actors with vaginas *and* standard-sized penises, capable of being penetrated at

the same time as doing the penetrating. This, of course, is an anatomic impossibility and plays to mythological urges without being accountable to embryological truth. Prenatal hormones, responsible for forming the penis, prevent the vagina from developing. What is seen on the video screen is accomplished through fakery.

83. Private communication from Cheryl Chase, January 1997.

84. Morgan Holmes makes a similar argument when she discusses what could happen if "phalloclits" were permitted to grow ("Re-membering a Queer Body," 12). Readers are encouraged to conduct a phenomenological bracketing exercise on themselves called "imaginative variation," whereby one alters some feature of an object to see what changes can be made without altering the object's essential nature. Imagine a change in a gender feature (for example the genitals) of a person one is attracted to in order to see if doing so extinguishes the attraction. This exercise is appropriate for people of any sexual persuasion.

85. Donahoe, 573.

86. Reported in Horowitz. This is not exclusive to physicians managing intersexuality. In one study, many physicians in a number of specialties admitted preferring to discuss physical symptoms rather than psychosocial issues, and, in fact, 25 percent of them reported not encouraging patients to talk about concerns (Clark and Snooks).

87. Reported in Ellen Hyun-Ju Lee.

88. E. T. Bradbury et al., "Decision-making by Parents and Children In Paediatric Hand Surgery," *British Journal of Plastic Surgery* 47 (1994):324.

89. In 1989, the "Children Act" was passed in England. Although the phrase "children's rights" is never mentioned (the act is mainly concerned with curbing professionals' power over the family), it does rule that children under sixteen who show a "sufficient understanding and intelligence to understand fully what is proposed are competent to give or withhold consent to treatment" (Bradbury et al., "Decision-making by Parents," 324). Given such a law, the intersexual movement in England might have more rapid success than its counterpart in the United States.

90. E. T. Bradbury et al., "The Psychological Impact of Microvascular Free Toe Transfer for Children and Their Parents," *The Journal of Hand Surgery* 19B, no. 6 (December 1994):690, 694.

91. Bradbury et al., "Decision-making by Parents," 328.

92. Of the thirty-four families whose children were missing fingers, twenty-seven decided, after counseling, to proceed with toe transfer surgery. Whether they elected surgery was unrelated to their distance from the hospital, social class, age of child, or the parents' adjustment to the hand deformity. It was related to whether they belonged to a support group for parents whose children were missing fingers. Those who were active members of the support group were *less* likely to proceed with surgery (Ibid.). The lesson from this is that the help that parents of intersexed infants receive from support groups may help in resisting the surgical tide.

93. Pediatric hand surgeons acknowledge that it is impossible to differentiate how much parents' adjustment is due to counseling and how much to surgery. On the basis of their research, researchers concluded that poorly adjusted parents who became more positive about their children after surgery had low levels of support from family and friends prior to the surgery (E. T. Bradbury et al., "The Psychological Impact").
94. Renshaw, 87–88.
95. This (r)evolution might start with just a few physicians who look at the data in a fresh way. Justine Schober, a brave pediatric urologist, has not only published articles critiquing medical practice in regard to intersexuality, she challenged the American Academy of Pediatric's policy on the treatment of intersexuality on a Dateline NBC program in June 1997. She sensibly distinguishes the need for "urgent, exacting diagnosis" of intersexuality from its treatment and asks whether physicians know if the best interest of the adult patient is served by the current management. "This knowledge is still obscure" (Justine M. Schober, "Long-Term Outcomes of Feminizing Genitoplasty for Intersex," in *Pediatric Surgery and Urology: Longterm Outcomes*, ed. Pierre Mouriquant [London: W. B. Saunders, forthcoming]). At the 1996 Lawson-Wilkins Pediatric Endocrinology Conference, Charmian Quigley, a highly published researcher and pediatric endocrinologist, gave credibility to positions taken by the Androgen/Insensitivity Syndrome Support Group by distributing the group's literature.
96. Theresa Quattrin, Susan Aronica, and Tom Mazur, "Management of Male Pseudohermaphroditism: A Case Report Spanning Twenty-One Years," *Journal of Pediatric Psychology* 15, no. 6 (1990):701.
97. That surgeries are performed as a way of avoiding speech is illustrated by a group of surgeons who explain that both the clitoral glans and shaft in girls must be reduced because "failure to do so will leave a button of unsightly tissue that *requires further explanation* at some point by the parent, child, and surgeon" (Stanley Kogan, Paul Smey, and Selwyn B. Levitt, "Reply by Authors," *The Journal of Urology* 130 [October 1983]: 748).
98. *ALIAS* 1, no. 5 (summer 1996):4.
99. Reilly and Woodhouse.
100. *ALIAS* 1, no. 5 (summer 1996):4.
101. Fichtner et al.
102. Some parents are advised to tell their XY daughters that one of her chromosomes has a short arm. Although this is an inventive, nongendered way of describing her "male-pattern" chromosomes, it is not exactly what I am advocating as a different script, since the physicians and parents both "know" it is XY (really male) and are collaborating in a way to obscure it from the daughter.
103. In cases of intersexuality, it is not guaranteed that parents will follow physicians' interpretations and advice. In one case, a couple was counseled that their fetus was most probably an XX male. Despite medical advice to continue the pregnancy (because physicians ex-

pected that the child would be normal, even though sterile), the "distressed" parents decided to terminate the pregnancy. Bernard LeFiblec, Author's Reply to "Termination of XX Male Fetus," *The Lancet* 343 (7 May 1994):1165.

104. Quattrin, Aronica, and Mazur.

105. One adult (nonintersexed) female, in reflecting upon her genitals, demonstrates that genital variability is available for analysis if we look and ask: "As a child I thought [I had] an unusual looking genital area. . . . [W]hile other little girls seemed to have a neat little crack in front, I had a wider crack and skin (labia) coming out. I was enormously relieved when pubic hair covered up this anomaly. . . . I never discussed this with anyone."

106. Using the verb *do* to emphasize the social-constructed nature of gender was introduced by Candace West and Don H. Zimmerman in the paper "Doing Gender," *Gender and Society* 1 (1987):125–51.

Glossary

Androgen-insensitivity syndrome (AIS): A genetic condition in which the cells of the body are unable to absorb either fetal or pubertal androgens. Thus, for example, an XY fetus with complete AIS would be born with typical external female genitals. This is the most common diagnosis of male pseudohermaphroditism.

Androgen Insensitivity Support Group (AISSG): An organization for people with androgen-insensitivity and their families. Its purpose is to reduce the secrecy and stigma about AIS. Publishes the newsletter *ALIAS*.

aposthia: The condition of being born without a foreskin.

clitoral plication: A surgical technique that reduces the apparent size of the clitoris by folding the clitoral shaft within the labia minora so that only the glans is visible.

clitoral recession: A surgical technique that reduces the apparent size of the clitoris by "burying" the erectile shaft under a fold of labia minora so that only the glans is visible.

clitorimegaly: The condition of having what physicians consider an enlarged clitoris.

clitoridectomy (or clitorectomy): A surgical technique involving removal of the clitoris.

clitoroplasty: Any surgery on the clitoris, usually to reduce its size.

congenital adrenal hyperplasia (CAH): An inherited enzyme deficiency condition, causing a malfunction of the fetus's adrenal gland, which results in the overproduction of fetal androgen. Thus, for example, an XX fetus with the severe form of CAH would be born with typical external male genitals. This is the most common diagnosis of female pseudohermaphroditism.

cultural genitals: The genitals one is assumed to have under one's clothing.

female pseudohermaphroditism: The condition in an XX person of having ovaries and "male" genitals. It represents about one-third of all cases of intersexuality.

fistula: A deep ulcer.

gender attribution: The gender others in the social world perceive you as being (female or male).

gender identity: One's sense of oneself as belonging to either the female or male category.

gender role: Cultural expectations of behavior as appropriate for a female or male.

genitoplasty: Any surgery on the genitals (female or male).

gonad: The gland (ovary or testis) that produces eggs or sperm and hormones.

gonadal dysgenesis: A form of intersexuality characterized by undifferentiated gonads, sometimes resulting in atypical external genitals. It represents about one-third of all cases of intersexuality.

human chorionic gonadotropin (HCG): A substance that stimulates the cells of the testes; used as a treatment to enlarge the micropenis.

hypertrophy: The "pathological" enlargement of an organ.

hypospadias: A condition of the penis characterized by a urethral opening on the underside of the shaft or considerably off the center of the glans. It is included by some as an intersex condition.

intersex: The condition of having genital, gonadal, or chromosomal characteristics that are neither all "female" nor all "male."

Intersex Society of North America (ISNA): An organization for intersexuals dedicated to providing support for one another and changing the medical management of intersexuality. Publishes the newsletter *Hermaphrodites with Attitude*.

introitus: The vaginal opening.

Klinefelter's syndrome: A condition, considered by some to be a form of intersexuality, caused by a chromosomal abnormality (an XXY pattern), sometimes resulting in the development of breasts at puberty in a person with a small penis and testes.

labia majora: Two large folds of skin that run along the sides of the vulva, enclosing the labia minora, clitoris, introitus, and urethral opening.

labia minora: Two smaller, hairless folds of skin located between the labia majora and meeting above the clitoris.

labioplasty: Any surgery on the labia; also monsplasty.

male pseudohermaphroditism: The condition in an XY person of having (usually undescended) testes and "female" genitals. It represents about one-third of all cases of intersexuality.

metoidioplasty: Technique that transforms the transsexual's clitoris into a penis by first treating it with testosterone and then cutting the suspensory ligaments that hold the clitoris under the pubic bone.

micropenis: A penis that has a stretched length of less than two and a half standard deviations below the mean for age or stage of development; a penis smaller than two centimeters at birth.

mixed gonadal dysgenesis: A common intersex condition characterized by an undeveloped gonad on one side and an abnormal testis on the other.

phalloplasty: Any surgery on the penis.

progestin virilization: A form of intersexuality caused by the mother's ingestion of synthetic androgens during pregnancy. The genitals of the XX fetus become "masculinized."

stenosis: The narrowing of a canal or cavity (e.g., the vagina).

true hermaphroditism: A form of intersexuality in which both ovarian and testicular tissue are present in either the same gonad or in opposite gonads. It is extremely rare.

urinary meatus: The external opening of the urethra through which urine passes out of the body.

vaginoplasty: Any plastic surgery on the vagina, especially to build, lengthen, or widen it.

5–alpha-reductase deficiency: A form of androgen-insensitivity caused by a genetic enzyme disorder that prevents testosterone from "masculinizing" the XY fetus's genitals before birth. The genitals "masculinize" at puberty.

Bibliography

Allen, Lawrence E., B. E. Hardy, and B. M. Churchill. "The Surgical Management of the Enlarged Clitoris." *The Journal of Urology* 128 (August 1982):351–354.

Alvarado, Donna. "Intersex." *San Jose Mercury News,* 10 July 1994, p. 1.

American Academy of Pediatrics. Position on Intersexuality News Release. *Chrysalis: The Journal of Transgressive Gender Identities* 2, no. 4 (fall 1997/winter 1998):1.

Angier, Natalie. "New Debate Over Surgery on Genitals." *New York Times,* 13 May 1997, pp. C1 and C6.

———. "Sexual Identity Not Pliable After All, Report Says." *New York Times,* 14 March 1997, pp. A1 and A18.

Anonymous. "Once a Dark Secret." *British Medical Journal* 308 (February 1994):542.

Ask Isadora. "I Yam What I Yam." *The Westchester County Weekly,* 14 September 1995, p. 28.

———. "Ongoing Conversations." *The Westchester County Weekly,* 21 December 1995, p. 28.

Belman, A. B. "Editorial Comment Re: One-Stage Repair of Hypospadias: Is There No Simple Method Universally Applicable To All Types of Hypospadias?" *The Journal of Urology* 152 (October 1994):1237.

Beheshti, Mojtaba, Brian E. Hardy, Bernard M. Churchill, and Denis Daneman. "Gender Assignment in Male Pseudohermaphrodite Children." *Urology* 22, no. 6 (December 1983):604–607.

Bigelow, Jim. *The Joy of Uncircumcising!* Aptos, Calif.: Hourglass Book Publishing, 1, 995.

Bing, Elizabeth, and Esselyn Rudikoff. "Divergent Ways of Parental Coping with Hermaphrodite Children." *Medical Aspects of Human Sexuality* (December 1970):73–88.

Blackless, Melanie, Anthony Charuvastra, Amanda Derryck, Anne Fausto-Sterling, Karl Lauzanne, and Ellen Lee. "How Sexually Dimorphic Are We?" Unpublished manuscript, 1997.

Bleier, Ruth. *Science and Gender: A Critique of Biology and Its Theories on Women.* New York: Pergamon Press, 1984.

Blum, Lucille Hollander. "Darkness in an Enlightened Era: Women's Drawings of their Sexual Organs." *Psychological Reports* 42 (1978):867–873.

Bolin, Anne. "Transcending and Transgendering: Male-to-Female Transsexuals, Dichotomy and Diversity." In *Third Sex, Third Gender:*

Beyond Sexual Dimorphism in Culture and History, edited by Gilbert Herdt, 447–485. New York: Zone, 1994.

Bolkenius, M., R. Daum, and E. Heinrich. "Paediatric Surgical Principles in the Management of Children with Intersex." *Progress in Pediatric Surgery* 17 (1984):33–38.

Bradbury, E. T., S.P.J. Kay, C. Tighe and J. Hewison. "Decision-making by Parents and Children in Paediatric Hand Surgery." *British Journal of Plastic Surgery* 47 (1994):324–330.

———. "The Psychological Impact of Microvascular Free Toe Transfer for Children and Their Parents." *The Journal of Hand Surgery* 19B, no. 6 (December 1994):689–695.

Braren, Victor, John J. Warner, Ian M. Burr, Alfred Slonim, James A. O'Neill Jr., and Robert K. Rhamy. "True Hermaphroditism: A Rational Approach to Diagnosis and Treatment." *Urology* 15 (June 1980):569–574.

Bullough, Vern. *Sexual Variance in Society and History*. New York: John Wiley and Sons, 1976.

Burr, Chandler. "Homosexuality and Biology." *The Atlantic Monthly* (March 1993):47–65.

Butler, Judith. *Gender Trouble: Feminism and the Subversion of Identity*. New York: Routledge, 1990.

Cairns, Kathleen V., and Mary Valentich. "Vaginal Reconstruction in Gynecologic Cancer: A Feminist Perspective." *The Journal of Sex Research* 22, no. 3 (August 1986):333–346.

Castro-Magana, Mariano, Moris Angulo, and Platon J. Collipp. "Management of the Child with Ambiguous Genitalia." *Medical Aspects of Human Sexuality* 18, no. 4 (April 1984):172–188.

Chase, Cheryl. "Affronting Reason." In *Looking Queer: Image and Identity in Lesbian, Bisexual, Gay, and Transgendered Communities*, edited by D. Atkins. Binghamton, N.Y.: Haworth, forthcoming.

———. "'Corrective' Surgery Unnecessary: Reply to 'Is It a Boy or a Girl?'" *Johns Hopkins Magazine* 46, no. 1 (February 1994):6–7.

———. "Letter to the Editor Re: Measurement Of Pudendal Evoked Potentials During Feminizing Genitoplasty: Technique and Applications." *The Journal of Urology* 156, no. 3 (1995):1139.

Chavis, William, John J. LaFerla, and Robert Niccolini. "Plastic Repair of Elongated, Hypertrophic Labia Minora." *The Journal of Reproductive Medicine* 34, no. 5 (1989):373–375.

Clark, C. I., and S. Snooks. "Objectives of Basic Surgical Training." *British Journal of Hospital Medicine* 50 (1993):477–479.

Collins, Patricia Hill. *Black Feminist Thought: Knowledge, Consciousness, and the Politics of Empowerment*. New York: Routledge, 1991.

Corney, R. H., H. Everett, A. Howells, and M. E. Crowther. "Psychosocial Adjustment Following Major Gynaecological Surgery for Carcinoma of the Cervix and Vulva." *Journal of Psychosomatic Research* 36, no. 6 (1992):561–568.

Cowley, Geoffrey. "Gender Limbo." *Newsweek*, 19 May 1997, 64–66.

Crooks, Robert, and Karla Baur. *Our Sexuality*. 6th ed. Pacific Grove, Calif.: Brooks/Cole Publishing, 1996.

Cruikshank, Stephen H. "Reconstructive procedures for the gynecologic surgeon." *American Journal of Obstetrics and Gynecology* 168, no. 2 (February 1993):469–475.

De Jong, Tom P.V.M., and Thomas M. L. Boemers. "Neonatal Management of Female Intersex by Clitorovaginoplasty." *The Journal Of Urology* 154 (August 1995):830–832.

Devor, Holly. "Female Gender Dysphoria in Context: Social Problems or Personal Problems." *Annual Review of Sex Research* 7 (1996):44–89.

———. *FTM: Female-to-Male Transsexuals in Society.* Bloomington: Indiana University Press, 1997.

———. *Gender Blending: Confronting the Limits of Duality.* Bloomington: Indiana University Press, 1989.

Dewhurst, J., and D. B. Grant. "Intersex Problems." *Archives of Disease in Childhood* 59 (July-December 1984):1191–1194.

Diamond, Jared. "Turning A Man." *Discover* 13, no. 6 (June 1992):71–77.

Diamond, Milton. "Human Sexual Development: Biological Foundations for Social Development." In *Human Sexuality in Four Perspectives,* edited by Frank A. Beach, 22–61. Baltimore: The Johns Hopkins University Press, 1976.

———. "Sexual Identity, Monozygotic Twins Reared in Discordant Sex Roles and a BBC Follow-Up." *Archives of Sexual Behavior* 11, no. 2 (1982):181–186.

———, and Keith Sigmundson. "Sex Reassignment at Birth: Long-term Review and Clinical Applications." *Archives of Pediatric and Adolescent Medicine* 151 (May 1997):298–304.

Donahoe, P. "Clinical Management of Intersex Abnormalities." *Current Problems in Surgery* 28 (1991):519–579.

Dorland's Illustrated Medical Dictionary. 28th ed. Philadelphia: W. B. Saunders, 1997.

Dreger, Alice Domurat. "Hermaphrodites in Love: The Truth of the Gonads." In *Science and Homosexualities,* edited by Vernon Rosario, 46–66. New York: Routledge, 1996.

———. *Hermaphrodites and the Medical Invention of Sex.* Cambridge: Harvard University Press, 1998.

Duckett, John W., and Laurence S. Baskin. "Genitoplasty for Intersex Anomalies." *European Journal of Pediatrics* 152 (1993):80–84.

Dull, Diana, and Candace West. "Accounting for Cosmetic Surgery: The Accomplishment of Gender." *Social Problems* 38, no. 1 (February 1991):54–70.

Ellis, Havelock. *The Psychology of Sex.* Garden City, N. J.: Garden City Books, 1933.

———. *Studies in the Psychology of Sex.* New York: Random House, 1942.

Epstein, Julia. "Either/Or—Neither/Both: Sexual Ambiguity and the Ideology of Gender." *Genders* 7 (spring 1990):99–142.

Exner, M. J. *The Sexual Side of Marriage.* New York: W. W. Norton and Co., 1932.

Fausto-Sterling, Anne. *Body-Building: How Biologists Construct Sexuality.* New York: HarperCollins, forthcoming.

———. "The Five Sexes." *The Sciences* (March/April 1993):20–24.

———. "Gender, Race, and Nation: The Comparative Anatomy of 'Hottentot' Women in Europe, 1815–1817." In *Deviant Bodies: Critical Perspectives on Difference in Science and Popular Culture*, edited by Jennifer Terry and Jacqueline Urla, 19–48. Bloomington: Indiana University Press, 1995.

———. "How Many Sexes Are There?" *New York Times*, 12 March 1993.

Feder, Ellen K. "Disciplining the Family: The Case of Gender Identity Disorder." *Philosophical Studies* 85 (1997):195–211.

Feldman, Kenneth W., and David W. Smith. "Fetal Phallic Growth and Penile Standards for Newborn Male Infants." *The Journal of Pediatrics* 86, no. 3 (March 1975):395–398.

Fichtner, Jan, D. Filipas, A. M. Mottrie, G. E. Voges, and R. Hohenfellner. "Analysis of Meatal Location in 500 Men: Wide Variation Questions Need for Meatal Advancement in All Pediatric Anterior Hypospadias Cases." *The Journal of Urology* 154 (August 1995):833–834.

Fiedler, Leslie. *Freaks: Myths and Images of the Second Self*. New York: Simon and Schuster, 1978.

Filardo, Thomas W. "Use of 'Normal' to Describe Penile Appearance after Circumcision." *American Family Physician* 53, no. 8 (June 1996):2440.

Findlay, Deborah. "Discovering Sex: Medical Science, Feminism, and Intersexuality." *The Canadian Review of Sociology and Anthropology* 32 (February 1995):25–52.

Flateau, E. "Penile size in the newborn infant." Letter to the Editor, *The Journal of Pediatrics* 87, no. 4 (October 1995):663–664.

Forel, August, and C. F. Marshall. *The Sexual Question*. Brooklyn, N.Y.: Physicians & Surgeons Book Co., 1906.

Foucault, Michel. *Herculine Barbin*. New York: Pantheon Books, 1978.

———. *History of Sexuality*. New York: Pantheon Books, 1980.

Freud, Sigmund. "Some Psychical Consequences of the Anatomical Distinctions between the Sexes" (1925). In *The Complete Psychological Works*, translated and edited by J. Strachy, vol. 18. New York: Norton, 1976.

Frey, P., and A. Bianchi. "One-Stage Preputial Pedicle Flap Repair for Hypospadias: Experience with 100 Patients." *Progress in Pediatric Surgery* 23 (1989):181–191.

Garber, Marjorie. "Spare Parts: The Surgical Construction of Gender." *Differences: A Journal of Feminist Cultural Studies* 1, no. 3 (fall 1989):137–159.

Garfinkel, Harold. *Studies in Ethnomethodology*. Englewood Cliffs, N.J.: Prentice Hall, 1967.

Garriques, Henry J. *A Textbook of the Diseases of Women*. Philadelphia: W. B. Saunders. 1894.

Gearhart, John P., Arthur Burnett, and Jeffrey H. Owen. "Measurement of Pudendal Evoked Potentials During Feminizing Genitoplasty: Technique and Applications." *The Journal of Urology* 153 (February 1995):486–487.

———. "Reply by Authors Re: Measurement of Pudendal Evoked Poten-

tials During Feminizing Genitoplasty: Technique and Applications."
The Journal of Urology 156, no. 3 (1995):1140.

Glassberg, Kenneth I. "Gender Assignment in Newborn Male Pseudoher-maphodites." *Urologic Clinics of North America* 7 (June 1980):409–421.

Goffman, Erving. *Stigma: Notes on the Management of Spoiled Identity.* Englewood Cliffs, N.J.: Prentice Hall, 1963.

Gooren, Louis, and Peggy T. Cohen-Kettenis. "Development of Male Gender Identity/Role and a Sexual Orientation Towards Women in a 46,XY Subject with an Incomplete Form of the Androgen Insensitivity Syndrome." *Archives of Sexual Behavior* 20, no. 5 (1991):459–470.

Green, James. "Getting Real about FTM Surgery." *Chrysalis: The Journal of Transgressive Gender Identities* 2, no. 2 (1995):27–32.

Greenfield, Saul P., Barry T. Sadler, and Julian Wan. "Two-Stage Repair for Severe Hypospadias." *The Journal of Urology* 152 (August 1994):498–501.

Gross, Robert E., Judson Randolph, and John F. Crigler Jr. "Clitorectomy for sexual abnormalities: Indications and technique." *Surgery* 59 (February 1966):300–308.

Guthrie, Robert D., David W. Smith, and C. Benjamin Graham. "Testosterone treatment for micropenis during early childhood." *The Journal of Pediatrics* 83, no. 2 (1973):247–252.

Hall, Winfield Scott. *Sexual Knowledge.* Philadelphia: The John C. Winston Co., 1916.

Hatch, Kenneth D. "Neovaginal Reconstruction." *CANCER* supplement 71, no. 4 (February 1993):1660–1663.

Hausman, Bernice L. *Changing Sex: Transsexualism, Technology, and the Idea of Gender.* Durham and London: Duke University Press, 1995.

Hecker, W. Ch. "Operative Correction of Intersexual Genitals in Children." *Progress in Pediatric Surgery* 17 (1984):21–31.

Hendren, W. Hardy, and Anthony Atala. "Repair of High Vagina in Girls With Severely Masculinized Anatomy From the Adrenogenital Syndrome." *Journal of Pediatric Surgery* 30, no. 1 (January 1995):91–94.

Hendricks, Melissa. "Is It a Boy or a Girl?" *Johns Hopkins Magazine* 45, no. 5 (November 1993):10–16.

Hermaphrodites with Attitude. Newsletter of the Intersex Society of North America. San Francisco.

Hinman, Frank Jr. "Microphallus: Characteristics and Choice of Treatment from a Study of 20 Cases." *The Journal of Urology* 107 (March 1972):499–505.

Holmes, Morgan. "Homophobia in Health Care: Abjection and the Treatment of Intersexuality." Paper presented at the Learned Societies CSAA meetings, Montreal, June 1995.

———. "Re-membering a Queer Body." *Undercurrents* (May 1994):11–14.

Holzaepfel, John H. *Marriage Manual.* Pamphlet distributed to physicians by Holland-Rantos Company, Inc. 1959.

Horowitz, Sarah. "The Middle Sex." *SF Weekly* 13, no. 5 (1 February 1995):11–12.

Hrdy, Sarah. *The Woman that Never Evolved*. Cambridge, Mass.: Harvard University Press, 1981.

Hubbard, Ruth, and Elijah Wald. *Exploding the Gene Myth*. Boston: Beacon Press, 1993.

Huffman, John W. "Some Facts about the Clitoris." *Post Graduate Medicine* 60, no. 5 (November 1976):245–247.

Irvine, Janice. *Disorders of Desire: Sex and Gender in Modern American Sexology*. Philadelphia: Temple University Press, 1990.

"Is Early Vaginal Reconstruction Wrong for Some Intersex Girls?" *Urology Times* (February 1997):10–12.

Jones, Howard W., and William Wallace Scott. *Hermaphroditism, Genital Anomalies, and Related Endocrine Disorders*. Baltimore: The Williams & Wilkins Co., 1958.

Kaplan, Morris. *Sexual Justice*. New York: Routledge, 1997.

Kessler, Suzanne J. "Creating Good-Looking Genitals in the Service of Gender." In *A Queer World: The Center for Lesbian and Gay Studies Reader*, edited by Martin Duberman, 153–173. New York: New York University Press, 1997.

———. "Meanings of Genital Variability." *Chrysalis: The Journal of Transgressive Gender Identities* 2, no. 4 (fall 1997/winter 1998):33–38.

———. Letter in response to Anne Fausto-Sterling's "The Five Sexes." *The Sciences* (July/August 1993):3.

———, and Wendy McKenna. *Gender: An Ethnomethodological Approach*. New York: Wiley-Interscience, 1978; Chicago: University of Chicago Press, 1985.

Kirk, Sheila. "It's Time For Your Medicine: Signs & Treatment For Intersexuality." *Tapestry Journal* 71 (spring 1995):11–13.

Kogan, Stanley J., Paul Smey, and Selwyn B. Levitt. "Reply by Authors." *The Journal of Urology* 130 (October 1983):748.

———. "Subtunical Total Reduction Clitoroplasty: A Safe Modification of Existing Techniques." *The Journal of Urology* 130 (October 1983):746–748.

Koyanagi, Tomohiko, Katsuya Nonomura, Tetsufumi Yamashita, Kouishi Kanagawa, and Hidehiro Kakizaki. "One-Stage Repair of Hypospadias: Is There No Simple Method Universally Applicable to All Types of Hypospadias?" *The Journal of Urology* 152 (October 1994):1232–1237.

Kremer, J., and H. P. den Daas. "Case Report: A Man with Breast Dysphoria." *Archives of Sexual Behavior* 19, no. 2 (1990):179–181.

Kuhnle, Ursula, Monika Bullinger, and H. P. Schwarz. "The Quality of Life in Adult Female Patients with Congenital Adrenal Hyperplasia: A comprehensive study of the impact of genital malformations and chronic disease on female patients' life." *European Journal of Pediatrics* 154 (1995):708–716.

Kumar, H., J. H. Kiefer, I. E. Rosenthal, and S. S. Clark. "Clitoroplasty: Experience During a 19–Year Period." *The Journal of Urology* 111, no. 1 (January 1974):81–84.

Lattimer, John K. "Editorial Comment on Stanley Kogan, et al's 'Subtunical

Total Reduction Clitoroplasty: A Safe Modification of Existing Techniques.'" *The Journal of Urology* 130 (October 1983):748.

———. "Relocation and Recession of the Enlarged Clitoris with Preservation of the Glans: An Alternative to Amputation." *The Journal of Urology* 81, no. 1 (1961):113–116.

Lee, Ellen Hyun-Ju. "Producing Sex: An Interdisciplinary Perspective on Sex Assignment Decisions for Intersexuals." Unpublished senior thesis, Brown University, April 1994.

Lee, Peter A., Thomas Mazur, Robert Danish, James Amrhein, Robert M. Blizzard, John Money, and Claude J. Migeon. "Micropenis: I. Criteria, Etiologies and Classification." *The Johns Hopkins Medical Journal* 146 (1980):156–163.

LeFiblec, Bernard. Author's reply to "Termination of XX Male Fetus." *The Lancet* 343 (7 May 1994):1165.

Lev-Ran, Arye. "Sex Reversal as Related to Clinical Syndromes in Human Beings." In *Handbook of Sexology II: Genetics, Hormones and Behavior*, edited by John Money and H. Musaph, 157–173. New York: Elsevier, 1978.

Lief, Harold I., and Lynn Hubschmann. "Orgasm in the Postoperative Transsexual." *Archives of Sexual Behavior* 22, no. 2 (1993):145–155.

Lindemalm, Cunnar, Dag Korlin, and Nils Uddenberg. "Long-term Follow-Up of 'Sex Change' in 13 Male-to-Female Transsexuals." *Archives of Sexual Behavior* 15, no. 3 (1996):187–209.

Lobe, Thom E., Diane L. Woodall, Gail E. Richards, Anita Cavallo, and Walter J. Meyer. "The Complications of Surgery For Changing Patterns Over Two Decades." *Journal of Pediatric Surgery* 22, no. 7 (July 1987):651–652.

Majeski, Tom. "Surgery Changes Russian Child's Sex." *San Jose Mercury News*, 25 July 1994.

Martin, June. "The Incidence, Frequency and Rate of Genital Satisfaction of Sixty-Four Post-Operative Male-to-Female Transsexuals Reported to be Experienced During Various Sexual Behaviors: A Descriptive Study." Ph.D. dissertation. Institute for Advanced Study of Human Sexuality, San Francisco, 1988.

Martinez-Mora, J., R. Isnard, A. Castellvi, and P. Lopez Ortiz. "Neovagina in Vaginal Agenesis: Surgical Methods and Long-Term Results." *Journal of Pediatric Surgery* 27, no. 1 (January 1992):10–14.

Mazur, Tom. "Ambiguous Genitalia: Detection and Counseling." *Pediatric Nursing* 9 (November/December 1983):417–431.

McGillivray, Barbara C. "The Newborn with Ambiguous Genitalia." *Seminars in Perinatology* 16, no. 6 (1992):365–368.

McKenna, Wendy, and Suzanne Kessler. "Who Needs Gender Theory?" *Signs: Journal of Women in Culture and Society* (spring 1997):687–691.

Meyer-Bahlburg, Heino F. L. "Gender Assignment from the Clinician's Perspective." Paper presented at the annual meeting of The Society for the Scientific Study of Sex, San Francisco, November 1995.

Mininberg, David T. "Phalloplasty in Congenital Adrenal Hyperplasia." *The Journal of Urology* 128 (August 1982):355–356.

Money, John. "Birth Defect of the Sex Organs: Telling the Parents and the Patient." *British Journal of Sexual Medicine* 10 (March 1983):14.

———. "Hermaphroditism and Pseudohermaphroditism." In *Gynecologic Endocrinology*, edited by Jay J. Gold, 449–464. New York: Hoeber, 1968.

———. "Psychologic Consideration of Sex Assignment in Intersexuality." *Clinics in Plastic Surgery* 1 (April 1974):215–222.

———. "Psychological Counseling: Hermaphroditism." In *Endocrine and Genetic Diseases of Childhood and Adolescence*, edited by L. I. Gardner, 609–618. Philadelphia: W. B. Saunders, 1975.

———. *Sex Errors of the Body: Dilemmas, Education, Counseling.* Baltimore: The Johns Hopkins University Press, 1968. Reprint, 1994.

———, and Anke A. Ehrhardt. *Man & Woman, Boy & Girl.* Baltimore: The Johns Hopkins University Press, 1972.

———, J. G. Hampson, and J. L. Hampson. "Hermaphroditism: Recommendations Concerning Assignment of Sex, Change of Sex, and Psychologic Management." *Bulletin of the Johns Hopkins Hospital* 97 (1955):284–300.

———, Gregory K. Lehne, and Frantz Pierre-Jerome. "Micropenis: Adult Follow-Up and Comparison of Size against New Norms." *Journal of Sex & Marital Therapy* 10, no. 2 (1984):105–114.

———, Tom Mazur, Charles Abrams, and Bernard F. Norman. "Micropenis, Family Mental Health, and Neonatal Management: A Report on Fourteen Patients Reared as Girls." *Journal of Preventive Psychiatry* 1, no. 1 (1981):17–27.

———, Reynolds Potter, and Clarice S. Stoll. "Sex Reannouncement in Hereditary Sex Deformity: Psychology and Sociology of Habilitation." *Social Science and Medicine* 3 (1969):207–216.

———, M. Schwartz, and V. G. Lewis. "Adult Erotosexual Status and Fetal Hormonal Masculinization and Demasculinization: 46, XX Congenital Virilizing Adrenal Hyperplasia and 46, XY Androgen-insensitivity Syndrome Compared." *Psychoneuroendocrinology* 9 (1984):405–414.

———, and Patricia Tucker. *Sexual Signatures: On Being a Man or a Woman.* Boston: Little Brown and Co., 1975.

Morgan, Kathryn Pauly. "Women and the Knife: Cosmetic Surgery and the Colonization of Women's Bodies." *Hypatia* 6, no. 3 (fall 1991):25–53.

Mulaikai, Rose M., Claude J. Migeon, and John A. Rock. "Fertility Rates in Female Patients with Congenital Adrenal Hyperplasia Due to 21-Hydroxylase Deficiency." *The New England Journal of Medicine* 316, no. 4 (22 January 1987):178–182.

Mureau, Mark A. M., Froukje M. E. Slijper, A. Koos Slob, and Frank C. Verhulst. "Genital Perception of Children, Adolescents and Adults Operated on for Hypospadias: A Comparative Study." *The Journal of Sex Research* 32, no. 4 (winter 1995):289–298.

Napheys, Geo. H. *The Physical Life of Women: Advice to the Maiden, Wife and Mother.* Philadelphia: George Maclean, 1870.

Newman, Kurt, Judson Randolph, and Kathryn Anderson. "The Surgical

Management of Infants and Children With Ambiguous Genitalia." *Ann. Surg.* 215, no. 6 (June 1992):644–653.

Oberfeld, Sharon E., Aurora Mondok, Farrokh Shahrivar, Janice F. Klein, and Lenore S. Levine. "Clitoral Size in Full-Term Infants." *American Journal of Perinatology* 6, no. 4 (October 1989):453–454.

Oesterling, Joseph E., John P. Gearhart, and Robert D. Jeffs. "A Unified Approach to Early Reconstructive Surgery of the Child With Ambiguous Genitalia." *The Journal of Urology* 138 (October 1987):1079–1084.

Oliven, John F. *Sexual Hygiene and Pathology: A Manual for the Physician.* Philadelphia: J. B. Lippincott Co., 1955.

Ortner, Sherry B. "Is Female to Male as Nature is to Culture?" In *Woman, Culture, and Society,* edited by Michelle Zimbalist Rosaldo and Louise Lamphere, 67–87. Stanford, Calif.: Stanford University Press, 1974.

Patil, U., and F. P. Hixson. "The Role of Tissue Expanders in Vaginoplasty for Congenital Malformations of the Vagina." *British Journal of Urology* 70 (1992):554–557.

Perlmutter, Alan, and Claude Reitelman. "Surgical Management of Intersexuality." In *Campbell's Urology,* edited by Patrick Walsh, 1951–1966. Philadelphia: W. B. Saunders, 1992.

Perovic, Sara. "Male to Female Surgery: A New Contribution to Operative Techniques." *Plastic and Reconstructive Surgery* 91, no. 4 (April 1993):704–710.

———. "Phalloplasty in Children and Adolescents Using the Extended Pedicle Island Groin Flap." *The Journal of Urology* 154 (August 1995):848–853.

Pinter, A., and G. Kosztolanyi. "Surgical Management of Neonates and Children with Ambiguous Genitalia." *University Children's Hospital of Pecs/Hungary* 30, no. 1 (1990):111–121.

Quattrin, Theresa, Susan Aronica, and Tom Mazur. "Management of Male Pseudohermaphroditism: A Case Report Spanning Twenty-One Years." *Journal of Pediatric Psychology* 15, no. 6 (1990):699–709.

Quigley, Charmian, and Frank French. "Androgen Receptor Defects: Historical, Clinical and Molecular Perspectives." *Endocrine Reviews* 16, no. 3 (1995):271–321.

Radman, Melvin H. "Hypertrophy of the Labia Minora." *Obstetrics and Gynecology* 48, no. 1 (July 1976):78–80.

Randolph, Judson, and Wellington Hung. "Reduction Clitoroplasty in Females with Hypertrophied Clitoris." *Journal of Pediatric Surgery* 5, no. 2 (April 1970):224–231.

Randolph, Judson, Wellington Hung, and Mary Colaianni Rathlev. "Clitoroplasty for Females Born with Ambiguous Genitalia: A Long-Term Study of 37 patients." *Journal of Pediatric Surgery* 16, no. 6 (December 1981):882–887.

"Read My Lips." *Taste of Latex* (9 November 1993):7.

Reilly, Justine M., and C.R.J. Woodhouse, "Small Penis and the Male Sexual Role." *The Journal of Urology* 142 (August 1989):569–571.

Renshaw, Domeena C. "Sexual Birth Defects: Telling The Parents." *Resident Staff Physician* 39, no. 2 (February 1993):87–89.

Rogan, Helen. "A Woman's Mag Masks Sleaze as Service." *Ms.* (September-October 1994):92–93.

Rohatgi, M. "Intersex Disorders: An Approach to Surgical Management." *Indian Journal of Pediatrics* 59 (1992):523–530.

Roslyn, Joel J., Eric W. Fonkalsrud, and Barbara Lippe. "Intersex Disorders in Adolescents and Adults." *The American Journal of Surgery* 146 (July 1983):138–144.

Rothblatt, Martine. "Gender Manifesto." *Tapestry Journal* 71 (spring 1995):31–36.

Rubin, Jeffrey, F. J. Provenzano, and Z. Luria. "The Eye of the Beholder: Parents' Views on Sex of Newborns." *American Journal of Orthopsychiatry* 44, no. 4 (1974):512–519.

Ruminjo, J. "Circumcision in Women." *East African Medical Journal* (September 1992):477–478.

Sane, Kumud, and Ora Hirsch Pescovitz. "The Clitoral Index: A determination of clitoral size in normal girls and in girls with abnormal sexual development." *The Journal of Pediatrics* 120 (2 Pt 1) (February 1992):264–266.

Schlussel, Richard. Lecture at Update in Pediatric Plastic and Reconstructive Surgery, a symposium at Mount Sinai Medical Center, New York, 17 May 1996.

Schober, Justine M. "Long-Term Outcomes of Feminizing Genitoplasty For Intersex." In *Pediatric Surgery and Urology: Longterm Outcomes*, edited by Pierre Mouriquant. London: W. B. Saunders, forthcoming.

Schonfeld, William A., and Gilbert W. Beebe. "Normal Growth and Variation in the Male Genitalia from Birth to Maturity." *The Journal of Urology* 48 (1942):759–777.

Schover, L. W., and M. Fife. "Sexual Counseling of Patients Undergoing Radical Surgery for Pelvic or Genital Cancer." *Journal of Psychosocial Oncology* 3 (1986):21–41.

Schultz, W.C.M. Weijmar, K. Wijma, H.B.M. Van de Wiel, J. Bouma, and J. Janssens. "Sexual Rehabilitation of Radical Vulvectomy Patients. A Pilot Study." *Journal of Psychosomatic Obstetrics and Gynecology* 5 (1986):119–126.

Slijper, F.M.E., H. J. van der Kamp, H. Branbenburg, S.M.P.F. de Muinck Keizer-Schrama, S.L.S. Drop, and J. C. Molenaar. "Evaluation of Psychosexual Development of Young Women with Congenital Adrenal Hyperplasia: A Pilot Study." *Journal of Sex Education and Therapy* 18, no. 2 (1992):200–207.

Slijper, F.M.E., S.L.S. Drop, J. C. Molenaar, and R. J. Scholtmeijer. "Neonates with Abnormal Genital Development Assigned the Female Sex: Parent Counseling." *Journal of Sex Education and Therapy* 20, no. 1 (1994):9–17.

Smith, Richard W. "What kind of sex is natural?" In *The Frontiers of Sex Research*, edited by Vern Bullough, 103–111. Buffalo: Prometheus, 1979.

Smyth, Cherry. "How Shall I Address You? *On Our Backs* (Jan./Feb. 1995):19–23.

Sotiropoulos, A., A. Morishima, Y. Homsy, and J. K. Lattimer. "Long-Term Assessment of Genital Reconstruction in Female Pseudohermaphrodites." *The Journal of Urology* 115 (May 1976):599–601.

Stecker, John F. Jr., Charles E. Horton, Charles J. Devine Jr., and John B. McCraw. "Hypospadias Cripples." Symposium on Hyspospadias. *Urologic Clinics of North America* 8, no. 3 (October 1981):539–544.

Stock, Jeffrey A., Jose Cortez, Hal C. Scherz, and George W. Kaplan. "The Management of Proximal Hypospadias Using a 1–Stage Hypospadias Repair with a Preputial Free Graft For Neourethral Construction and a Preputial Pedicle Flap for Ventral Skin Coverage." *The Journal of Urology* 152 (December 1994):2335–2337.

Stoll, Clarice Stasz, ed. *Sexism: Scientific Debates*. Reading, Mass.: Addison-Wesley Publishing Company, 1973.

Stoller, Robert J. *Sex and Gender*. Vol. 1. New York: J. Aronson, 1968.

Teague, J. L., D. R. Roth, and E. T. Gonzales. "Repair of Hypospadias Complications Using the Meatal Based Flap Urethroplasty." *The Journal of Urology* 151 (February 1994):470–472.

Tiefer, Leonore. "The Medicalization of Impotence—Normalizing Phallocentrism." *Gender & Society* 8, no. 3 (September 1994):363–377.

———. "Might Premature Ejaculation Be Organic? The Perfect Penis Takes a Giant Step Forward." *Journal of Sex Education and Therapy* 20, no. 1 (1994):7–8.

Toby. *Finding Our Own Ways*. Self-published newsletter. 1987.

Tong, Steven Y. C., Karen Donaldson, and John M. Hutson. "When Is Hypospadias Not Hypospadias?" *MJA* 164 (5 February 1996):153–154.

Van Seters, A. P., and A. K. Slob. "Mutually Gratifying Heterosexual Relationship with Micropenis of Husband." *Journal of Sex & Marital Therapy* 14, no. 2 (1988):98–107.

Walker, Alice. *Possessing the Secret of Joy*. New York: Pocket Star Books, 1992.

Walker, Kenneth M. *Preparation for Marriage*. New York: W. W. Norton, 1933.

Wesley, John R., and Arnold G. Coran. "Intestinal Vaginoplasty for Congenital Absence of the Vagina." *Journal of Pediatric Surgery* 27, no. 1 (July 1992):885–889.

West, Candace, and Don H. Zimmerman. "Doing Gender." *Gender and Society* 1 (1987):125–151.

Woodward, L. T. *Sophisticated Sex Techniques in Marriage*. New York: Lancer Books, 1968.

Wright, Helena. *The Sex Factor in Marriage*. New York: The Vanguard Press, 1931.

Zucker, Kenneth J. "Commentary on Diamond's Prenatal Predisposition and the Clinical Management of Some Pediatric Conditions." *Sex and Marital Treatment* 22, no. 3 (1996):148–160.

———, Susan Bradley, Gillan Oliver, Jennifer Blake, Susan Fleming, and Jane Hood. "Psychosexual Development of Women with Congenital Adrenal Hyperplasia." *Hormones and Behavior* 30 (1996):300–318.

Index

abortion
    candor about own, 35
    as control of own body, 82
    of XX male fetus, 162–163n.103
abuse, sexual
    children's postoperative care perceived as, 63
    repeated genital exams as, 59–60
adhesions, 39
adolescents, intersexed, 12, 140n.45
    counseling of, 28–30
aesthetics and surgery, 34. *See also* cosmetic surgery
aesthetic vaginal labioplasty, 114
Africa, female genital surgery in. *See* female genital mutilation
AIDS status, candor about own, 35
ALIAS (AISSG newsletter), 79, 165
ambiguity, genital, 3, 33
    as natural option, 32
    and parents of intersexed children, 20, 21–24
American Academy of Pediatrics, 83, 162n.95
    picketed by ISNA, 78, 159n.58
amputations, 107
anatomy as destiny, 108

androcentrism, 109
androgen
    prenatal exposure to, 138n.30
    production of, at puberty, 44
    synthetic, 168
    as therapy, 19, 20, 25
androgen-insensitivity syndrome (AIS), 29, 61, 78, 86–87, 95, 97, 135n.7, 140n.1, 165
    parental responses to, 130
Androgen-Insensitivity Syndrome Support Group (AISSG), 79, 86, 87, 122, 123, 154n.26, 162n.95, 165
anxieties, of parents of intersexed children, 32, 55, 92
aposthia, 39, 165
appearance *vs.* function, of genitals, 126, 136n.8
asexual person, self-characterization as, 77, 78
authority
    gender, grounds of, 120
    of medicine, 97–98, 120

Bartmann, Sarah, 158n.38
Berkowitz, Gary, 75
Bigelow, Jim, 82–83
Bill of Gender Rights, transgenderist, 160n.73
birth certificate, and gender announcement, 21

sexual pleasure, 53; versus
social adjustment, 37
sexual responsivity, women's,
and genital surgery, 55–58
shame, 5, 84. *See also* embarrassment
reduced through support
groups, 79–80
Short, Roger, 143n.38
Sigmundson, Keith, 6
silicone breasts, 51
slavery, and bodily violation, 82
social acceptance, and genitals,
53
stenosis, 61, 68, 168
stent, 63. *See also* dilation,
vaginal
steroid
evaluation, 18
treatments, 96
stigma, 35, 37
reduced through support
groups, 79
stimulation, genital, and
subsequent pain, 57
suicide, 69
support groups, 77–80
ISNA, 129
for parents of intersexed
children, 99, 131
surgery, 14, 23, 140n.45
for aesthetic reasons. *See also*
cosmetic surgery
and avoidance of speech,
162n.97
complications in women, 61–
64
cosmetic, *see* cosmetic
surgery
to create vagina, 2, 3. *See also*
vaginoplasty
degrees of urgency of, 141n.6
as discipline, 39
elective, 111
evaluation of, *see* evaluation

of surgery
hand reconstruction, 125–
128, 161n.92, 162n.93
and health insurance, 153n.8
to improve quality of life, 34
intersexed adults' reflections
on, 53
and intersexual identity, 86
lay views of, 100–103
lifesaving, 34
on male-to female transsexuals, 64–68
marriage as proof of success
of, 106
motivations for, 73–76
multiple, 61, 62, 69, 71, 98,
116, 152n.95
options for transgender
community, 121
perceived as punishment, 127
reconstructive, after genital
cancer, 10, 46, 54, 107,
109–110, 148–49n.29,
151n.67, 155n.45
to reduce phallus size, 18
ritual *vs.* clinical, 81
statistical reporting, 82
success criteria for, 10
on unacceptible genitals, 8,
46–51

Taste of Latex (periodical), 115
teasing, 34–35
testicle implants, 116
testosterone, ability of Y-
chromosome infant to
make, 18
testosterone therapy, 1, 2, 19,
38, 41, 44, 68–69, 95, 124,
167
Tiefer, Leonore, 116, 142–
143n.32, 144n.43
tissue sloughing, 47
toe transfer, 125–28
tomboyish behavior, in girls, 26

About the Author

Suzanne J. Kessler is a professor of psychology at Purchase College, State University of New York. She has written articles on intersexuality and is coauthor, with Wendy McKenna, of *Gender: An Ethnomethodological Approach*, the book that laid the foundation for much of the scholarship in gender studies.